Perfectly Average

Perfectly Average

The Pursuit of Normality in Postwar America

ANNA G. CREADICK

University of Massachusetts Press
Amherst & Boston

Copyright © 2010 by University of Massachusetts Press
All rights reserved
Printed in the United States of America
LC 2010019127
ISBN 978-1-55849-806-8 (paper); 805-1 (library cloth)

Designed by Jack Harrison
Set in Adobe Garamond Pro
Printed and bound by Thomson-Shore, Inc.

Library of Congress Cataloging-in-Publication Data
Creadick, Anna G., 1967–
Perfectly average : the pursuit of normality in postwar America /
Anna G. Creadick.
p. cm. — (Culture, politics, and the Cold War)
Includes bibliographical references and index.
ISBN 978-1-55849-806-8 (pbk. : alk. paper) —
ISBN 978-1-55849-805-1 (library cloth : alk. paper)
1. United States—Civilization—1945–
2. United States—Social conditions—1945–
3. National characteristics, American.
4. Body image—Social aspects—United States—History—20th century.
5. Middle class—United States—History—20th century.
6. Sex in popular culture—United States—History—20th century.
7. Community life—United States—History—20th century.   I. Title.
E169.12.C67 2010
973.918—dc22
2010019127

British Library Cataloguing in Publication data are available.

For two little girls, 2 and 4.

Contents

Illustrations

Acknowledgments

First, my deepest gratitude to Christian Appy, series editor, and Clark Dougan, senior editor, at the University of Massachusetts Press, whose hands-on approach is rare and rewarding and whose patience, care, good cheer, and faith in this project have been deeply sustaining. For critical assistance in helping me untangle ideas and arguments as I developed the manuscript, I am grateful to my trusted readers, Ardis Cameron, Judith E. Smith, Kevin C. Dunn, and T. J. Boisseau. For their patience, wit, and wisdom as they nurtured this project in its earliest stages, I am indebted to Margo Culley, Kathy Peiss, and Randall Knoper, as well as Lisa Henderson and Deborah Carlin. For excellent editorial assistance in the final stages, I thank Mary Bellino and Carol Betsch.

Other colleagues who have supported me in large and small ways include Laurel Allen, Cerri Banks, Betty Bayer, Wendy Bergoffen, Nora Blake, Lara Blanchard, Fay Botham, Monica Brown, Lucy Mae San Pablo Burns, Bahar Davary, Jodi Dean, Christine de Denus, Cama Duke, Robin Fordham, Walter Gruenzweig, Chris Hanlon, Susan Henking, Mary Hess, Kirk Hoppé, Cedric Johnson, Lisa Kaenzig, Heidi Kaufman, Kristy Kenyon, Carol A. Mason, the N.P.P. Academy, Lee Quinby, Alison Redick, Doug Reilly, Kevin S. Reilly, Arlene Rodriguez, Richard Salter, Nic Sammond, Lisa Tetrault, and Margaret Weitekamp. I am especially deeply indebted to Kathy Peiss and Judy Smith, who inspired me, and whose rigorous training provided a solid foundation. And my thanks are overdue to the fine faculty of the English Department at Appalachian State University—Cece Conway, E. T. Arnold, Tom McGowan, Mark Vogel, Bruce Dick, Robert Lysiak, and most especially J. W. Williamson. My apologetic thanks to all the others who helped along the way whom I have neglected to mention here. Special gratitude to Jo and Ian Taylor (and to their house and the Kingdom of Fife) for the final stretch.

The support and warmth of my community of colleagues at Hobart and William Smith Colleges has been crucial. I am especially grateful to the faculty in the

English Department and Women's Studies Program, and to the Provost's Office for its consistent support of junior faculty scholarship. I am grateful as well to the Hobart and William Smith librarians, reference assistants, and InterLibrary Loan staff. Michael Hunter and Joseph Chmura deserve special mention. My thanks to the indefatigable Tina Phillip, who managed to find innumerable last-minute sources lickety-split even internationally, and also to Cindy Warren and our student workers for their kind assistance. My smart and lively students, especially in my Popular Fiction, Women's Studies, and Sexuality and American Literature classes at Hobart and William Smith, have pushed my thinking, proved (and disproved) my hunches, and added fresh insights.

I am grateful for research funding from the Hobart and William Smith Provost's Office as well as a well-timed Faculty Research Grant. This work has benefited from the vast resources of the W. E. B. Du Bois Library at the University of Massachusetts; the expertise of assistants at the Francis A. Countway Library at Harvard University; the generosity of the staff at the Laconia Public Library in Laconia, N.H.; the surprising collection at the Royal Albert Library in Brussels, Belgium, and the kind assistance of Thomas Bills at the Cleveland Health Museum.

An early version of some of the material in Chapter 3 first appeared as "Postwar Sign, Symbol, and Symptom: *The Man in the Gray Flannel Suit*," in *Cultures of Commerce: Representation and American Business Culture, 1877–1960,* edited by Elspeth Brown, Catherine Guidis, and Marina Moskovitz (New York: Palgrave/Macmillan, 2006) 277–93. Some of the ideas in Chapter 5 first appeared as "The Erasure of Grace: Reconnecting *Peyton Place* to Its Author," *Mosaic: A Journal for the Interdisciplinary Study of Literature* 42.4 (December 2009): 165–80. I am grateful to Palgrave and to the editors of *Mosaic* for permission to reuse this material.

Thanks to my beloved if far-flung extended family, Creadick-Winters-Sengel-Cook-Boswell-Vellani-Evans-Rogowski-Sherman-Holt-Dunn, who have been kind and patient with me during the seemingly interminable task of producing a book, and who have been especially tolerant of my ideas about a cultural history which some of them, in fact, lived through. I am especially grateful for my mother Susie's contagious grace with language, my father Nowell's intellectual energy, and my sister Mae's clear-eyed sense of justice.

Loving thanks, finally, to my own precious family. To Barrow and Strummer, the two little girls I wished for when I started this, you are my sweet rewards for finishing it. And most of all, to handsome Kevin, whose loving support in all things, but especially in this, has been unwavering and utterly crucial (at this very minute, he is vacuuming so I can finish): Thank you for believing this book into being. It is for you.

Perfectly Average

Introduction
Situation Normal

SNAFU

In the 1955 best seller *The Man in the Gray Flannel Suit*, the protagonist, Tom Rath, a white, middle-class, suburban commuter, experiences multiple flashbacks to his time as a paratrooper in World War II. His first recovered memory raises the notion that "normality" was something the war itself had destroyed: "It had been snafu from the beginning—situation normal, all fouled up, only they hadn't used the word 'fouled' in those days; no word had been anywhere near bad enough to express the way they felt. They had jumped at the wrong time at the wrong place, and a quarter of the company had been killed by rifle and machine-gun fire before they hit the ground."[1] The expression "SNAFU" was taken up widely during World War II: the War Office produced a series of animated short, educational/morale films starring an inept soldier named Private SNAFU; the Glenn Miller Service Orchestra released an infectious little number called "SNAFU Jump"; one hastily assembled combat force of the 9th U.S. Armored Division—culled from cooks, clerks, drivers, and other noncombatants—christened themselves "Team SNAFU" before going off to join the bloody Battle of the Bulge.[2] The term permeated civilian and postwar lexicons as well. But it is ironic to consider that during wartime, "situation normal" referred not to an absence of war but to a temporary suspension of mayhem within a constant state of warfare. This detail emphasizes the inextricable links between "normality" and war, as well as the utter relativity of the term itself.[3] Normality was, and remains, situational: it is an idea that reveals more about *when* it describes than about *what* it describes.

1

What, then, does normality reveal about postwar America? The immediate postwar decades constitute a moment when normality was most fully articulated and deeply inscribed into everyday American life. Although the "regime of the normal" certainly did not begin in 1943 nor end in 1963, I propose that normality was reified and entrenched in national discourse during this pivotal time.[4] The embrace of normality was a post-traumatic response to World War II, with Cold War consequences. Even as it was being employed at this time, however, normality was also being questioned and critiqued. The concept shifted from describing an average to prescribing an ideal; from claiming the authoritative discourse of scientific rationality to voicing a contradictory discourse of popular psychology; from offering a source of security to being a metonym for conformity and danger to "progress." But despite such contradictions, normality functioned to soothe wartime and emergent Cold War anxieties through the construction of a new "ideal for which to strive."[5]

Although the term *normality* emerged in the mid-nineteenth century, World War II was a critical moment for its linguistic redeployment.[6] The war itself had been experienced as a kind of snafu (to understate the matter), and so the pervasive felt need was to construct "situation normal," whatever that was, after decades of depression and war. Between the years 1943 and 1963, *normality* thus emerged as a "keyword" of American culture,[7] broadly disseminated through the increasingly porous domains of science, medicine, and psychiatry and an increasingly nationalized popular culture. In the postwar decades, the convergence of wartime statistics, mass media, and a pressing need to reconstitute the "social body" made normality no longer something innate or inborn, but rather a quality to be actively *pursued*. Normality was a condition that anyone could (and should) strive to achieve.[8] The painful irony was that for all Americans normality proved to be not only highly desirable but also completely beyond reach, no matter how close to it they seemed. Normality presented an impossible combination of the typical and the ideal: to achieve it, one would have to become perfectly average.

"Normal person: *See* Normality."

The hefty green library reference books known as the *Readers' Guide to Periodical Literature* are a product of their time—the 1945 volume was compiled and published in 1946, the 1946–47 volume appeared in 1948, and so on. As such, its pages document some of the significant keywords of

cultural history. In 1945, the word *normality* began to appear as a regular subject heading in the *Readers' Guide* for the first time. From then on, it is continuously listed, with varying numbers of articles cited, virtually every year until 1963. The proliferation of articles in this index allows us to chart normality's lifespan through the mass culture of the postwar era.[9]

Between the mid-1940s and the early 1960s, *normality* was characterized by a tension between its quantitative—medical, mathematical, statistical—and its qualitative—psychological, sociological, ideological—meanings and applications. Was normality to be translated as the "average," as the absence of abnormality, or as a kind of "optimum functionality"? A tug-of-war over the meaning of normality ensued in the periodical discourse, and over the course of the postwar decades the definition shifted from quantitative toward qualitative, from statistical description to psychological condition.

Most of the earliest articles indexed in the *Readers' Guide* focus explicitly on the definition of the term or at least the problem of defining it, with titles such as "Note on the Meaning of Normal," "Who Is Normal?" and "What Is Normal?" These entries, many from scientific journals, are articles that construct normality as measurable, exact, and concretely definable. Yet these articles are also characterized by a lively debate over the increasingly incompatible applications of the term in the fields of statistics, biology, medicine, and psychology—a debate which suggests that the word as well as its meaning was becoming unmoored.

In 1945, for example, the neuroanatomist C. Daly King published an essay in the *Yale Journal of Biological Medicine* proposing an "objective" and "proper" definition for the term: "In the whole field of psychology and to a lesser but increasing extent in the biological fields, we find a prevalent misuse and misapplication of the basic term, normal. . . . The misuse of the term, normal, in a sense synonymous with 'average' or 'ordinary' is a case in point, for no such identity exists. The average may be, and very often is, abnormal. The normal, on the other hand, is objectively, and properly, to be defined as *that which functions in accordance with its design.*"

King asserts that the "medical profession" remains "unconfused about the distinction" but that psychologists and mathematicians have misused the term. "What is in fact normal can never be ascertained simply by the use of any mathematical tool," he argues, "because its essential dependence is upon qualitative considerations, and mathematics deals with quantitative data." That statistical methods had "bloomed mightily" in the field of psychology meant that the same problem was transferred to new fields, so

"none of this" expansion would alter "the current misuse of the term," nor would it suddenly undo entrenched habits of its "misemployment, now hardened into scientific and even popular vocabulary."[10] King's analysis suggests that by 1945 *normality* had infiltrated popular discourse, but that its prevalence there was seen by some as a sign of mass "misemployment" or, alternatively, as the beginning of a metamorphosis in meaning.

In the late 1940s and early 1950s, as the pressures of postwar readjustment eased and a period of "affluence and anxiety" began for the American middle class, the conversation about normality became more anxious and critical.[11] Entries in the *Readers' Guide* shifted toward the fields of sociology and psychology in mass-market publications such as *Collier's* and *National Parent Teacher*. The attempt to attach scientific weight to normality persisted, but with titles such as "Is Your Child Normal?" the articles reached more profoundly into American homes and lives.

In the mid-1950s, normality moved fully into mainstream discourse. Articles in *Ladies' Home Journal, Look,* and *America* address normality in distinctly psychological terms and maintain a more prescriptive air, asking, then answering, "What *is* normal?" The distressed tone of one 1955 *Look* feature and the bleak imagery of the photo illustrating it (fig. 1) reveal that at this stage the popular media approach was serious and probing, addressing postwar issues that remained unsettled, whether sexual, psychological, financial, or physical. "Because man is driven by sex and anger impulses," the caption reads, "emotional taxes must be as inevitable in his life as fiscal ones."[12] Such articles hooked readers with worrisome questions and photographs of "real" subjects—always white and middle class.

After a decade of scientific, quantitative debates over the definition of "normal" and didactic features targeting middle-class readers with psychological or sociological strategies for achieving it, the category of normality began to be questioned. The *Readers' Guide* for 1955–57 indexes two articles—"Normal Isn't as Normal Does" and "The Coming Crisis in Psychiatry"—that signal a turning point in public attitude. In his two-part 1957 piece "The Coming Crisis in Psychiatry," Dr. Walker Percy (who went on to write several bleak novels of middle-class alienation, beginning with *The Moviegoer* in 1961), describes a ground shift in the field of psychiatry, which was increasingly "functional" in orientation and thus utterly "*unable* to take account of the predicament of modern man." The "coming crisis," he argues, was whether psychiatry would be seen as "a biological science . . . [or] a humanistic discipline." Drawing on the theories of Kierkegaard and Jung, Percy mulls over the existential "alienation" of "many

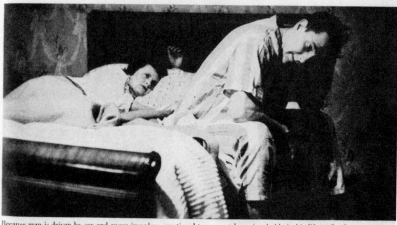

WHAT IS NORMAL?

Because man is driven by sex and anger impulses, emotional taxes must be as inevitable in his life as fiscal ones

FIGURE 1. "What Is Normal?" photograph by James Hansen, *Look*, May 1955.

a man" who nevertheless meets "every biological and cultural norm." This alienation, he suggests, cannot be accounted for by biology. He concludes that "God is absent," which means one of two things: "Either we have outgrown monotheism, and good riddance; or modern man is estranged from [all] being. . . . He has lost something, what he does not know; he knows only that he is sick unto death with it."[13] Describing the existential crisis of even the most "normal" of postwar individuals, Percy establishes what will become a major critique of normality as a hollow pursuit.

Much of the rhetoric and imagery of postwar culture was coercive—telling Americans how to be men, how to be women, how to be parents, how to be sexual, how to be political, how to dress, what to buy, where to live, how to seem: normal. The chorus of "experts" spoke in new ways during the postwar decades, and at greater volume. Advice literature, produced by churches, schools, the government, and the media, was ubiquitous. *Dr. Spock's Baby and Child Care*, for example, had sold twice as many copies by 1965 as had the all-time fiction best seller, *Peyton Place*.[14] Pamphlets and paperbacks with titles like *On Becoming a Woman*, *How to Deal with Your Tensions*, and *Making the Grade as Dad* swamped Americans readjusting to life after the war.

By the early 1960s, the popular articles on normality begin to push back against the cultural dominance of this advice literature. *Readers' Guide* entries from *Life*, *Ladies' Home Journal*, and *Science Digest* reach peak numbers and range in tone from questioning to ironic to outright parody. Where earlier features had been accompanied by the drama of photographs, these articles are illustrated exclusively with cartoons, as though normality can no longer be represented by "real" bodies. Titles ask "Who's Normal?" and answer, "Nobody, but We All Keep on Trying" or teasingly offer "How to Be Perfectly Normal without Really Trying." The author of "Who's Normal?" (*Life*, August 1960) sounded an exasperated critique of "the pamphleteers" who had urged readers "onward and upward to psychological perfection" but "have had a long turn at the rostrum." He praises a Mental Health Education conference which two years earlier had produced "an agonizing reappraisal of the barrage of advice to which the U.S. citizen has been subjected during all these post-Freudian years" and asks, "Just what is a 'normal' person? Are you, am I, is anybody normal? If we are not normal, what should we do about it? Study the pamphlets? See a psychiatrist? Shoot ourselves? Or—just possibly—relax and enjoy it?"[15]

In 1961 and 1962, both *Science Digest* and the *Atlantic Monthly* reported with bemusement and suspicion that the American Psychiatric Association had set new standards for the "normal control subject." *Science Digest*'s "Normal Man Pictured as a Contented Bore" cast normality as a distinctly negative quality (cf. fig. 2), while the *Atlantic Monthly*, in "Normal as a Fox," saw it as a put-on, a ruse. An illustration accompanying the *Atlantic* article shows an ordinary-looking man holding a sign that reads "Certified Psychiatrically Normal," but his shadow, seen on the wall behind him. is that of a wild fox:

> The normal American male is giving the psychiatrists precisely what they are looking for: a picture of a steady, loving, faithful, trustworthy, contented sap. . . . I submit that only an entire nation of men waiting for their chance to pick up a big bundle of the firm's dough and scoot with the boodle and a blonde to Brazil would attempt to put over this incredible picture of themselves. . . . [W]hat I see is . . . a crowd of perfectly foxy characters just waiting patiently. As for the psychiatrists, *I* wonder a lot about *them*.[16]

Clearly, Americans had reached a saturation point: the idea of normality had so deeply embedded itself in postwar culture that it had generated a backlash.

The new skepticism is signaled by the addition of quotation marks around the term: "Baffling Search for the 'Normal' Man," reads the title of

FIGURE 2. "100% Normal," illustration by Roy Doty, *New York Times Magazine*, 1962. Reprinted by permission of Roy Doty.

one *New York Times Magazine* feature. The authors cite a Cornell psychiatric study which found that a majority of residents in a midtown Manhattan neighborhood—fully 80 percent—"showed signs of some mental disturbance." Such statistics led them to question the "classic scientific" approach to defining mental health in the same terms as physical health: "A man is considered physically healthy, or normal, when there is an absence of disease. Similarly, a man enjoys mental health (or normality) when there is an absence of mental disease." The Cornell study had defined normality as synonymous with psychological stability, with "mental health," and yet had shown mental instability to be norm, at least in midtown Manhattan. The *Times Magazine* feature lists a dozen "baffling" and contradictory "definitions" of normality from "psychiatrists and . . . scientific journals" before its authors conclude that the search for a definition of the "normal man" had become "a safari, the quarry seemingly always on the other side of someone's booby trap. There are many definitions, almost no agreement. Variations on a theme seem infinite. There is optimism and pessimism, certainty and uncertainty."[17]

A damning discussion of normality in another *New York Times Magazine* feature, published in September 1963, marks the beginning of the end

FIGURE 3. "Home,
Normal Home,"
illustration by Roy
Doty, *New York Times
Magazine*, 1963.
Reprinted by permis-
sion of Roy Doty.

FIGURE 3. "Home, Normal Home," illustration by Roy Doty, *New York Times Magazine*, 1963. Reprinted by permission of Roy Doty.

of its life in the *Readers' Guide.* Accompanied by startling illustrations (fig. 3), the piece, titled "Close-up of the 'Normal' Wife," asserts that "a study of some perfectly adjusted Americans married to same raises a variety of questions." According to what the author calls "our scientific scrutinizers," the "normal wives" of the study can be described as "stable, contented homebodies—blithely conventional, cheerfully unambitious, happily in a rut. But can this be normality? Is this the ideal of mental health toward which we strive even in today's enlightened era?" Her conclusion is that, like the "illiterate peasant women of an earlier age," these "golden few" average American housewives must "die out," for although they, like the peasant women, were "the backbone of their society, . . . progress was made by the malcontent."[18] This "Close-up" found that the quest for normality had produced a new set of more serious problems. Comfort and stability had led to "mediocrity." Normality, particularly where embodied by "unambitious" American women, had become the enemy of progress, a threat to modernity.

At first normality was an organizing concept that spoke to the needs of Americans seeking a return to "normal"—to orthodoxy, uniformity, even conformity—after the deep disruptions of war. From the specialized realm of medical, statistical, and scientific debates about its definition ("balanced, harmonious blending of function that produce[s] good integration"), normality emerged as the standard for the mental, physical, and social well-being of the nation. Promulgated by advice literature in countless popular magazines, normality as a psychological concept became more deeply internalized in the culture. A tension emerged, however, between normality as a descriptive category, a synonym for the "average" or most usual, and normality as a prescriptive category, the embodiment of an ideal. Was normality appealing or confining? The immediate postwar desire for comfort through sameness began to clash with the growing mainstream ideology of anticommunism: normality began to seem too much like uniformity, or worse, conformity—that dangerous quality of totalitarian societies. A certain need for conformity in 1945 had become a fear of conformity by 1951. By the early 1960s normality could be invoked with a sneer: It was a concept whose instability had been exposed.

Theorizing Normality

The politics of exclusion—McCarthyism, Cold War containment, the status of women, anti-unionism, the oppression of gays and lesbians, and life under Jim Crow, for example—have been deeply analyzed by scholars of the postwar period. Fewer, however, have theorized the politics of inclusion, or the homogenizing forces of culture. How is it that some groups of people are able to imagine themselves as the same rather than different, as part of a center in relation to which all else becomes periphery? In this book, I explore how such a process can occur and—more important—how it can fail.

As a homogenizing force, normality complicates the categories of difference that have been so central to the study of culture and identity. Normality invokes race, gender, class, sexuality—but it also transcends these categories to incorporate others, such as body, mind, health, morality, location, and nation. At the same time, however, a study of normality could have been imagined only from within a context of the study of difference, as they are two sides of the same coin. Categories of "sameness" are, after all, the categories against which all "difference" has been measured.

To investigate homogenizing categories of culture requires that we ask a new set of questions: How do individuals or populations imagine themselves, or become imagined, as the *same*? What are the forces that allow people to imagine themselves as the Self against which all else becomes Other? How successful, or complete, can that process ever be? To probe these questions, I look closely at the ideological content and form of several postwar texts that coalesce around particular themes. In each chapter I approach the broad topic of normality from a different location: the science of the body; the social science of character; the material culture of class; the literary construction of sexuality; the geographies of community. I begin from the premise that these texts are not mere representations of normality but rather *constitutive* of normality in its postwar guise. Furthermore, as cultural forms, the texts are inseparable from cultural practices. In the postwar context, normality became a pursuit, garnering astonishing support and cooperation of the very individuals it seemed to oppress. Normality was generated both inside the bounds of "disciplinary institutions" such as hospitals, schools, courthouses, and prisons,[19] and outside them, as the broader cultural discourse worked to circulate and reinforce its message. Normality was most effectively disseminated and translated into the everyday lives of postwar Americans through the vehicle of mass culture.

Why *normality* and not *normalcy*, *normativity*, or *social norm*? While President Warren G. Harding had famously promised a "return to *normalcy*" after World War I, I have isolated *normality* here, rather than other shades of a similar concept, because *normality* was the specific term taken up during the post-World War II decades. Such semantics are significant in reattaching ideas about the "normal" to the historical moment that produced them.[20] In the *Readers' Guide to Periodical Literature*, these vocabularies are made visible in the form of subject headings that literally organize, index, and structure the way a culture thinks about itself. After World War II, *normality* emerged explicitly as a keyword of American culture, but more important, normality functioned as a way of ordering the world.

In contrast to conceptualizing the "normal" as an identity or a regime, then, I suggest that normality operated as an epistemological category, one enlisted to organize and make meaning of postwar experience.[21] It was more than a category of identity at times used to describe or define a particular population. Its binary logic functioned as a system, a way of knowing. Although it indeed at times exercised a kind of tyranny, at other times normality exhibited a democratizing potential. My subject, then, is not normality per se—something that cannot truly be said to exist—but rather the process by which "what looked like" normality inserted itself into American life at this time.[22]

One of the few places where normality has been specifically theorized is the growing field of disability studies.[23] There is logic to this phenomenon, of course, given that power relations are more visible to those who are positioned outside them. As Marta Russell notes, "the 19th century construction of the 'norm' is one of the most dangerous notions that the disability movement has had to confront."[24] Lennard Davis argues in his groundbreaking work, *Enforcing Normalcy: Disability, Deafness, and the Body*, that the study of normality is a necessary part of the disability studies project, just as the notion of disability had been necessary to the construction of the "normal": "Normality has to protect itself by looking into the maw of disability and then recovering from that glance. . . . One of the tasks for a developing consciousness of disability issues is . . . to reverse the hegemony of the normal and to institute alternative ways of thinking about the abnormal."[25] The "disabled" mind/body has historically been normality's constitutive Other—but not its only Other.

A second effort to theorize normality has come from the overlapping fields of lesbian and gay studies, queer theory, and the history of sexuality. Cultivating the ground prepared by Gayle Rubin, Adrienne Rich, and others, Michael Warner has examined the "unmarked category" he terms "heteronormativity."[26] Beyond showing that heterosexuality has been institutionalized as normative, Warner argues that normality's logic has seeped into lesbian and gay politics repeatedly, and dangerously. The most recent example, he proposes, is the way gay marriage initiatives threaten to divide the queer community into the "normal" (married, monogamous couples) and the deviant (all others). Again, while "normal" sexuality regularly produces "queer" as its constitutive Other, historians of sexuality have shown that this process has changed over time, and the results are always uneven. Which particular homosexuality is being produced? Which heterosexuality? And which "normal"?[27]

In his work *The Heart of Whiteness: Normal Sexuality and Race in America, 1880–1940*, Julian Carter has extended queer theory's investigations of normality to intersect with whiteness studies.[28] Carter argues that early twentieth-century American cultural discourses produced a new concept of the "normal" to help signify American civilization. Fusing "whiteness" and "heterosexuality," he argues, the "normal" became a substitute for both while also "eliding" both. Carter's work is historically situated, suggesting how normality functioned in U.S. culture between its nineteenth-century origins discussed by Lennard Davis and the post–World War II period under discussion here. Although his argument forges a critical link between race theory and queer theory, because his interwar historical evidence does not invoke the "normal" per se, Carter's work seems to imprint the past with a more contemporary conception of heteronormativity.

From this scholarly work on normality I draw two insights. First, we cannot adequately theorize normality through the lenses of ability, class, gender, sexuality, or race alone—or even in combination—because normality's epistemological sweep and capacity to organize experience extends far beyond these categories. And second, we can never fully understand the power and influence of normality without a rigorous evaluation of how the concept is generated and disseminated in its own historically specific contexts.

Historicizing Normality

Scholarly reevaluations of the private lives of such public midcentury American figures as Betty Friedan and Alfred Kinsey demonstrate the deep investments in "keeping up appearances" people made in the postwar world. Daniel Horowitz illustrates how Friedan erased her own radical past as a labor journalist in the 1940s and '50s to construct her alienated-suburban-housewife persona for *The Feminine Mystique*.[29] Sex researcher Alfred Kinsey's public image as a "tweedy academic and family man" was, his biographer James H. Jones argues, "carefully controlled" to obscure his own "secret life [as] a homosexual and . . . masochist who . . . pursued an interest in extreme sexuality with increasing compulsiveness."[30] What does it mean that two of the most forward-thinking intellectuals of the time felt compelled to do their work behind carefully constructed facades?

One of the most important discoveries I made during this project is that normality proved to be impossible to achieve—not only for those tacitly excluded from its parameters by race, class, body, or other "difference," but also for those who purportedly should have embodied it most completely. This discovery casts a new light on the imagined postwar populace: the alienation of those white, middle-class suburban-dwellers may have stemmed not from their "fantasies" of victimization, not from their "affluence and anxiety," but from the utter impossibility of achieving normality no matter how close to it they seemed.[31] This "history of an idea," then, requires a rethinking of the history of the postwar period and beyond. For though the concept of the "normal" certainly predated World War II, it appears that something in the postwar milieu placed normality under the lens.

The years between 1945 and 1963 constitute a distinctive historical moment bracketed by the end of World War II on one side and the assassination of President John F. Kennedy on the other. These years cohere as an era, an idea supported by the 1945 appearance and 1963 disappearance of *normality* in the *Readers' Guide*. The end of the war had brought a need for a "return to normal"—but a return for whom? Returning African American veterans, through the Double V Campaign, had hoped for a better postwar life, yet it would be 1948 before President Harry S. Truman made the first symbolic move toward civil rights by desegregating the Armed Forces. The mechanism of the GI Bill was also marked by uneven, unequal application, reinforcing the exclusion of many women, poor, and minority Americans while circumscribing a wide and diverse group of white American males with a new "sameness." Jewish Americans continued to confront an anti-Semitic America: a spate of postwar narratives about American anti-Semitism (such as the novel and film *Gentleman's Agreement*) and a major Jewish literary renaissance in the 1950s expressed the desire for change. World War II was an important watershed for gays and lesbians as well, launching a "coming out" process that continued to build, despite repression during the Cold War. For many American gays and lesbians, then, a "return" to a prewar "normality" was neither desirable nor possible after such a seismic shift. Many American women who had experienced new work lives as a crucial part of the war effort also felt conflicted about a "return" to "normal" roles. And even that white, heterosexual, middle-class "man in the gray flannel suit" who had spent the prewar years struggling to make a living experienced ambivalence about the breadwinner role to which he was expected to return.

What was at stake, then, in the impulse to "normalize"? When was normality enforced or coerced, and when was it embraced for its productive or democratizing potential? What power did "normality" have that would lead thousands of women to voluntarily scrutinize their own bodies for a "Norma Look-Alike Contest" or hundreds of undergraduates to offer themselves to be measured for the "Harvard Study of Normal Men"? How did "normality" make meaning in ways that were worth the cost? In the following chapters I explore these questions to reveal the equally intriguing phenomenon that normality always existed alongside its own critique.

The trajectory I have documented in the postwar periodical literature—from the scientific to the broadly popular—is mirrored in the loosely chronological structure of this book. The following chapters parallel shifting attitudes toward normality and at the same time work to reveal the range of texts and sites from which and on which this potent idea was generated. Folding together scientific studies, material culture, social sciences research, film and television, public policies, statistics, and a variety of literary forms, I trace the way normality was both implicitly and explicitly constituted around body, character, class, sex, and community—some of the most pressing issues for postwar Americans eager to construct a renewed nation.[32] By isolating normality as a subject of history, and by acknowledging that it is, in fact, subject *to* history, I aim to destabilize its continuing function as a powerful organizer of ideas and identities.

1

Model Bodies, Normal Curves

In late April of 1999, I stepped off a streetcar in Dresden, Germany, and walked down a long driveway to face a looming brick and plate-glass structure. Its facade was intimidating: four-story columns reached up to a broad white frieze emblazoned with huge gold letters: DEUTSCHES HYGIENE-MUSEUM. A long banner falling from the top of the front read *Der Neue Mensch: Obsessionen des 20. Jahrhunderts*—"The New Man: Obsessions of the Twentieth Century." I had come here to see "Normman and Norma," sculptures of the "average" American male and female body, which had been shipped over from Cleveland to Dresden for this special exhibit.

Norma and Normman were designed in 1942 by the sexologist Robert L. Dickinson, using "anthropometric" measurements, incorporating "the most exhaustive data ever assembled" following "a lifetime of research." The models were sculpted by Abram Belskie, who had collaborated with Dickinson on a larger collection of reproductive models in the 1930s which, along with Norm and Norma, were donated to the Cleveland Health Museum in 1945.[1] As I neared the entrance of the German Hygiene Museum, I noticed the white paint was peeling, the brick grimy, the gold letters mottled, the modern edges dented and worn with age and disrepair.

On the way to Dresden I had been reading, morbidly, Kurt Vonnegut's *Slaughterhouse Five*. And so as our train slowly wound its way toward the station, I found myself looking out the windows trying to reconstruct another Dresden, the one before the infamous Allied firebombing in World War II, which I had just read about in the novel. The German Hygiene Museum had opened in 1930 but was destroyed in the bombing; after the war it was reconstructed as the brick and glass structure now towering before me.

15

Norm and Norma were much smaller than I had expected. Sculpted at half life-size, they stood on one of several large, slowly revolving display tables filled with exhibits of skulls, jawbones, and racial phenotype charts. The statues were positioned just after phrenology, just before glossy photos of lithe young Aryan bodies doing calisthenics, and alongside the original maps and plans for Auschwitz. According to the exhibit's catalog, "the fundamental contradiction of '*der neue mensch*,' the role model for dictators as well as revolutionists, men of enlightenment, and humanists, is the subject of [this] exhibit. . . . The German Hygiene Museum . . . is inextricably linked with the shape of the image of *der neue mensch*, and that's why it is its duty to come closer to the history they have in common."[2] Like me, Norm and Norma were a bit dislocated and far from home. But their sojourn in Dresden and their integration into this chronology had a certain logic.

Divine Average

Despite their diminutive stature, the figures of Norm and Norma make a striking impression: they are strong, youthful, hard bodies that do not seem average at all but, rather, more of a *divine* average. An übermensch and his überwench (fig. 4). The bodies themselves—young, hairless, erect, and smooth, Norma's with pert breasts and Norm's with broad shoulders—are far more eroticized, perfected, and fetishized than "medical models" might be expected to be. Their poses are barely differentiated, formal and rigid, as if in a military at-attention stance. Together, they suggest a combination of the militarized tone of wartime iconography and the strapping, idealized worker-bodies seen in the public art and sculpture of the New Deal era. But it is their calm, forward-staring glances, their classical features beneath 1940s wigs, that are the most unsettling, and the most startlingly reminiscent of the bodies and faces constructed by the totalitarian propaganda of Nazi Germany and Stalinist Russia. The Aryan look and eugenicist overtones of Norm and Norma were not aberrations, but signs of a midcentury obsession. Their boldly European features, their alabaster whiteness, their youthful, able bodies reveal what "normality" had been designed to include and exclude.

Anyone considering Norm and Norma would immediately be struck by the significance of their names. "Normman" was purposefully spelled with two *m*'s, emphasizing that he signified the Norm(al)-man. If the statues began as symbolic representations of an average—composite figures of a

FIGURE 4. "Norma" and "Normman" models, Dickinson-Belskie collection, Cleveland Health Museum photographs. Images used by permission of The Cleveland Museum of Natural History.

particularly large sample—their names began a process of recasting them
as the embodiments of normality, a much more problematic notion. An
average is drawn from a set of figures that may change over time, while
normality is characterized by an inherent dichotomy: one is *either* normal
or abnormal. The slippage in meanings attached to these model bodies par-
allels the postwar shifts in normality itself as an epistemological category.

Feminist and postmodernist scholars have theorized the body as a sign,
as a site for relations of power, and as a locus for the "performance" of gender. Historians have revealed that the body is subject *to* as well as subject
of history: recent histories of beauty, medicine, physical culture, sexuality,
and science explore how humans have redefined themselves at the most
corporeal levels across time. I build from the position that our understandings of the body are "mediated" through language and culture and are
always "subject to historical change."[3]

What historical forces made normal bodies a subject of interest at this
time? How do we explain the impulse to measure, quantify, and define
normality with such purported scientific precision? Who was included—
and excluded—in compiling this norm? What would be the lingering effects of a normality cast in a tangible, material form? Norm and Norma
were compiled from anthropometric measurements, sculpted as part of
a series of a sexologist's reproductive models, and framed, in part, by eugenicist politics. What anthropometry, sexology, and eugenics shared was
an interest in bringing scientific methods to problems of the social body.
Since World War I, but especially during and after World War II, science,
government, and commerce made use of GI measurements and statistics
in their efforts to construct a "standard" American body, extending the
ongoing project of the "mismeasure of man."[4]

Eugenics, a theory of the scientific perfectibility of the human race, was
first defined by the British biologist Francis Galton in 1883 and widely
accepted and applied in the United States as well as in Germany throughout the early twentieth century (and after). In the pre-Nazi era, German
eugenicists expressed admiration for "American leadership" in eugenicist
sterilization programs and "communicated" with American colleagues
about "strategies."[5] The field of eugenics developed in two directions, "positive eugenics," which encouraged the birthrate of the "fit," and "negative
eugenics," which discouraged the birthrate of the "unfit." As part of a set
of reproductive models, and as "perfect" specimens, Norm and Norma
reflected a positive eugenics agenda.[6]

An examination of Dickinson and Belskie's methods reveals that their
models represented only a specific kind of body. There was a not-seeing in

their sampling, a blindness to other kinds of bodies—bodies that trouble normality but that, according to the theorist Judith Butler, are utterly *necessary* for bodies like Norm's and Norma's to become "bodies that matter."[7] Because they were so tangible, Norm and Norma materialized the notion of a normal body and inscribed its boundaries for all to see.

First, according to these model bodies, normality includes only the youthful and the beautiful. Norm and Norma's bodies are muscular and fit largely because only eighteen to twenty-four year olds were measured. These were the "average American male and female in the full flush of early maturity," explained the physical anthropologist Harry L. Shapiro, who chaperoned Norm and Norma through the national media. "The female figure," he wrote in *Natural History*, "represents the norm or average American woman of 18 to 20 years of age. 'Normman,' her male counterpart, is modeled on averages for 20-year-old males."[8] Yet Norm and Norma were said to be unprecedented in their representativeness, because they were compiled from such a vast pool of data including, according to Shapiro, "men in the army during the first World War, special studies of the old American stock, series of college men and women from various parts of the country, a sample measured at the recent World's Fair in Chicago, insurance company records, and extensive data obtained by the Bureau of Home Economics on 15,000 American women who were measured in detail . . . for sizing women's ready-made garments."[9]

The use of large numbers of college students' measurements bespeaks the limited age range of the sample. Youthfulness was intrinsic to their beauty, as Henry Shapiro reported: "Norma and Normman, although they were designed to conform with the average adult before the onset of the ravages of age, exhibit a harmony of proportion that seems far indeed from the usual or average." Shapiro concludes that both the statues and the measurements "leave little doubt that the [American] figure is improving esthetically."[10] Shapiro's choice of words is suggestive of the links between normality and war: the "ravages of age" echoes "ravages of war," while a bodily "harmony of proportion" invokes the "harmony of peace." These youthful, beautiful bodies—compiled, notably, largely from prewar subjects—stand strong, unscathed by war or by the shortages on the home front.

Second, Dickinson and Belskie's construction of fully developed male and female bodies—the simple division of bodies into Norms and Normas—communicated the importance of gender in defining normality (and subtly encoded reproductive heterosexuality into the definition as well). In the face of the destabilization of gender roles during the war, Dickinson and Belskie helped to reinscribe and reify a binary gender system. Furthermore, as "reproductive models," Norm and Norma worked as medical metonyms for the male and female reproductive organs, which Dickinson and Belskie also measured, quantified, and sculpted in detail (though these models were not so easy to display).[11] Norm and Norma were somewhat peripheral to the bulk of the Dickinson-Belskie collection of birth and reproductive models, and they were sculpted later. But it would be Norm and Norma who would spend the longest time in the public eye.

Third, a glance at these two statues reveals that normality was both implicitly and explicitly constructed as *white*. Subtly cast into the design of their features, figured from the disproportionate thousands of white subjects in the sample, normality's whiteness was also manifest in their polished white plaster surfaces, then declared by the labels Dickinson affixed to them: "Native White American."[12] This overtly racialized nationalism lent scientific credibility to nativist and eugenicist sentiments of the times.

The whiteness of the measured subjects was also regularly emphasized in Shapiro's comments: "[Norma] is modeled from . . . thousands of native white Americans," he writes, carefully linking the nation to the Anglo-Saxon body.[13] Such remarks can be read as throwbacks to racial taxonomies of the late nineteenth century, although some coverage made claims for the statues' racial and ethnic inclusiveness at the same time: "Norma is the product of the American melting pot," Josephine Robertson asserted in the *Cleveland Plain Dealer*.[14] By coding normality white, Dickinson and Belskie may have been enacting the "melting pot" assimilation of white ethnics, but by the same stroke they simultaneously perpetuated the segregation of other groups by excluding them from definitions of both "American" and "normal."

Finally, Norm and Norma were clearly defined as able-bodied. "Norma has a good constitution and mental stability," Health Museum director Dr. Bruno Gebhard reported in the *Cleveland Plain Dealer*. Animating the inanimate, he elaborated on her "great mental adaptability": "During the war she indicated some of her potentialities when she undertook work previously done almost exclusively by men. Whether she would go so far as to use a bayonet, as did the Russian women, I am not sure, but I believe she will do well what is required of her. For certainly she is a strong-bodied, competent young lady."[15] An emphasis on the strength and capability of these normal bodies emerges here again, but with nascent Cold War overtones. Against the bayonet-wielding Russian women, the "strong-bodied"

Norma remains a "lady." Such attention to the strength and competence of these normal bodies signals the link between normality and the need to remake American society.

Norm and Norma, although specifically defined as white, youthful, and strong, were held up as the correct bodies, the ideal bodies to breed an American future. As one headline read, "Evolution Outlook Bright if Model Girl Weds Wisely." Dr. Daniel Quiring, a professor of comparative anatomy at Case Western Reserve, explained this vision in boldly eugenicist terms: "By proper selection in matrimony many of the ills that human flesh is heir to can be virtually eradicated. . . . We can, by taking thought and using the same selective methods as with plants and lower animals, insure this country a stronger, healthier population." Quiring also calmed fears that Norma's increased height in comparison to her "Victorian Grandmother" was a sign of anything "freakish": "Dr. Quiring said that he didn't believe that Norma . . . would grow much taller, for according to studies by Galton of tall persons mating, and tall and short persons mating, the offspring tended to stay within the normal range. . . . That [Norma] will just keep on improving physically and mentally is in the forecast."[16] Normality, then, meant being superior in function but average in form.

This discourse of strong, able bodies seems deeply ironic, even cruel, in light of the return of millions of veterans, many of whom were wounded, at the very moment when "demobilization" and reintegration were the "hottest postwar problem plaguing legislators."[17] According to David A. Gerber, by the war's end, approximately 671,000 Americans had been wounded, 300,000 of them requiring long-term hospitalization and often systematic rehabilitation. As for mental injuries, "as many as 500,000 men were said to have been hospitalized for neuropsychiatric causes in the last year of the war alone."[18] Lennard Davis writes in *Enforcing Normalcy* that "to be visibly disabled was to lose one's full nationality, which should be an invisibility, a neutrality, a degree zero of citizenly existence."[19] William Wyler's 1946 film *The Best Years of Our Lives* attempted to address this contradiction by featuring a visibly disabled veteran on film.

Based on a *Time* magazine article about the problems facing returning veterans and their families, the story was filmed "on location" in Cincinnati, Ohio. The film featured an amateur actor, Harold Russell, a real-life double amputee who had lost his hands in an explosives accident at military training camp. Despite fears that viewers would not accept a "real disability," Wyler conducted audience research and insisted on including Russell in the film. The film won seven Oscars, including Best Picture. Russell

won two—one for Best Supporting Actor and a "special" Oscar for giving
hope and inspiration to other veterans through his performance. In this,
the Academy reflected what Gerber calls the "sharply divided consciousness" in postwar America, which "both honored the veteran and feared his
potential to disrupt society."[20] Continued anxieties about masculinity and
the disabled body help to explain the surprising tendency in most local and
national publicity to discuss *Norma*, not Normman, as the representative
postwar citizen.

The statues themselves became a tangible sign, object signifiers of the
idea of a normal body: white, youthful, reproductive, able, and intact. All
"Other" bodies then became a kind of absent presence: the bodies of "minority" veterans, the bodies of returning disabled veterans, bodies (such
as President Roosevelt's) crippled by polio, the emaciated or incinerated
bodies of holocaust and war, the laboring bodies of African Americans who
had migrated to northern cities, the displaced bodies turned out of Japanese internment camps, the bodies of newly arrived Asian "war brides"—
the list is long. In the face of all of these "Other" bodies, America instead
chose to define, cast in plaster, and parade a definition of the normal body
that was explicitly young, able, white, and strong.[21] The normality Norm
and Norma purported to represent, then, was imaginary. Even with such
"comprehensive" data supporting them, what they truly embodied was a
fantasy, a way for Americans to imagine a perfect postwar citizenship.

Sound Bodies

In July of 1945, Norm and Norma, along with the larger collection of
Dickinson-Belskie medical reproductive models, were acquired "for display and distribution" by the Cleveland Health Museum. Their acquisition
was front-page news, along with the latest war horrors and struggles on the
home front: war headlines—"Goering Notebook Intrigue," stark images
of a U.S. destroyer left "Battered but Afloat" after attacks by "Jap Suicide
Planes," the federal takeover of a striking Goodyear plant. In the midst of
such chaos, "Nation's Ideal Boy and Girl Come to City—In Sculpture"
creates a striking contrast.[22]

The language of war had permeated everyday life. Part of the reason for
the interest in the normal body, then, seems to have been fear: fear that
being "soft" of body was what had made Americans vulnerable to the attack on Pearl Harbor, and fear that Americans might still be unprepared
for whatever the future would hold. The turn to normality spoke of a need

for stability after six years of war, while the sense of victory led Americans to see themselves as a people against whom others should be measured: the norm.

Robert Latou Dickinson was one of the most renowned sex researchers of the early twentieth century. A practicing obstetrician/gynecologist for forty years at Brooklyn Hospital, he was a president of the American Gynecological Society, a secretary of the National Committee on Maternal Health from its 1923 founding, and its honorary chair after 1937. Dickinson primarily saw himself as a crusader against the prudery and shame associated with human reproduction. An active promoter of birth control (he cofounded the Planned Parenthood Association), for some he brought "respectability and an aura of solid professional authority" to a controversial movement that had been dominated largely by "feminists and lay organizers."[23] Well before Kinsey's studies were published, R. L. Dickinson aimed to treat sexual reproduction with the kind of frankness that only science could give it: "In sex education, more important than *information* is *attitude*. To hide, to hush, to hurry past is giving way to a modern directness of approach and dignity of speech. . . . [W]e have never scientifically studied sex behavior until now."[24] Dickinson made national headlines with his dramatic plaster life models of the stages of birth and other aspects of human reproduction when portions of that collection were exhibited at the 1939 New York World's Fair. He saw his medical models as an especially effective way of making the processes of human reproduction more public, of educating people about their own bodies not just with visual aids but with tactile scale models rendered from live studies: "What no picture or movie can show, *the model can*," he claimed. "Why should not the highest art serve medicine and health teaching?"[25]

Norm and Norma were designed using anthropometric methods. Anthropometry, or the science of comparative measuring of human bodies, dates from the late eighteenth century. Systematic anthropometric studies began to increase rapidly in the nineteenth century, as a method employed by the burgeoning field of anthropology. By 1875, medical and scientific anthropometric organizations were established, concurrent with the rise of standardization as an international concern. Dudley A. Sargent had produced "scientifically constructed" figures of the "average young man and woman of the Gay Nineties," compiling them from his measurements of Harvard and Radcliffe students in the late 1900s.[26] And similar practices continue today for "human engineering" projects such as seating, helmets, and uniforms.[27] But anthropometry saw a marked increase in popularity in the 1940s.[28] Although anthropomorphic methods were first standardized in Europe, in 1941 Harry L. Shapiro founded a small, short-lived methods journal in America.[29] Because the normal body was tied to anthropometry, it was highly quantified, a body based on measuring and charting, as in the notion of a "normal curve."[30] The wartime military had itself been a normalizing force, dividing its members into "fits" and "misfits," while deriving from both populations a massive set of statistics that would be put to postwar uses.[31]

Scientists and social scientists found multiple opportunities for the application of anthropometrics, and soldiers became the ready-made subjects from whom they could extrapolate fresh claims about the "national average."[32] For example, one 1945 *New York Times* feature describes the army's Chemical Warfare Service's measuring the heads of more than three thousand GIs to establish "three gas mask sizes which [would] fit every soldier in the Army." The authors of the head-size study note that the results would be applied in "civilian life after the war" in designing products that would "accommodate the body of the average man."[33] Yet the particulars of recruiting strategies combined with "a host of sociological variables" render military populations more specialized than representative: "[they are] neither biological populations nor random samples of biological populations represented in the U.S. and its territories."[34] Anthropometry, therefore, was not so much accommodating as inventive of the "body of the average man."

A related practice that sheds further light the scientific search for the normal body is somatotyping. First introduced by W. H. Sheldon in 1940, somatotyping is, essentially, anthropometry using photographs of nude subjects instead of live ones. Sheldon devised quantitative methods for describing and assessing the morphology of the human form, dividing it into three shape and composition scales: endomorph, mesomorph, and ectomorph. By the late forties and early fifties, "Sheldonism" was mainstream.[35] Thousands of men and women enrolled at Ivy League and Seven Sisters colleges throughout the 1940s, 1950s, and 1960s were photographed nude as part of such research projects (and many of the more famous ones—Madeleine Albright, George W. Bush, and Hillary Rodham Clinton reportedly among them—live in not a little terror of those images coming back to haunt them).[36] From these photographs and others, Sheldon produced an oversized volume, *Atlas of Men*, which opens with the complaint that "the medical profession has never had available satisfactory norms even for such an elemental datum, for example, as bodily weight. . . . [A] doctor has been in a position to tell the patient only what the *average* happens to be for men of the same age and stature," but "the average weight of men your age and stature may miss your own normal or optimal weight by seventy pounds."[37]

Sheldon sought to define "norms" for the human body, which he saw as distinct from the "average." Norms were "optimal," or ideal, figures. Sheldon, himself a eugenicist, also believed that somatotypes were genetic marks, "unwavering determinants of character regardless of transitory weight change."[38] The *Atlas* included volumes of "standard somatotype photographs" of nude male subjects, their faces and genitalia blotted out, all taken from Sheldon's total sample of 46,000 men, including "Negroes or Negro-White mixtures" and "Jewish" subjects, but omitting the few "Orientals" in hopes of later conducting a "satisfactory comparative study . . . in their native settings."[39] These images, along with accompanying essays and appendixes, were intended to promote and standardize somatotyping methods, but they were also, clearly, echoes of such nineteenth-century race science methods as phenotyping and phrenology. For Sheldon, somatotypes would produce a much-needed "biological identification tag" for researchers, "a general human taxonomy."[40] This context of midcentury pseudoscience is important to remember when considering Norm and Norma. The public and private uses to which these "medical" models were put were bound up with the rhetoric of evolution and race, class and character, and investments in the perfectibility of the human race.

The earliest large public exhibition of the Dickinson-Belskie reproductive models was held at the 1939 World's Fair, although Norm and Norma were not yet among them. Some seven hundred thousand people filed by to see the mysteries of the human fetus in utero, represented in three dimensions and sculpted by Dickinson's colleague Abram Belskie.[41] According to Bruno Gebhard, who worked as a "technical consultant" for the Medical and Public Health Exhibit at the fair, the number of people in attendance made this exhibit "the most successful attempt in mass health education."[42] One of the most popular 1939 World's Fair features was the "Typical American Family" contest, a promotion held in forty-seven states, which culminated almost two decades of "Fitter Family" contests. These contests, writes Christina Cogdell, "upheld healthy, native-born white families with two or more children as the proper eugenic norm to which American couples should aspire."[43]

The Cleveland Health Museum itself was an institution invested in the production and dissemination of discourses on normal bodies. Founded as the first permanent museum of health in the United States, it opened its doors in November of 1940, with a distinctive "emphasis . . . on education and not on collection." According to its first director, Dr. Bruno Gebhard, the museum featured "man's normal growth and development," and its aim was "better health for more people, it being understood that health is a state of physical and mental ease." By 1950, according to Gebhard, a half dozen museums of hygiene existed, working to address "something which medical museums had neglected: preventative medicine, or hygiene."[44] Gebhard mentions as a "milestone" in these efforts the 1930 International Hygiene Exposition held in Dresden, where the "Transparent Man" was first exhibited.

Gebhard had been curator of the German Hygiene Museum from 1927 to 1935 and had helped organize the Transparent Man exhibit before taking up his post in Cleveland.[45] The Transparent Man—a clear plastic sculpture of a human male body, with visible circulatory and nervous systems, organs, etc.—was part of the exhibit I attended in Dresden, and had originated there. His counterpart, "Juno" the Transparent Woman, was installed in the Cleveland Health Museum in 1950. The construction of both models was overseen by Franz Tschakert, a former German Hygiene Museum worker who had fled to Cologne and established a workshop to produce such models for new institutions. Although Gebhard refused to join the Nazi Party, in 1934–35 as curator he accompanied one of his "positive eugenics" exhibits on a U.S. tour, promoting the Third Reich's race hygiene and sterilization programs to audiences in at least six American cities.[46] When Gebhard became director of the Cleveland Health Museum in 1940, he had just met Robert L. Dickinson at the New York World's Fair the year before. The two men shared an interest in public health and a background in eugenics. As a gesture of respect for Gebhard, Dickinson . donated his entire collection of models (then valued at $25,000) to the Cleveland museum for display as well as reproduction.[47]

The Cleveland Health Museum, like the German Hygiene Museum and others of its kind, combined education, edification, and aesthetics in representing the human form to its human visitors. Celebrating the acquisition of the new collection in a luncheon address, Dickinson reported that "the Dickinson-Belskie collection includes 100 models with 300 parts now possessed by Cleveland Health Museum for distribution to marriage counselors, clinics, medical schools, and elsewhere."[48] Norm and Norma were aesthetic objects designed to be put on display in the public space of a museum. But they were also designed to be disseminated (fig. 5). They

CLEVELAND HEALTH MUSEUM
8811 Euclid Avenue   Cleveland 6, Ohio
R.L. DICKINSON COLLECTION

"Norma" (No. 100)   "Normman" (No. 101)

We are happy to announce that these two fine
statuettes are now available.

Years of research preceeded the sculpturing of
these masterpieces demonstrating the average
male and female between the ages of 18 and 25.
Dr. R. L. Dickinson and Mr. Abram Belskie are
recognized as the world's two outstanding
geniuses in reproducing, scientifically accur-
ate in every detail, the human body. Figures
are one-half life size and portable.

You will admire the fine finish which may be
had in white, terra cotta, or old bronze, highlighting the beautiful body curves. Composition
of the finest art plaster, heavily reinforced
with two steel bars running from the head to the
base, insuring safety in handling.

We can supply three different types of display
pedestals, either square or circular
in design finished to your specifications in
enamel, stained or varnished wood. The pedestal
also will serve as a packing case.

Weight of statuettes   —25 pounds.
Weight of pedestal -- case - 30 pounds.

Prices:
"Norma"........$75.00..."Normman"........$85.00
Pedestal Case...................$15.00-$20.00

F.O.B. Cleveland, Ohio   November, 1945

FIGURE 5. Order form for "Norma" and "Normman," Cleveland Health Museum, Nov. 1945. Images used by permission of The Cleveland Museum of Natural
History.

were reproduced, recast in plaster, and sold to doctors and teachers across
America—$75.00 for a Norma, but $85.00 for a Norm. They were available in "white, terra cotta, or old bronze" to highlight the "beautiful body
curves."

Norm and Norma were presented to the public, then, as embodiments
of normality, as representatives of a "whole," and as aesthetic objects to be
purchased, studied, and emulated. The sculpting of these statistical ab-
stractions into pleasing forms, the acquisition and display of them by the

Cleveland Health Museum, the physical reproduction and distribution of them to "medical, nursing and health groups,"[49] and their eventual reproduction through media coverage helped to reify them as more representative of the "real" than any previous body models had been. At the same time, such practices fetishized Norm and Norma as embodiments of an ideal.

On November 27, 1945, the fifth anniversary of the founding of the Cleveland Health Museum, a reception was held for more than six hundred guests at the Rainbow Room of the Hotel Carter. Dr. Robert Latou Dickinson spoke briefly as the guest of honor. "Norma," recently acquired, was "one of the Luncheon decorations."[50] The use of Norma as a decoration reveals that even within the context of a public health agenda, the female figure was singled out to be eroticized and objectified in not-so-subtle ways. And yet a yawning silence surrounds the subject of Norm in most of the publicity about the models. Published statistics from the study were precise regarding Norma and either vague or "unavailable" for Norm. Such inattention is noteworthy, because the male body had historically been the representative for "humanity" in cultural anthropology, medicine, and other contexts. But now, the female body, Norma's body, became the stand-in for the postwar citizen, the focus for attention and objectification in the public eye.

A Hypothetical Individual

If Norm and Norma were produced in a sexologist's context of educating Americans about reproduction, they were consumed in a different context. As Norm and Norma went public, they found an environment in which American citizens, focused on a return to normal, were easily seduced by the idea of the measurement, discipline, and perfectibility of the human form.

On August 6, 1945, the first of two atomic bombs dropped on Japan signaled the imminent end of World War II. A month later, on September 9, the *Cleveland Plain Dealer* announced a "Norma Look-Alike Contest" (fig. 6). Jointly sponsored by the paper, the Cleveland Health Museum, the YWCA, and other local organizations, the contest was promoted in the *Plain Dealer* through September 23—the first two weeks following VJ Day. The winner would receive $100 in war bonds.

Inspiring weeks of running coverage in the *Plain Dealer*, feature stories in national publications, and even a guest appearance on television, Norm partment, the British government and the Allied military command in the India-Burma theater, while (Continued on Page 2. Column 1)

ARGENTINA O. K.'S CHARTER
BUENOS AIRES, Sept. 8—(P)—
The Argentine cabinet ratified the United Nations charter today.

fied unofficially as a B-29, approximately five miles from here last night.

J. H. Kerr, editor of the Randolph Press, said 10 bodies had been removed from the plane and taken to Fort McClellan, Ala.

Kerr said the ship appeared to "explode before it struck."

He was taken to St. John's Hospital where physicians said he had suffered a possible skull fracture and chest injuries. His condition is serious.

Other attendants jacked up the car to get him out before arrival of a fire rescue squad, which took him to the hospital.

Are You Norma, Typical Woman?
Search to Reward Ohio Winners

BY JOSEPHINE ROBERTSON

A search for Norma, the typical American woman, will begin today in Ohio in order to discover whether there is actually a woman whose measurements coincide with those of an average computed from measurements of 18,000 women all over the United States and represented by the statue Norma at the Cleveland Health Museum, 8811 Euclid Avenue.

The search is sponsored by the Cleveland Plain Dealer and Cleveland Health Museum with the cooperation of the Academy of Medicine of Cleveland, the School of Medicine and Flora Stone Mather College of Western Reserve University, the Cleveland Board of Education and the Y. W. C. A. The chief motive of the search is to stimulate interest in the physical

development of the American people.

Awards of $100, $50 and $25 War Bonds will go to those women who most closely approximate the average as indicated by the statue. There in addition are 10 awards of $10 each in war stamps.

Although the statue Norma represents the composite of measurements of women from 18 to 20, the search includes all women from 18 to 80, for it is believed that if there is a mother or grandmother or great-grandmother within these ages who has kept her figure through the years so that she approximates Norma she certainly deserves an award.

The figure, Norma, is the result of collaboration by Dr. Robert L. Dickinson, physician, and Abram Belskie, sculptor, of New York, who have produced a series of anatomical models valued at $25,000, which

has been purchased by Cleveland Health Museum. The 15,000 young women whom Norma typifies include college students and representatives of farming, business, industry and many other walks of life.

Norma is the product of the American melting pot. In the beginning of this country's history there was no truly typical American woman unless in was Pocahontas. Settlements were made largely according to European nationalities and there was not much intermingling. In the latter part of the 18th century certain European scientists began to think of Americans as a distinctive type, but as an inferior one due to what they termed inferior environment.

Thomas Jefferson refuted these critics with tables of comparative weights. But he wasn't believed very generally abroad.

(Continued on Page 8, Column 3)

FIGURE 6. "Are You Norma, Typical Woman?" *Cleveland Plain Dealer,* 9 Sept. 1945, 1. ©1945 The Plain Dealer. All rights reserved. Reprinted with permission.

and Norma became two of the "most celebrated and widely publicized" model bodies of the midcentury.[51] Details of the contest and later national publicity about the model bodies suggest the degree to which Americans were willing to discipline their own bodies in pursuit of normality.

The entry form itself (fig. 7) was prescriptive, a grid with a limited range of body measurements preprinted. Rather than writing in their actual measurements, contestants had to check the box closest to the one they matched. Normality, it seemed, had strict parameters: though theoretically the contest was open to any woman from "18 to 80," only those with a waist between 25 and 35 inches and a weight between 118 and 139 pounds were candidates. Nevertheless, thousands of women measured themselves—or allowed others to measure them, as the sponsors recommended. The article "Here Are Tips on Measuring Figure for 'Norma' Contest" ran the second day of the contest. Front-page copy suggested that

SEARCH-FOR-NORMA ENTRY

Norma Editor: Please enter my dimensions as given below in the "Search for Norma:"

NAME _____

ADDRESS _____

CITY _____ ZONE_____

OCCUPATION _____

AGE _____ SINGLE or MARRIED   Number of CHILDREN_____
                (circle which)

Dimensions Table in Inches and Pounds

HEIGHT	58	59	60	61	62	63	64	65	66	67	68
	58½	59½	60½	61½	62½	63½	64½	65½	66½	67½	68½
BUST	30	31	32	33	34	35	36	37	38	39	40
	30½	31½	32½	33½	34½	35½	36½	37½	38½	39½	40½
WAIST	25	26	27	28	29	30	31	32	33	34	35
	25½	26½	27½	28½	29½	30½	31½	32½	33½	34½	35½
HIPS	34	35	36	37	38	39	40	41	42	43	44
	34½	35½	36½	37½	38½	39½	40½	41½	42½	43½	44½
THIGH	15	16	17	18	19	20	21	22	23	24	25
	15½	16½	17½	18½	19½	20½	21½	22½	23½	24½	25½
CALF	10	10½	11	11½	12	12½	13	13½	14	14½	15
ANKLE	8¼	8½	8¾	9	9¼	9½	9¾	10	10¼	10½	10¾
FOOT	7¾	8	8¼	8½	8¾	9	9¼	9½	9¾	10	10¼
WEIGHT	118	120	122	124	126	128	130	132	134	136	138
	119	121	123	125	127	129	131	133	135	137	139

INSTRUCTIONS:

MEASURE bust at the fullest point, waist at the narrowest, hips at the top of the bone just below the waist, thigh midway between hip bone and knee joint, calf at the fullest when the foot is flat, ankle on the inside bulge, foot (right) from heel to big toe with the feet flat. Keep your tape parallel to the floor in all measurements.

MARK your dimensions, using nearest number, on the table above by blacking out the blocks containing each of your dimensions.

MAIL ENTRY at once to Norma Editor, 568 Plain Dealer Building, Cleveland 14, O., using this coupon or exact facsimile.

FIGURE 7. "Search-for-Norma" entry form, *Cleveland Plain Dealer,* 9 Sept. 1945, 8. ©1945 The Plain Dealer. All rights reserved. Used with permission.

"it takes a second person to measure your figure accurately. Get a friend to read the tape," while an accompanying series of photographs on page 3 illustrated "Miss Frances Stein tak[ing] the tape readings on Mrs. W. G. Blassingame at the Y.W.C.A." In the photos, Miss Stein is shown holding the tape measure against the bathing-suited Mrs. Blassingame's bust, waist, hips, ankle, and thigh.[52]

These two scientific models thus gave rise to particular, traceable, and public social practices. That nearly four thousand women voluntarily scrutinized their own bodies in this way suggests that an element of pleasure and power was derived not only from judging the normality of others, but from the literal and figurative surveying of the self. More important, this contest reveals the degree to which postwar individuals cooperated with normalizing practices.

Every day for two weeks, the *Plain Dealer* ran the entry form, photographs, and front-page features written by the "Norma Editor," Josephine Robertson, who miraculously found a fresh angle every time: from "Norma in 1945 Fashions" to "Comparisons of Norma with the Physical Education Models of the 1890s." As time passed, both the editorial staff and *Plain Dealer* readers seem to have become quite taken with the contest and its subject. Early on, the articles were descriptive, focusing on science and health, genetics debates, and the evolution of the human form. Later, articles were comparative, measuring "Norma," who had at this point become completely anthropomorphized, against her Victorian "Grandmother." "Norma" made appearances in editorial cartoons (one features a voluptuous woman standing on a scale marked "Thirty Days of Peace" with the caption, "Gosh, Norma, You're Gaining Already!") and nonsequiturs elsewhere in the paper ("World Ending So Soon? Poor Norma!" reads a headline about a doomsday prediction).[53] Norma was becoming a stand-in for "Americans today," a personification of the postwar condition.

Disturbing incongruities emerged, then, between the contest features and the news of the day, which reveal the links between the tumult of war and the desire for a return to normal. The shadow of World War II was heavy with memories of Pearl Harbor and a new understanding of totalitarianism with its "war machines" driven by propaganda and resulting in the genocidal crimes of the Holocaust. One way Americans could begin to come to grips with the such horrors was to juxtapose themselves against those grim images in order to seem normal by comparison. On one day, a headline announces "Five Troopships Bring 5,000 More Yanks Home Today," while the header next to it reads "Norma Wants Her Posture to Be Perfect." While the "House Puts [a] Lens on Pearl Harbor," we learn that "Norma's Gym Suit in '90s Covered All." And although Britain asks for "Three to Six Billions in Aid" and "Tokyo Rose [Is] Indicted by Own Words," it seems "Perfect Posture Is Goal of Norma."[54] In other words, while the surrounding articles described meat rationings and labor strikes, joblessness, massive demobilization, and the scars of war, the contest articles focused on Norma's strong, improved body, her perseverance, and her aesthetic perfection.

On one photo page of the *Plain Dealer*, a bathing-suited Norma con-
testant looking over her shoulder in a Betty Grable pose is placed directly
above a large head-and-shoulders shot of a thuggish Nazi war criminal
identified as the "Beast of Belsen." This juxtaposition creates a literal beauty and the beast effect, as the bright, blonde, idealized American woman's
body is contrasted against the brutal German criminal's dark, scarred, "foreign" face.[55] And on September 17, twin headlines, in the same typeface,
announce "Jap Manhunt Is Nearly Complete," and "Hunt for Norma Ends
Wednesday," the two columns separated by an artist's rendering of Norma
in various 1945 fashion styles.[56] At the end of the war, such juxtapositions
constructed a clear contrast: "Our" bodies against "Theirs."

These impulses had nationalistic and xenophobic roots, to be sure. The
most pressing agenda was the need to restore and improve the American
social body, in contrast to all these "Others" (Britain, Tokyo Rose, Nazis,
"Japs"). This rationale is mentioned explicitly by one local biologist, quoted
in a *Plain Dealer* feature on the contest: "All we need is to make better use
of what we have, our splendid bodies and brains. War has taught men and
women the value of sound bodies and our people are beginning to take
pride in physical development. We can . . . insure this country a stronger,
healthier population."[57] Another contest-inspired article notes the trend
toward "more strenuous physical fitness" programs in high schools, since
"the toughening of Norma's muscles and the increasing of her endurance,
which received special emphasis after Pearl Harbor to enable her to go to
school and hold a part-time job, too, will not only be continued but be
increased in its scope" after the war's end.[58] These later *Plain Dealer* contest
articles had become solidly prescriptive, sealing Norma's status not as the
average, but as a new ideal.

When Martha Skidmore, a slim, brunette "former war worker"–turned–
theater cashier, was declared the winner of the Norma Look-Alike Contest
on Sunday, November 23, 1945, the *Plain Dealer* published a front-page
photograph of her alongside an image of Norma at the same scale (fig. 8).
Presumably the reading public would want scrutinize the winner's body for
themselves. Skidmore, who had worked as a "gauge grinder for the Parker
Appliance Co." during the war, had gone back to her job as a theater cashier after being "let out after V-J Day." Lending a normality of spirit to
her normality of form, the *Plain Dealer* reported that Skidmore "liked to
swim, dance, and bowl [and] indicated that she was an average individual
in her tastes and that nothing out of the ordinary had ever happened to her
until the Norma Search came along."[59]

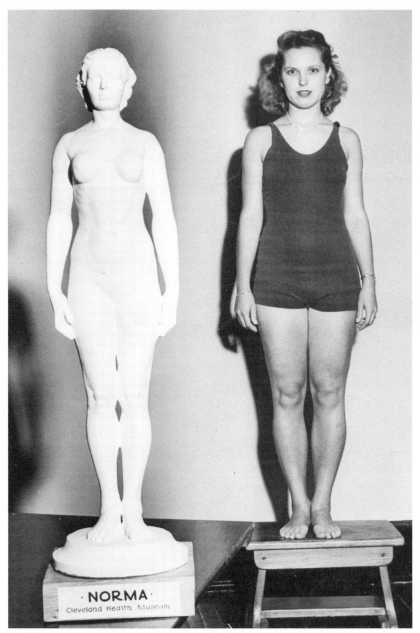

FIGURE 8. Martha Skidmore, "Norma" Contest Winner, front-page photograph, *Cleveland Plain Dealer*, 23 Sept. 1945. Used by permission of The Cleveland Museum of Natural History.

What was most surprising about the contest winner, however, was the revelation that Martha Skidmore's measurements "did not coincide with those of the statue"—hers simply came the *closest*. Although the statue was based on measurements of living women, only "about one percent" of the nearly four thousand Norma contestants even came close. This one percent had been summoned to the YWCA, where they were measured again "by medical and physical education experts. One expert measured all waists, another all busts, and so on." Although no one matched Norma's "mathematical average," the paper finally printed her model measurements, in the front-page feature, for the public record: "Height, 63 1/2 inches; bust, 33 1/4 inches; waist, 29 inches; hips, 39 inches; thigh, 20 inches; calf, 13 1/2 inches; ankle, 9 1/2 inches; foot, 9 inches, and weight, 123 pounds."[60]

Ironically, the contest ultimately proved normality to be both highly desirable and impossible to achieve, even for those self-selected, entry-form-fitting contestants who should have embodied it most. "After assessment of the measurements of 3,864 women who entered the search," reporter Josephine Robertson concluded, "Norma remained a hypothetical individual."[61]

Continuing publicity about the models from the late 1940s through the early 1950s repeatedly positioned Norma's figure as normal by comparing her 33-29-39 measurements against the "fashion ideal." One story, titled "Portrait of the American People," which appeared in the July 1945 edition of *Natural History* magazine, featured the tall, lithe fashion model Rosemary Sankey wearing a glamorous sheer gown opposite the comparatively short, muscular Norma. These fashion models, according to the story's author, Harry L. Shapiro, "constitut[e] a very uniform physical type" but are "eagerly sought after as dress models and . . . much admired by the public." In this group, the measurements 34-24-34 were considered "ideal." The "mean dimensions" of a surveyed group of female Powers fashion models were "stature 5 feet 8 inches, . . . bust 33.5 inches, waist 24 inches, hips 34.5 inches . . . and weight 120 pounds."[62] In another venue, Shapiro describes Normman, but in much less explicit terms than Norma: "Normman is about 5 feet 8 inches and weighs 145 pounds. He is the tallest of all white groups, exceeding the national averages of the various European people who have contributed to his origin."[63]

Generally, the visibility of Norma's body sharply contrasts the absences, silences—and censorship—attending Norm's. A February 1946 feature in the national news magazine *American Weekly*, for example, included full-page photographs of both Norm and Norma but carefully placed a fig leaf over Normman's genitals. Norma, again, was offered fully nude.[64] Titled "Figure Figured Out by Science," the feature made Norma's body, again, the focus of the viewer's gaze. Norma was enlarged to full page-height and made fully available for consumption, while Normman was reduced to half her height and partially obscured. One of the *Plain Dealer's* running features on the contest even displayed the nude Norma from four different angles above the daily contest call and entry form. To represent Norm the same way, publishers would have to reveal the naked male body in all its particulars.

Before settling into relative obscurity in her exhibit at the Cleveland Health Museum, Norma made an appearance on CBS television's *Adventure*. In "The American Look," originally airing on November 15, 1953, the narrator, again Harry L. Shapiro, examined "the historical development and nature of the American physical type" by focusing in on changes in fashion ideals for women. After a parade of female figures, each sculpted to "match" the fashions of their era, Norma appears as the "surprise" guest whose (purportedly more attainable) "average" figure contrasts the exaggerations of Victorian, Gibson Girl, and Flapper "bodies." To emphasize Norma's representation of all American bodies, the episode concludes with a shadow play in which various "immigrant" silhouettes (imagine grossly exaggerated "Ellis Island" figures slouching beneath rucksacks or sporting Chinese hats and braids) step up behind a screen to be absorbed/erased into the central silhouette: a curvy female "America" with arms uplifted. The melting-pot fantasy is enacted once again, as all "difference" dissolves into a white, Anglo form. Fittingly, the episode concludes with the revelation of Norma's measurements. The host even asks Shapiro to repeat them twice, so that viewers at home can "find a measuring tape and see for themselves" whether or not they possess "normal" American bodies.

The Norm and Norma statues constitute one of the most "scientific" and quantitative efforts to describe normality during this period. But through them we can also trace the shift of normality from the realm of science and medicine, to public promotion and display, to individual participation and cooperation. Through this process, the claim to know what normal meant was subtly transferred from experts such as Dickinson, to institutions such as museums and schools, to individuals reading the paper in Cleveland or watching television and whipping out the tape measure. Normality moved from an external, projected quality to an internalized one.

What Norm and Norma were purported to represent was the normal postwar body. What they came closer to representing was the unwounded, intact, healthy, youthful, Caucasian, reproductive, heterosexualized, "perfectly" average American body—in other words, a body that did not, could not, exist. The ironic results of the 1945 Norma Look-Alike Contest inadvertently proved normality to be a "hypothetical" quality, one that only the unreal could embody. As Harry Shapiro acknowledged in 1945, "the average American figure approaches a kind of *perfection* of bodily form and proportion: the average is excessively rare."[65] Nevertheless, normality retained its power, and Americans continue to pursue it.

Inanimate Yet Superior

In the article announcing the winner of the Norma Look-Alike Contest, Bruno Gebhard expressed distress about the implications of the new "data" obtained from the thousands of contest registrants, claiming that "if a national inventory of the female population of this country were taken there would be as many '4Fs' among the women as were revealed among the men in the draft." Postwar women, he feared, were largely unfit for service, and the solution was physical fitness. "The unfit are both bad producers and bad consumers," Gebhard concluded. "One of the outstanding needs in this country is more emphasis everywhere on physical fitness. And you can't make that statement too strong."[66]

In a curious reversal of signification, one *Plain Dealer* story in the issue of September 18, 1945, subtitled "Perfect Norma Is High School Goal," reported that "Norma, the typical American girl, as exemplified by pupils of Cleveland high schools, will be given a more strenuous physical fitness program this year than ever before."[67] Rather than Norma symbolizing living subjects, Cleveland's high school students now had to "exemplify" Norma. The prescriptive turn extended even further in an article two days later:

> Yesterday the Central Y.W.C.A. at its open house for approximately 1,000 women featured Norma and measured several hundred women for comparison of their proportions with hers. At Flora Stone Mather College the department of physical education, headed by Miss Emily R. Andrews, expects to establish measurements as norms for various heights and chart them so that students who need to lose or gain in spots or generally may have a mark to shoot at. At the end of the year Normas for the various classes will be determined. In his Sunday sermon, Dr. B. C. Clausen, pastor of Euclid Avenue Baptist Church, will take Norma's spiritual measurements, speaking on the subject, "Norma's Religion."[68]

That local physical education teachers would construct these "Normas," supposed reflections of an average, and turn them into projections of an ideal for students to "shoot at" reveals the way normality itself had moved from average to ideal, from descriptive to prescriptive.[69] The concluding remark regarding Norma's "spiritual measurements," as with the detail that contest-winner Martha Skidmore liked to bowl, shows a tendency to slip from physical normality into mental, cultural, and even spiritual realms— all of which were areas of postwar anxiety. One physical education teacher, for example, expressed the hope that "Cleveland high school girls would never again be so soft as they were before the war."[70]

The focus on Norma in the media coverage of the models suggests a public accustomed to expecting perfection of the female form, and accustomed to viewing it as well. The sexualization and objectification of women's bodies that is identified with 1950s beauty contests was well underway in the '40s, with the "pin-up girl" culture that made stars of actresses such as Rita Hayworth, Betty Grable, and Hedy Lamarr. The war had sanctified jovial masculine sexual self-expression—soldiers plastered their barracks with inviting pinups of their favorite film stars. "Conditioning" classes at local YWCAs helped young women trying to develop an hourglass figure. Miss Emily Keefe, head of health education for the Greater Cleveland YWCA, who was interviewed in the *Plain Dealer*, noted that most of her students "still usually prefer slimness to curves, having in mind Katharine Hepburn rather than Mae West. But they seem to look more favorably on bust development than in the past."[71]

Postwar health textbooks, such as Eleanor Metheny's *Body Dynamics* (1952), were rife with instruction about bodily normality, aimed particularly at female readers. Metheny's goal was to provide "scientifically sound information" about the functioning of the human body and "how it may be improved" in "fitness and efficiency."[72] *Body Dynamics* informed readers of "the conditions which must be met for maximum efficiency in normal walking," while the racialized illustrations put a Norma-like figure to different purposes (fig. 9). This evidence suggests that *women* were the ones whose bodies were in need of surveillance and control after World War II—not surprising given the upending of women's gender roles during the war. And yet women were also caught up in the impossible tension between va-va-voom and fitness cultures. When such bodies couldn't be had by diet or exercise, they could be bought: by 1950, 85 percent of women over fifteen wore bras, girdles, or both, and corsets had become a $500,000,000 annual business.[73]

FIG. 19. The gorilla "walks with his back."

FIG. 50. Bizarre positions of legs, arms, and shoulders are both fatiguing and unattractive.

FIGURE 9. "The gorilla 'walks with his back'"; "Bizarre position of legs, arms, and shoulders are both fatiguing and unattractive." Illustrations from Eleanor Metheny, *Body Dynamics* (1952), 184. © The McGraw-Hill Companies, Inc.

The body would continue to be a site for anxieties over normality into the 1950s. Science fiction films such as *The Incredible Shrinking Man*, *The Amazing Colossal Man*, and *Attack of the 50-Foot Woman* worked through troubling fears and existential questions about the body in the face of an increasingly atomic age. In *The Incredible Shrinking Man*, Scott Carey, a white middle-class "organization man," starts out as the figure of post-war normality. After exposure to a combination of radioactive fallout and chemical pesticides, he begins to shrink, to become different from everyone else. From that position of difference, he questions the meaning of "normal": "Sometimes I begin to think that it's the *world* that's changed, that *I'm* the normal one," he remarks to a beautiful female dwarf, a circus performer he meets in a bar.[74] Challenging the "containment" thesis about Cold War culture, these films repeatedly leave their protagonists' crises uncontained and their audiences unsettled.

Two pivotal scenes in a best-selling pulp novel published only one year after Norm and Norma's Cleveland debut speak to the lingering power of inanimate bodies. At the beginning of Irving Schulman's infamous 1946 "juvenile delinquency" tale *Amboy Dukes*, the tough, teenaged protagonist, Frank Goldfarb, treats his beloved younger sister, Alice, to a bus ride along Fifth Avenue, where she becomes mesmerized by the "postured manne-quins" in shop windows. The mannequins wear furs and gowns "with a grace that no girl or woman could ever hope to equal. In their inanimate yet superior faces were fixed for all time the expressions of women accus-tomed to the adulation of many men, and these slender inanimate dolls seemed to Alice to have partaken of more wonderful experiences than would ever befall her."[75] Young Alice sees these "dolls" especially in terms of their femininity: their "grace," their "slender" bodies, and their "supe-rior faces . . . accustomed to . . . adulation." White, inanimate, false and yet hyperreal, these sculpted figures become potent symbols for qualities that Alice desires, but can never "hope to equal."

In the context of a story focused on teenagers dislocated by the World War II "home front," this scene poignantly evokes both the allure of a burgeoning postwar consumer culture and the pressure of these "postured" bodies, so ambiguous in their claim to represent. Shulman's novel plays up the wartime tensions within this (significantly) Jewish family: both parents work doggedly to rise out of their working-class "ethnic" neighborhood of Brooklyn's Pitkin Avenue, while their two teenagers grow increasingly isolated, angry, and desperate in their parents' absence. Just before the novel's tragic conclusion, Schulman once again has Frank and Alice travel uptown. What had earlier been Alice's longing looks into shop windows now become bitter judgments in which she and all of Pitkin Avenue come up short:

> The season depicted in the windows was summer and the mannequins por-trayed the average citizen and his family, clad in expensive cottons, tending their victory garden and flower beds; . . . a carefree, light-hearted group pic-nicking on a terrace, their set faces were fixed in an eternal smile; . . . bright people at the beach, at the country club, strolling to the badminton courts.

> There were windows featuring the correct dress for the junior miss, and
> Alice covertly glanced at the suit which her mother had purchased for her
> in Klein's better store, and the suit now appeared drab and uninteresting,
> without charm or smartness.

Here Shulman explicitly highlights the WASPish quality of these manne-
quin lives, spent in "country clubs" and "expensive cottons," in stark contrast to Alice's "drab" suit bought from Klein's. These concluding visions of
a plate-glassed suburban middle class extend beyond the earlier encounter
focused solely on femininity of form. Now these model bodies successfully
evoke an entire world—the world of "the average citizen and his family"
in their "correct" dress, who live, Frank assures Alice, "around."[76] For these
two characters, the "average" was visible everywhere, and yet—as for the
Ohio contestants—always just beyond their reach.

In the 1940s and 50s, storefront mannequins, which, like Norm and
Norma, had largely been sculpted from wood, wax, or plaster in the past,
began to be made from plastics and fiberglass. In the postwar period, experimentation with these materials made mannequins less sculptural and
more easily mass-produced, to keep up with the booming clothing industry. Mannequins became more "plastic" in their appearance as well:
in 1947, when Christian Dior introduced the New Look, live models began to emulate mannequins, rather than the reverse. With "wasp waists
and emphasized busts, they took on mechanical poses similar to plastic
dolls with rounded shoulders." This "plastic doll look" remained prevalent
throughout the early '50s, with female models remaining "stilted in body
attitude."[77]

No less a model body than Barbie herself would appear in 1959, with
her infamous measurements of 36-18-38. The first "teenage fashion doll,"
Barbie was designed by Ruth Handler, co-founder of Mattel, and named
after Handler's own daughter. Over 350,000 were sold in 1959 alone, setting a new sales record for Mattel. Originally, Handler apparently wanted to create a fully developed doll—specifically, a doll with breasts—to
function as a different kind of role model for young girls, so they might
imagine futures beyond carrying "baby" dolls. Ironically enough, while
Norm and Norma were exported to Germany, Barbie's body was originally
imported from Germany—her form was reportedly based on a 1955 German doll named Lilli, produced for adults after a popular vampish cartoon
character. Handler had seen the doll on a trip to Germany, and rights to
reproduce the Lilli doll's body were purchased to put Barbie into mass
production (notably, prominent nipples had to be filed off the first mold

before she was cast). Barbie would go on to become the one of the most popular model bodies in history: the doll is currently marketed in more than 150 countries, and three Barbie dolls are reportedly sold somewhere in the world every second.[78]

Again, this train leads back to Dresden and the logic of Norm and Norma displayed beside maps of Auschwitz. As bizarre as the Norm and Norma statues may seem, they were part of a broader and largely successful construction of normal bodies, one attached to racialized definition of ideal Americanness. The fact that the Norm and Norma case happened *when* it happened tells us much: in the immediate postwar moment, normality was offered as the antithesis to war, but it had to remain intrinsically tied to wartime in order to make sense. The architects of the normal body were not only the eugenicists, anthropologists, and sexologists, but also the postwar populace who embraced, internalized, and emulated the model bodies put on display.

$$2$$

Normalizing the Nation

The Study of American Character

In the publicity surrounding the "Norm and Norma" sculptures in the late 1940s, anthropologist Harry L. Shapiro and others had slipped frequently and easily from descriptions of the "normality" of the models' bodies to assertions about their normality of *character*.[1] Journalists and scientists regularly anthropomorphized the plaster figures, moving beyond their surfaces to hypothesize about their interiors. Such slippage from bodies to minds was not surprising; inquiry into the "normal" American character was another significant academic project of the interwar and early postwar years. In 1949, for example, a *Collier's* article spotlighted the news that the Rockefeller Foundation had funded a scholarly investigation of "normal, happy people." This announcement was illustrated with an image of a presumably "normal" man being analyzed under a microscope (fig. 10).[2] Indeed, by the early 1940s the search to describe "normal" Americans was being conducted on many fronts: Did Americans constitute a distinctive physical "type"? Could they defend themselves in time of war? And who was included in this category of Americans?[3] This wave of scholarship forged a critical link in the midcentury epistemology of normality: the leap from investigating the normal body to investigating a kind of normality of spirit.

Scholars of "normal" American character moved beyond Dickinson and Belskie's medical/anthropometric models to build newly interdisciplinary models, weaving quantitative and qualitative methods into new typologies. Scientific inquiries like the Harvard Grant Study of Normal Men (1945) attempted to define and quantify normality itself. Scholars of American "national character," from Margaret Mead to David Riesman and others, had in common the presumption that a "normal" American character existed, even when their purpose was to critique its habits. Inextricable from all these efforts was the midcentury entrenchment of the field of American Studies, which would make an institutional project of "understanding the national culture holistically."[4] Like the Dickinson-Belskie models, these overlapping strands of scholarship ultimately helped to concretize "normality" as a way of seeing.

In this chapter I argue that postwar scholarship aimed at defining the normal American worked to normalize Americanness itself, in a way that ultimately cooperated with politics of the emerging Cold War and notions of American exceptionalism. Hygiene studies of "normal men," midcentury

FIGURE 10. "Getting Back to Normal," illustration by Harry Devlin (image accompanying news of recent Rockefeller grant to fund Berkeley study of "normal" personality), *Collier's*, 20 Aug. 1949, 74. Used by permission of the Harry and Wende Devlin Artistic and Literary Trust.

GETTING BACK TO NORMAL

investigations of "national character," and early American Studies scholarship on "American civilization" began from different places, but were
eventually put to similar and increasingly nationalistic uses, and helped to
gather individual postwar bodies into a national, social, and political body.
In their collective pursuit of American character, they effectively "normalized" a nation.

Studying Normal Men:
"Your carcass is the clue to your character"

In 1945, the preliminary results of a six-year Harvard University study of
"normal young men" were published twice, first in an academic monograph titled *What People Are: A Study of Normal Young Men*, and then again
in a popular interest volume penned by Ernest A. Hooton titled *"Young
Man, You Are Normal": Findings from a Study of Students*.[5] While Dickinson and his colleagues had combed the greater Cleveland area to find their
"Norma," an interdisciplinary team at Harvard looked no further than to
the "young men at [their] own doorstep" (Heath et al., vii). The subjects
of the Grant Study, as it came to be called, were 268 Harvard sophomores
selected for their "normality" and studied over a four-year period, from
1939 to 1942. Though the first results were published in 1945, the study
was designed to be longitudinal, to continue for "fifteen or twenty years"
at least. An interdisciplinary research team applied a range of methodolo-
gies to gather information on the social class, religious life, physiology,
health, intelligence, and personality of these "normal men." Like the Norm
and Norma case, the Harvard Grant Study epitomized the impulse to measure, quantify, and define normality in the 1940s and to project it into the
future. But unlike the Dickinson-Belskie models, the Grant Study moved
beyond investigations of the normal body's exteriors to more detailed questions about its interiors. The Grant Study set out to measure the normal
man, body and soul.

What they found was made clear by Hooton's title: "Young Man, You
Are Normal." As one *New York Times* reviewer noted, the study's "results, as
might be foreseen, are not spectacular and seldom depart from the expec-
tations of common sense. The subjects were 'normal' to begin with, pretty
much in tune with life and 'free from gross physical and psychic defects.'"[6]
Ultimately, all the voices involved in the project shared a basic sense that
all of these red-blooded American males were normal, and by implication,
that normality itself was, and would continue to be, all-American.

The Grant Study was launched in 1938, when two physicians and professors in Harvard's Department of Hygiene, Clark W. Heath and Arlie V. Bock, received a gift from a former patient, the dime-store magnate and budding philanthropist William T. Grant, to study the fit, the well, the "normal." Grant had created his foundation in 1936 with the aim of supporting "strong social science research, the object of which was . . . 'the enrichment of life, with a primary interest in people and in their adjustment to the world in which they live.'" The Grant Foundation supported the Harvard study from 1938 to 1947 and again from 1957 to 1977.[7] For the first five years, the Grant funding allowed the study to have "specially equipped headquarters" adjacent to the Hygiene Building on the Harvard campus, and a staff that included four physicians, a psychologist, an anthropologist, a social worker, and two secretaries.[8]

In a press release dated September 30, 1938, Arlie Bock described the study's aims: "Doctors traditionally have dealt with their patients after troubles of many sorts have arisen. The Department of Hygiene . . . proposes to revise this procedure and will attempt to analyze the forces that have produced normal young men. . . . A body of facts is needed to replace current suppositions."[9] As Bock would argue, "the time [was] ripe to attempt the work."[10] The dust jacket of Heath's monograph, *What People Are*, emphasized the importance of studying "the well . . . not the ill, the normal, not the abnormal," because "hitherto little attention has been paid to well people upon whom depend the leadership and work of the world." (The fact that a current world leader, President Franklin Roosevelt, had been stricken by polio was not common knowledge, but lends special irony to such claims nevertheless.) "Knowledge of normality," the jacket proclaimed, was necessary for "social planning today" and "of great concern to medicine, education, business, and government."[11]

The authors anticipated skepticism: "From the very first," Heath wrote, "the reader will ask, 'What do you mean by *normal?*' For our present purposes, 'normal' is defined as the *balanced*, harmonious blending of function that produces good integration" (3–4). Heath contrasted this definition of normality as a kind of optimal functionality against three others: the statistical sense of normality as the "average"; "the vain search for the normal person in the sense of a 'perfect' one"; and the medical habit of using "normal" as a kind of "clinical shorthand for 'nothing abnormal found upon examination.'"[12] But their apparent clarity of definition was soon muddied by the authors' shifting sense of who or what it was they were studying. Within the first two paragraphs of his preface to the Heath volume, Arlie

Bock described the study's subjects as "normal human beings," as "effective people," and as leader "types" (vii), signaling a tension between their typicality and their distinctiveness. Bock carefully placed quotation marks around "the 'well' person"—the "diagnosis and classification" of whom was the study's project (vii), but he did not emphasize the word *normal* in the same way: "Through the exclusion of the presence of disease, the doctor calls the person normal. What is normal? How can we establish the nature of this entity we call normal, and through this understanding aid a young man in the direction that will produce his most effective responses? . . . It is actually easier to make a diagnosis of illness than it is to make a diagnosis of the interests, potentialities, and other vital qualities of the well young man" (viii–ix).

In his discussion of the selection of participants, Heath claimed, confoundingly, that they sought "as wide a group of '*normal*,' *healthy*, and *superior* young men as was possible in the college setting" (110, emphasis added). The epistemological slipperiness of normality surfaces here, as ever. With the Norm and Norma case, the science of determining an average slid quickly into a popular discourse about the quest for an ideal. For the Harvard researchers, *normal* was both average and "superior"; their aims, then, were both descriptive and prescriptive from the outset.

These problems of definition did not go unnoticed. As soon as the first results were published, the Grant Study was criticized by the biologist C. Daly King, whose definition of normality the study had adopted. King zeroed in on what he saw as a fundamental flaw the authors' application of concept of normality: they thought they were choosing "normal" men to study, when in fact, he argued, they were choosing "average" ones:

> The Grant Study claims to be investigating normal young men. . . . [but] their use of the term normal is a clear example of the very looseness against which [I protest]; indeed, it has the further appearance of involving self-contradiction. . . . [The Grant Study] . . . did choose a typical cross-section of the usual Harvard undergraduate population, neither the extraordinary geniuses nor the unusually incapable, neither the most remarkable physical specimens nor the most ailing—in short, the average. Then why not call them so?

King bemoans the confusion of the "average" with the "normal," a concept he continued to insist should be more strictly defined as "the efficient functioning inherent in the design."[13] His concerns sprang not only from the Grant Study's conception of normality but also, implicitly, from its selection process.

Over a four-year period from 1939 to 1942, the 268 Harvard men were chosen through a highly biased selection process, which also varied from year to year. First, fully 40 percent of each Harvard class (numbering roughly a thousand) were excluded for having a freshman grade average of C or lower; these students were considered to be at risk of failing to graduate, which would interfere with plans for a longitudinal study. The remaining students were then screened, and half were excluded for any "physical disability which might interfere with physiological . . . tests"; for "foreign language and culture" (for the sake of "uniformity" in psychological measurements in English); or for physical or psychological afflictions ranging from diabetes to "the combination of marked acne, visual defect and obesity" (Heath 111; 113–14). Each year, the names of the sophomores left standing were submitted to the Harvard deans, who personally selected out a smaller group of "boys" whom they recognized as "sound." Arlie Bock resorted to metaphor to explain the concept: "sound" subjects were those who were able "to paddle their own canoe."[14]

Selecting 268 Harvard sophomores by such means and calling them "normal men" may seem laughable today, but the authors of the study vigorously defended the subjects as a perfectly democratic sample that was "not too heterogeneous" (Hooton 8). Moreover, Bock's definition of the "sound" individual raises what is rarely acknowledged in the minimal secondary literature that exists on this study: its openly eugenicist elements. Eugenics remained a vital ideology in American culture throughout the 1930s and 40s (and beyond). The physical anthropologist Earnest A. Hooton was a well-known, if controversial, public intellectual and voice of eugenicist thinking when he was chosen to write *Young Man, You Are Normal*, the popular press monograph that would summarize the Grant Study's results to the general public.[15] The design of the Grant Study was explicitly eugenicist: in the middle of the 1930s, Harvard's Department of Hygiene established a system that cast the Harvard undergraduate as "the person who is fit for his service to society" (Heath, ix). As George Vaillant, one of later authors of the longitudinal study, notes, in 1940 men who went to Harvard were not always wealthy or privileged, but they were almost all white and native-born.[16] Moreover, the study itself employed eugenicist discourse, even in the most banal of contexts. Take, for example, this discussion of the problem of hiring: "Selection of the wrong person for the job harms at least three people, the one selected, the one rejected, and the employer. The negative approach through elimination of the unfit has proceeded faster than the positive approach through selection of the

fit" (Heath 6). Finally, the context of the Grant Study is telling, as the
authors parse distinctions between men of "strong" and "weak masculine
component," or between physical features and mental "adjustment," or between Catholics and Jews—right in the midst of the Holocaust. "Leaders
of the people should rise from among those who are well and fit," Heath
and his colleagues plainly announce in their introduction (5). And, not
surprisingly, rise they did. Four of the original participants went on to run
for the U.S. Senate, and one of them—John F. Kennedy—would become
president.[17]

The methods of the Grant Study were remarkable for their interdisci-
plinarity, combining quantitative and qualitative approaches to tackle "the
problem of the diagnosis of the normal person" (Heath 7). As Arlie Bock
explained, "The Study proposes no innovation in the technique of medicine. It proposes merely to use existing and generally accepted methods,
applying them to the study of the total constitution and personality of
well, successful young men."[18] The research team specifically included a
physician of internal medicine, a physiologist, a physical anthropologist,
a psychologist, two psychiatrists (though no psychoanalysts, since, as the
authors note with some derision, the study was interested in the subjects'
mental health, but not the root causes of it), and a "personnel worker"
(family social worker), Lewise Gregory (later Davies), who conducted
qualitative sociological interviews with the subjects and their families. Together, the researchers threw everything they had at their subjects, including somatotyping, personality testing, Rorschach inkblot tests, intelligence
and aptitude tests, and physical and medical evaluations. The Grant Study
thus provides a window into the midcentury impulse to measure, quantify,
bring multiple instruments into use to pursue normality with full force,
and with the fact-finding sheen of "a clinical approach" (Heath 9).

Considering the scope of the project, the resulting monograph, *What
People Are: A Study of Normal Young Men*, was a fairly slim volume of some
hundred pages, with another few dozen more of appendixes, including
sample charts and graphs and some glossy black and white photographs.
What People Are presented a straightforward summary of the study's findings organized by discipline, beginning with "personality" and "adjustment strategies" and moving on to "socio-economic," "morphological"
(body type), "physiological," "medical," and "mental" (intelligence) measurements. Embedded within each broad and clinical-sounding category
is surprisingly specific data about such details as masturbatory frequency,
insulin tolerance, athleticism, anti-Semitism, attitudes toward God and

the existence of an afterlife, class position, "home situation," nail-biting, diet, and SAT scores. Each of the co-authors simultaneously published results, or planned to, in top journals in their own fields. All of these authors regularly emphasized the need for "further research," as their experiments had raised more questions than they answered.

The Grant Study was heavily concerned with normal bodies—using somatotyping to divide the men's bodies along "morphological" lines and then correlating physical appearance with spiritual health.[19] Faced with the small sample size, the physical anthropologist of the study, Carl Seltzer, decided to focus his study of body build on "two aspects" that lent themselves to "simpler classifications": "strength or weakness in the masculine component" and "proportions" (Hooton 81; Heath 59–60). The study used a continuum gradation, from "Strong Masculine Component" to "Moderate" to "Weak" and "Very Weak" (figs. 11–14), while the evaluation of "proportion" was determined through measurements of "breadth of chest relative to breadth of shoulders, calf circumference relative to breadth of shoulders, head circumference relative to chest circumference," and the like (Heath 60).

The subjects' faces are blocked out, but their genitalia are on full display. These illustrations are significant because of the study's most overt claim, that normality of form could be correlated with normality of spirit. As Hooton quipped, "Your carcass is the clue to your character" (102). The photographs emphasized this point, inviting the viewer to draw such correlations as well. Somatotype illustrations were also included in Hooton's mass-market version of the Grant Study report, but genitals as well as faces were obscured for the broader reading public since, as Hooton had argued in *Young Man, You Are Normal*, bodily masculinity could be easily graded "without reference to the primary sex organs" (82). The emphasis on physical appearance was surely overdetermined by the influence of the physical anthropologist onboard, and this bias is especially strong in Hooton's version of the narrative in *Young Man, You Are Normal*. For example, he argues that the somatic findings of the anthropologists are more discrete and numerical, more objective, and therefore better science than the results of the psychiatric and personality testing.

With or without full frontal nudity, however, the photographs amplify another deep assumption of the study: normality is implicitly gendered male. As the sequence of photographs (and particularly their captions) makes clear, the "weaker" the masculine component, the stronger the "feminine" component, and thus the presence of the feminine signifies a

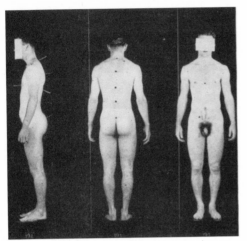
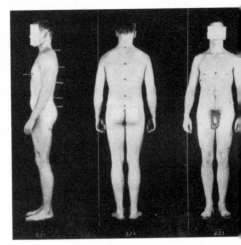

FIGURE 11. "Strong" Masculine Component, Harvard Grant Study of Normal Men. Figures 11–14 are reproduced from *What People Are: A Study of Normal Young Men* by Clark W. Heath, in collaboration with Lucien Brouha, Lewise W. Gregory, Carl C. Seltzer, Frederic L. Wells, and William L. Woods, Cambridge, Mass.: Harvard University Press, copyright © 1945 by the President and Fellows of Harvard College, copyright © renewed 1973 by Clark Wright Heath.

FIGURE 12. "Moderate" Masculine Component, Harvard Grant Study of Normal Men.

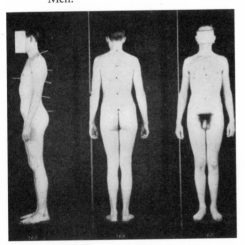
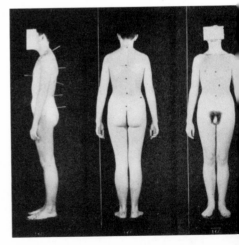

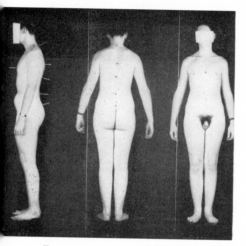

FIGURE 13. "Weak" Masculine Component, Harvard Grant Study of Normal Men.

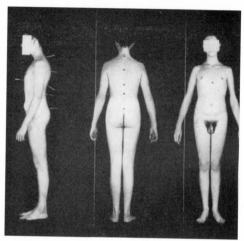

FIGURE 14. "Very Weak" Masculine Component, Harvard Grant Study of Normal Men.

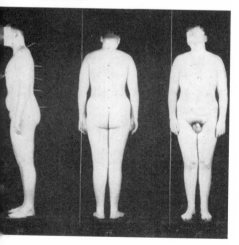

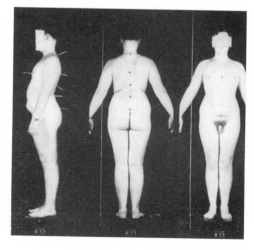

departure from normality. In her discussion of the scientific pursuit of the "homosexual body," Jennifer Terry discusses similar photographic studies as a kind of "scientific scopophilia," noting that the blotting out of faces itself has a "homogenizing effect" that "renders the photographed individual as a specimen." Such photographs of homosexual bodies at this time, Terry writes, were "encoded as morbid" and invited viewers "to look for and find pathology."[20] With the Grant Study photographs, the scopophilia is similar, though the homogenizing function is less so. Viewers attempting to look for and see normality were likely frustrated, since all of the bodies are technically labeled as normal, yet all of the bodies except for the "strong masculine component" models are described as flawed in every respect. Significantly, the "norm" in the Harvard sample, then, was not the middle of the spectrum (the "moderate masculine component"), but rather the ideal. The "strong" masculine component was the form that occurred in the majority (80%) of the Harvard subjects. Further exaggerating their findings, the authors applied the label "weakness in the masculine component" to *all* the remaining 20 percent, whether those individuals were classified as moderate, weak, or very weak. In this way, the authors casually normalized the ideal and pathologized the rest.[21]

The subjects were also tested, prodded, and probed by physicians, who charted such details as blood counts, diet, and insulin tolerance, as well as blood pressure, heart, and respiratory rates at rest and on a treadmill. The physiological and medical reports readily acknowledge the fact that "not one [of the subjects] could be considered strictly 'normal' in a medical sense. . . . For if we are studying 'normal' people in the sense of the medically perfect, it will be in vain—such a thing does not exist" (Heath 78). The authors remind the reader of the study's definition of normal as "the balanced harmonious blending of functions that produce good integration" (Heath 3; Hooton 12), and turn instead to reportage of banal details:

"[I]t is worthy of note that not more than 18 percent of individuals had a temperature of [the usually accepted average of] 98.60° (Heath 78)

"The average number of glasses of milk per day for each boy was four, and the number varied from none, in a boy who was believed to be allergic to it, to about twelve" (81)

"Some crowding or spacing of the teeth was present in 57 per cent of the group, and malocclusions were common" (81)

"In the matter of operations, tonsillectomy was most frequent" (81)

The authors' primary claim regarding the medical data is simply that "a great deal of biological variation is discoverable from the routine medical examination of selected healthy young men" (Heath 82). The physiological and medical variation they found frustrated attempts to draw any other conclusions about their subjects, so the doctors at that point seem to throw up their hands: "It seems obvious that to describe a person as 'healthy' and 'normal' is not enough" (82). Foiled, to some extent, in their attempts to chart a normal physiology, the Grant Study team turned to the measurement of personality, intelligence, and something they termed "adjustment."

To measure the "character" of these students, the Grant Study team deployed an arsenal of "personality tests." Each subject was seen by a psychiatrist for six to eight hours, in sessions focused on family background, career ambitions, and personal beliefs and values. While the psychiatric information on the subjects included mood, affect, motivations, and attitudes, the authors resisted over-quantifying their findings, noting that "the present aim is to lay the groundwork for a permanent and useful clinical classification of normal personality" (Heath 22). Predictably, they mapped their conclusions about the "soundness" of participants onto detailed charts (fig. 15).

While Heath's *What People Are* had a serious, Harvard University Press air about it, the subsequent popular press book, Hooton's *Young Man, You Are Normal*, brought more humor and skepticism to the subject, though Hooton nonetheless communicated great respect and enthusiasm for the study. At the time, Hooton's name was a significant selling point: "Not all Grant Studies and Grantees have the inestimable advantage of being presented to the public by Professor Earnest Hooton, whose erudition and irrepressible humor are familiar," one reviewer wrote.[22] Part I of Hooton's text, "What the 'Normal' Young Men Are Like," presents a fairly dry summary of the study's findings divided into several sections: "Their Physiques," "Their Health," "Their Social and Economic Backgrounds," "Their Personalities," and so on. One ten-page section simply reproduces statistical "trait associations" having to do with personality (for example, "Social Traits: Sociable, Asocial, Shy"), but arranges the data two different ways, so that "the enthusiastic trait analyzer" can make comparisons (Hooton 61–62; 57). After rehearsing the data, Hooton turns to his true passion: drawing correlations.

Hooton is occasionally critical of the study, particularly the "somewhat foggy and indistinct" (63) categories the psychiatrists used to measure

APPENDIX B

PSYCHIATRIC DATA: DISTRIBUTION OF PERSONALITY TRAITS OF GRANT STUDY PARTICIPANTS

General "Soundness" Classification		No. Individuals	Per Cent
Group A (most "sound")		93	37
Group B (intermediate)		113	45
Group C (less "sound")		46	18
	Totals	252	100
Not classified		16	
	Total	268	

Classification by Traits (257 Individuals)
(Arranged in order of frequency)

Well Integrated Basic Personality	153	60
Pragmatic	99	38
Motivations towards Practical Organizing	95	37
Self-conscious and Introspective	65	25
Lack of Purpose and Values	55	22
Friendly	55	21
Motivations towards the Ideational	54	21
Motivations towards the Cultural	54	21
Vital Affect	52	20
Inhibited	49	19
Shy	47	18
Bland Affect	46	18
Verbalistic	46	18
Sensitive Affect	44	17
Political	44	17
Mood Fluctuations	41	16
Humanistic	40	16
Incompletely Integrated Basic Personality	38	15
Unstable Autonomic Functions	36	14
Self-driving	36	14
Inarticulate	36	14
Just-So	35	14
Motivations towards Physical Science	32	12
Asocial	24	9
Motivations towards the Creative and Intuitive	16	6

FIGURE 15. Psychiatric Data, Harvard Grant Study of Normal Men. From Heath, *What People Are.* Harvard University Press, copyright © 1945 by the President and Fellows of Harvard College, copyright © renewed 1973 by Clark Wright Heath.

personality, and the "psychometrics" of intelligence testing. Hooton (a eugenicist, remember) is more than willing to highlight differences in religion and to make bold hypotheses about the links between physiognomy and character. Where striking correlations are found, he casts the results as significant and relevant; where no correlation is found where one was expected, he blames the small sample size. To cite a few among many examples:

> "It is thus suggested that relatively flat chests go with the less expansive and rounded personality traits" (97)

> "In the Scholastic Aptitude Test also, the men with weakness in the masculine component score on the average nearly 30 points higher than the larger and more strongly masculine group, but here again the difference is not certainly significant" (112)

> "Altogether, in spite of the inadequate sizes of the subseries with which we have been forced to work, there can be little doubt that the Jews are strikingly different from the total series of the Grant Study group in personality traits and the Catholics less markedly, but still perceptibly different" (164)

More than Heath and his coauthors, Hooton regularly emphasizes the Grant group's paradoxical representativeness and uniqueness. His "Fitness" chapter is especially revealing, as are the "masculine component" sections. Regarding intelligence, for example, Hooton carefully emphasizes that one can be *too* intellectual, yet one can never have a strong enough "masculine component." The Harvard subjects are regularly idealized, especially as their normality is measured against what the author sets up as larger "average" samples—Harvard Hygiene Department freshman statistics, World War I Army records, or other statistics on hand (Hooton 82).

While Hooton goes to great pains to produce scores of correlations, the most convincing common denominators in this sample were the ones the scientists either downplayed or were blind to: the subjects' maleness, their whiteness, their able-bodiedness, and their youth.[23] The variations that were striking enough to be emphasized by the authors—social class, religious affiliation, athleticism, personality—attest to the ideological weight attached to "wellness" at this time.[24]

The study also reported on subjects' social status. The team's social worker, Lewise Gregory Davies, took a social history from each subject, and then "traveled the length and breadth of the United States to meet their parents," according to Vaillant. In his report, Hooton calls "Miss Lewise Gregory" a "tactful and sympathetic social researcher," but adds that "[w]omen are probably better than men in ... these ... activities—snooping and social research interviewing" (24). In the subjects' family homes, Davies took down histories that included "characterizations of grandparents, aunts, uncles," and "an estimate of social status." From the mothers she took "a history of each boy's infant-and-child development and any family history of mental illness."[25] The "indefatigable" Davies recorded religious beliefs, parental relationships, and childrearing practices. This information, gleaned from hours of face-to-face interviews, was not quoted (never is the "voice" of any of these "Normal Men" heard in either text);[26] rather, her findings are also turned into charts and graphs, proportions and percentages (fig. 16).

In relating what normal men are like socioeconomically, Hooton, Heath, and later Vaillant continually emphasize their "surprising" variation. People with tragic family lives, poverty, lack of religion, even poor grades and poor fitness—all these had somehow made it into the study in large numbers. Hooton concludes that "'normal' boys spring from every sort of a familial background—rich and poor, favored and underprivileged, socially select and proletarian. They come from families that are harmonious and happy,

FIGURE 16. Sociological Data—Problems of Childhood, Harvard Grant Study of Normal Men. From Heath, *What People Are*. Harvard University Press, copyright © 1945 by the President and Fellows of Harvard College, copyright © renewed 1973 by Clark Wright Heath.

TABLE III

GENERAL TYPES OF PROBLEMS CONFRONTING PARENTS IN RAISING CHILDREN
(*200 families*)

	No. of families	Per cent
General problems of social adjustment	81	40.5
Financial	30	15.0
Discipline	42	21.0
Problems arising from discord in homes	24	12.0
Health	9	4.5
How to present the subject of sex	8	4.0
Academic	7	3.5
Eating	8	4.0
Religion	5	2.5
Bed wetting	2	1.0
Fingernail biting	1	0.5
Others	19	9.5
"None of importance"	58	29.0

but also, in many cases, from homes that are discordant and disrupted" (30). Such variation was celebrated for its democratic implications, but it signals what would be a nagging theme in the study of "normal men": their difference.

A distinct pattern occurs in almost every report from the "different disciplines" in the Grant study. The psychiatrists' comment on studying the normal "personality" is a representative example: "The more one gets away from the pathological, the more numerous and subtle become the variations, and the more inadequate are attempts to classify individuals in to a few standard 'types'" (Heath 18). While typologies of "abnormal" subjects, the authors suggest, are perfectly easy to construct, these normal men were simply too differentiated for the scientists to make any claims about them that would stick. A collective hand-wringing over the heterogeneity of the "normal young men" ensues, occurring in every section (emphasis added throughout):

> "There is perhaps no realm of behavior in which this group showed a *greater variation* in ability, interest, and time devoted than athletics" (Heath 39)

> "The variety of religious belief displayed by these students was one of the most impressive features of the data. The nature of what was actually believed was *so varied* in its quality and nuance as to constitute an all but uniquely distinctive expression of the person in whom it appeared" (41)

> "*Considerable discrepancy* exists in rate of growth within both physique and personality" (48)

> "The *differences* between normal young men are, however, much greater than those which have been outlined" (51)

> "The visits and interviews in the homes of the parents disclosed a *great, at times even confusing, variety* in the home life" (53)

> "Although it is common knowledge that healthy young men vary greatly in characteristics of body build, it is noteworthy under the present circumstances that these *variations are so extensive*. Stature, for example, varies 35 cm. in the group, and there is nearly 100 per cent difference in weight. Other findings show corresponding ranges. When one considers the rather strict selectional criteria of this group of normal individuals, one cannot dismiss this fact easily" (58)

> "[There is] *considerable variability* in the group with respect to medical, physiologic, and psychometric data" (58)

Again and again, the scientists seem shocked to find so many differences among this group of carefully selected normal men. One likely explanation is that the investigators were simply able to perceive variation in the normal subject, while they were unable to see anything but sameness—lowest common denominators—in the "abnormal." Perhaps more easily projecting themselves onto their subjects, the scientists individuate "normal" men, but collectivize the "abnormal" in order to (re)produce them as deviants.

The true "discovery" of the Harvard Grant Study, then, was that when investigations of mind and body were integrated, differences among normal men made their collection into one category virtually impossible. The only thing, in fact, that made them "normal" was their a priori selection into a category with that label. What is most striking is that this flaw was perfectly visible to at least some of the authors' contemporaries. As one 1946 reviewer remarked of Hooton's text, "From the fetching title you will have guessed correctly that the professors are going to resolve that perplexing question: what is a normal young man? You have in all probability been bumbling along assuming there is no such thing. We hate to give it away, but that is just what the professors prove."[27]

The first years of the Grant Study coincided with the U.S. entry into World War II. The war, then, became part of the data to be analyzed by the first reports from the study, both of which were published early in 1945, before the bombing of Japan and the war's end. Only 11 out of 268, instead of a "statistically expected" 77, were rejected for service because of physical defects. And only three, rather than the expected 36, were rejected for "psychiatric reasons."[28] Fully 85 percent of the Grant Study subjects entered the military, and of these, 70.8 percent were commissioned officers, and only 4.1 percent "ordinary G.I.'s or 'gobs'" (Hooton 171–72). Their post-collegiate "adjustment" was rated "excellent," "normal," or "difficult" by Lewise Davies through "careful scrutiny" of the follow-up letters and data she received from them (Hooton 173). This first follow-up data allowed for the first longitudinal conclusions to be reached by Hooton at the end of *Young Man, You Are Normal*: "It is evident, then, that the ability of a man to adjust himself easily and successfully to the requirements of a military life . . . or to a civilian occupation . . . is to a considerable degree predictable from the personality traits he manifests in college" (177).

Despite this effort to align normal personality with future "adjustment," Hooton concluded his survey of the Grant Study with a final critique of the "limitation of 'normality'" which "considerably cramps the investigation of the relations between manifold aspects of the human organism." The "extremes" must be considered as well, Hooton argued: "Nature directs our attention to the composition and balance necessary for achieving the 'normal' by the gross caricatures drawn in the pathological" (181).

When George Vaillant joined the Grant Study as a psychiatrist and re-searcher in 1967, he seemed to respond to Hooton's critique by combin-ing the Grant Study data with data from two other longitudinal studies, one of "delinquent" and "non-delinquent" youth and the other of "gifted" women. In so doing, Vaillant shifted the study's focus away from normality and toward the category that these three distinct data pools held in com-mon: "adult development."

Twelve of the original Grant Study subjects withdrew while they were still in college, and eight more withdrew over the next half-century. But "for nearly sixty years (or until their deaths), the remaining 248 men have continued to participate with remarkable loyalty," answering question-naires approximately every two years, providing medical records every five years, and undergoing interviews "about every fifteen years." The men's wives and children have also been interviewed over time, to measure their impressions of the subjects' growth and "development."[29] The subjects lived well, lived long, and remained involved in the project, making it one of the most successful longitudinal studies of adult development ever undertaken. Remarkably, then, the Grant Study, while it has dropped its reference to "Normal Men," is still under way.

While the explicit focus on normality in the original Grant Study was significant, the scholarly effort was not unique. In 1949, the Rockefeller Foundation funded the investigation of "normal personality" at the newly established Institute for Personality Assessment and Research at the Uni-versity of California at Berkeley (see fig. 10).[30] By 1956, William Whyte's *Organization Man* engaged the culture of personality testing that had tak-en hold in the two decades since the conception of the Grant Study. Such testing had intensified a broader postwar culture of "normality," a term Whyte critiqued as a "mutual deception we practice on one another":

> Who is normal? All of us to some degree have a built-in urge to adjust to what we conceive as the norm, and in our search we can come to feel that in the vast ocean of normality that surrounds us only we are different. We are the victims of one another's facades.
>
> And now, with the norm formally enshrined in figures, we are more vul-nerable than ever to this tyrant. "Science" seems its ally, and thus, faulty or not, the diagnosis can provoke a sense of guilt or inadequacy; for we can forget that the norm is often the result of the instinctive striving of previous test takers to answer as they think everyone else would answer.[31]

At first glance, the Grant Study may seem an amusing relic of postwar wrong-headedness, classic "pseudoscience," a waste of time and resources—

but it was part of a burgeoning postwar industry that itself might be considered a kind of *scientia normalis*: institutes of personality assessment, mental health publications, "atlases" of the human form, diagnostic statistical manuals, and more.[32] Furthermore, its findings remain part of contemporary science. Integrating the Grant Study with two other studies in the late 1960s, Vaillant built his career on this research, publishing a major monograph on the longitudinal study every couple of decades. The work now has the status of the longest-running study of "adult development" ever undertaken, a claim that obscures its roots as three studies: the original study of 268 Harvard students; a study of 456 "inner city" Boston juveniles and delinquents; and a study of a group of 90 "gifted children" from California private schools. Data gleaned from the Grant Study is still applied and citied today, in clinical manuals, nursing series, textbooks, and other works.[33] It is, in fact, the data behind George Vaillant's recent self-help pop-science tome *Aging Well* (Little, Brown, 2002; paperback, 2003), complete with New-Agey dew-moistened fern frond on the cover. While normality has disappeared as a category for this research, its logic remains embedded in these projects.

For the Harvard Grant Study, normality was not standing in for a simplistic attribute or even a set of attributes; rather, it functioned as a way to structure knowledge: a way to semantically control an unstable and unsettling world. The message was that we don't have to worry about American men, because, as Earnest Hooton assured them, "Young man, you are normal." To the degree they were not "normal," they were "un-American."[34] Beyond their whiteness, maleness, able-bodiedness, and youth, then, the least acknowledged common ground of these embodiments of normality was their national origin. While the Americanness of normality was left unspoken by the Harvard scientists, it was the normality of "Americanness" that would inspire further discourse from a different set of midcentury scholars.

Studying National Character: "We *are* our culture."

While the Grant Study team investigated "normal men," scholars from many different corners were working to try to pin down a sense of the "national character." These parallel efforts are intrinsically related. Writing for *American Quarterly* in 1964, the historian Michael McGiffert compiled a bibliography of over 150 English-language works on the subject of the American "national character" published between 1940 and 1963.

McGiffert clustered the works under the subheadings "Culture and Personality," "National Character: Concepts and Methods," "American Character," and "The Uses of National Character Studies," but the "American Character" segment accounts for more than half of the entries. Later, McGiffert even edited an American Studies textbook on the topic. Dedicated to another midcentury scholar of American character, David Potter, *The Character of Americans: A Book of Readings* ranged from Crèvecoeur and Tocqueville through Turner, Mead, and Hsu, to Riesman, Potter, and Lipset. While the foreword argues that "for nearly two centuries Americans have been trying to explain themselves to themselves," after Frederick Jackson Turner appears, on page 100, the remainder of the more than 400-page anthology is devoted entirely to national character scholarship from the postwar decades.[35]

Why did a near-obsession with "American character" emerge during and after World War II? The war itself was crucial, if not causal, in this shift; government agencies like the OSS had called on scholars such as Margaret Mead and Ruth Benedict to apply their culture-and-personality school insights to military dilemmas: "How could civilian morale be maintained? What kind of propaganda could be most effectively employed against the enemy? How should American troops should conduct themselves in foreign lands?"[36] Social scientists pursued this work with what Mead later described as "kind of fervor," as the war had made the study of national character a matter of "grave practical importance," according to Benedict. Benedict worked for two years for the Office of War Information, but Mead was the best-known proponent of national character studies.[37] Her 1942 book *And Keep Your Powder Dry* ushered in the study of American character as a scholarly project. John Hingham dates the revival of scholarly national character studies from Mead's book and Arthur M. Schlesinger's 1942 presidential address to the American Historical Association, "What Then Is the American, This New Man?"[38] Margaret Mead had understood democracy as "a type of behavior and an attitude of mind which runs through our whole culture." Furthermore, she felt democracy could be defined and exported by determining the "American personality structure."[39] This early anthropology of the self thus went hand-in-hand with the Grant Study's discovery that "normal men" shared a "well-integrated basic personality," which is "stable, dependable, thorough, sincere, trustworthy" (Hooton 42). Once defined, the American character, like the Harvard "normal men," and like the Norm and Norma models, would be one against which any individual citizen could be measured. "We *are* our culture," Mead proclaimed.[40]

As Michael Denning and others have shown, in the early 1930s scholars, artists, and other cultural workers began to struggle over the meaning of America, of civilization, and of democracy. This "popular front" Americanism was characterized by "militant trade unionism; antiracist ethnic pluralism. . . ; and an antifascist politics of international solidarity."[41] But by the early 1950s the cultural and political logics of the Cold War helped a "generic model of ethnicity" take hold, one that, according to Nikhil Singh, "rewrote" earlier pluralist visions and substituted "a racially and ethnically unmarked national subject" in their place.[42] The "anthropological turn" was making *culture* the foundational concept for the social sciences, and thus for some scholars America itself, as Phil Gleason argues, "became normative—that is, America as a practical instance of democracy came to be equated with the abstract ideal of democracy." If America was a synecdoche for democracy, then Americans, according to dominant "culture and personality" theories of society, must exhibit inherent democratic traits.

What did postwar scholars find when they pursued "the American character"? In 1954 the sociologist Reuel Denny wrote that "observers of the American national character agree with each other in ascribing certain traits to that character [and] despite their differences in aims and methods, arrive at overlapping conclusions."[43] Margaret Mead, whose study bookmarked the turn to national character as a subject, argued that the features of the American character were a drive toward success, ambivalence about aggression, quantitative measurement of success, moral interpretation of success/failure, disinterest in the past, focus on the future, and ambivalence toward other cultures.[44] Other major social scientific texts on the topic included Riesman's extremely popular *The Lonely Crowd: A Study of the Changing American Character* (1950) and David Potter's *People of Plenty: Economic Abundance and the American Character* (1954). Both works announced their interest in national "character," but—in a post-Holocaust context,—were careful to do so without incorporating race (Potter mentions this aim explicitly). Both authors expressed anxiety about affluence, and both revealed the impact of behaviorism in social science research. In many ways, these texts were also deeply gendered in their analysis of Americans' weakness of character: both Reisman's "other-direction" and Potter's "consumerism" are cast as feminine qualities, so that anxieties about American character translate as anxieties about an increasingly feminized populace.

More significant than the content of their findings is the fact that these scholars had set up American character as a problem, and as a subject.

Postwar "American character" studies inevitably reified American character through their voluminous writings on the subject. The contours of this "character" were actively contested: Rupert Wilkinson, in a study of some twenty postwar monographs on the subject, found that over half of the them were explicitly critical of American character.[45] Nevertheless, all were in agreement that there was such a thing as a national character, and their work subtly inscribed it. In time, this "American character" would be held up as the measure of other nations' "characters" as well.

The rise of American Studies as an academic discipline is a third thread tightly interwoven with these midcentury investigations of normality and the American character. American Studies locates its "birth" in the late 1920s and early 1930s as part of a Great Depression/FDR/New Deal crisis response: a return to "bedrock" ideals and promises and a renewed political commitment to building true "cultural democracy in America."[46] The 1920s and 1930s texts that have been marked as the foundational ones for American Studies—works by V. L. Parrington, Constance Rourke, and Perry Miller, among others—worked across disciplines to achieve a synthesis of visions of America as a historical and contemporary world culture. Theirs was a quest for the "American Mind."[47] This impulse was visible in the status of American literature in the interwar years as well. In 1929, the journal *American Literature* was founded, and the Modern Language Association sponsored its first convention session on American literature; by the early 1930s, Yale was offering courses in American Civilization, and one of the first American Studies readers, *The American Mind*, was published in 1937.[48]

At this time, popular front efforts continued to define American democracy as deeply pluralistic and multivocal,[49] and work on the American national character was different in its attitude toward its subject, as well as in its scale and scope. In 1931, for example, Constance Rourke's *American Humor: A Study of National Character* emerged as a foundational and model American Studies text; W. T. Lhamon calls it "the first *theory* of American culture, conceived as such."[50] But unlike the major social science studies of American character in the 1950s, *American Humor* conceptualized American character in relatively value-neutral terms. In her foreword, Rourke describes American character as the very ground in which American folk culture (and thereafter, American literature) took root: "This book has no quarrel with the American character; one might as well dispute with some established feature in the natural landscape."[51] Furthermore, in the 1930s and '40s, the lines between American Studies and national character studies were difficult to map. David Riesman's early work on the national character, like that of many other social scientists with qualitative tendencies, was published in American Studies journals. David Potter was the first Coe Professor of American Studies at Yale. Scholarship on the American character thus emerged precisely at the intersection of American Studies and the "culture and personality" experiments of social science. The outbreak of World War II, however, would be a crucial factor in the institutionalization and politicization of American Studies.

As the United States approached World War II, a conviction took hold that democracy was "a real, dynamic, burning creed worth fighting for."[52] On the one hand, the war sparked and sustained an anti-fascist, anti-racist vision for American democracy. On the other hand, it spawned an atmosphere of "excessive nationalism" that spurred scholarly interest in charting national history, literature, and culture. As U.S. involvement in the conflict deepened, American Studies burgeoned into a full-fledged field of its own. The war proved to be an impetus for the institutionalization of American Studies, for the turn to the study of "American character," and for the export and dissemination of these ideals via work on democracy and the establishment of American Studies programs abroad.

The years between 1945 and 1960 have thus been described as a "golden age" for American Studies. This period saw the production of a library of "classical" monographs that developed a lasting template for the interdisciplinary cultural study of the United States. Major, well-funded programs were chartered and proved highly popular with scholars and their students; the *American Quarterly* and the American Studies Association were founded; and the first doctoral degrees granted.[53]

By 1950, a shift had also taken place in American Studies scholarship, from individualized, satellite efforts to more cooperative, institutional efforts with corporate and governmental support. At this moment, the project of American Studies (on the surface, at least) meshed well enough with Cold War politics to secure government funding necessary to allow it to flourish. Often the political and intellectual crossover was explicit: some scholars had direct OSS ties, and later American Studies programs became fertile recruiting grounds for the CIA.[54] Early letters regarding the foundation of the American Studies program at Yale, for example, were unambiguous about the program's foreign policy and political mission: "In the international scene it is clear that our government has not been too effective in blazoning to Europe and Asia, as a weapon in the 'cold war,' the merits of our way of thinking and living in America."[55] American Studies was positioned to be at the very least a kind of boosterism, and at best, according to the Yale program's prospectus, a "safeguard against totalitarianism." To further this aim, American Studies programs would eventually begin to produce experts for export: graduates could enter government service and "set out to another shore . . . to articulate, if they can, what we stand for."[56]

As much as the Grant Study and the national character studies, then, around midcentury the discipline of American Studies helped to construct a dominant ideology of what "America" meant. While critiques of the United States as an unfinished democracy continued after the war,[57] the emergence of the Cold War simplified the terms of debate. As the United States and the USSR were constructed as ideologically opposed superpowers, the definition of "the American way" needed to be streamlined for export. In Cold War discourse, the USSR posed a challenge to the United States precisely on the terms that social scientists and humanities scholars had posited. From the exemplary moment of the Kitchen Debates onward, "American character" and something called the "American way of life" would be constantly reified through the struggle to win "hearts and minds."

In the introduction to the volume *What People Are: A Study of Normal Young Men*, Clark Heath had argued that "the great questions" of his time were those "concerning people themselves: how to produce in them self-respect and self-reliance; how to influence them through better home situations, better schooling, suitable occupations, and the development of routines in government, business, and social life in which all may have confidence" (6). Here the pursuit of "normality" was deeply tied to a need for more "confidence" in the character of Americans—qualities such as self-respect and self-reliance—as well as confidence in the nation itself—institutions such as home, school, government, business, social life. In the postwar decades, the ideas that America "stood for" became normative, and postwar American Studies became, for a time, a "fundamentally nationalist project."[58] Normalizing the nation meant that to be American was to be normal; to be normal was to be American.

3

Passing for Normal
Fashioning a Postwar Middle Class

Part of the seductive power of normality was its statistical alignment with the middle: the "normal" curve plotting out the midpoint on a continuum. For postwar Americans, the middle seemed a safe place—secure and solid—not a life on the social or economic fringes. If "normal" meant the middle, the pursuit of "normality" meant becoming, or remaining, middle class. But the postwar middle was shifting ground.

A 1959 *Look* magazine cartoon by Ned Hilton (fig. 17) both acknowledges and lampoons postwar Americans' obsessions with their own status. A white, suburban housewife is sitting on a couch reading. She pauses to asks her pipe-smoking husband, "Are we in the uppermost upper part of the lower middle class, or the mid-lower part of the *upper* middle class?" These questions suggest that even in the late 1950s, the most bourgeois Americans were still struggling over their own socioeconomic standing. But the most telling implication of the cartoon was that everyone, at least everyone who read *Look* magazine, was *somewhere* in the middle class.

In the past, class status might have been determined by a combination of income and occupation, education, and place of residence, but post–World War II economic shifts and public policies brought all of these factors into uneven relation. As affluence became more widespread in the 1950s, income and occupation became less reliable as predictors of class status. The GI Bill made a college education available to a much wider cross-section of Americans, so higher education was no longer a clear mark of income or status. And as millions of GIs flocked with their families to become homeowners in the suburbs, older geographies of class were up-

66

ended as well. Thus while millions of Americans may have been passing into a middle-income range economically, their class status could remain uncertain. For example, census figures show that between 1947 and 1959 median family incomes rose more than twice as fast as living costs—from $4,000 to $5,400, after taking inflation into account—and that by 1959 roughly 40 percent of the nation's families were in the $5,000 to $10,000 bracket. *Fortune* magazine found, however, that in 1953, when the median income was $4,242, fully 60 percent of the 15.5 million families in the $4,000–$7,000 income bracket were headed by "blue-collar workers." A rising income, in other words, did not necessarily signify a move into the middle class in terms of status. A 1950 Chicago study found that clerical workers, who were typically lumped in with professional, managerial, and sales workers as "white collar," had the education level of managerial workers, but the income level and "residential distribution" of craftsmen and operatives.[1] Nevertheless, just as the facts of being middle class were in transition, the *feeling* of being middle class was solidifying.

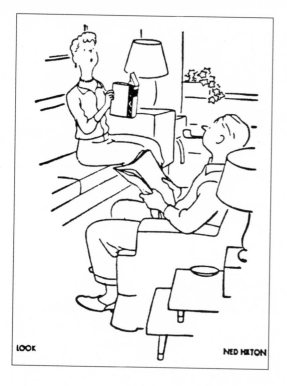

Figure 17. "Are we in the uppermost upper part of the lower middle class, or the mid-lower part of the *upper* middle class?" cartoon by Ned Hilton, *Look*, Aug. 1959.

The historian Beth Bailey has therefore argued for a "cultural" definition of middle-class in postwar America. She cites statistics that support the notion that a broadening spectrum postwar Americans claimed middle-class status out of a need to be affiliated with the "middle." One 1953 Purdue University survey, for example, asked a large, representative sample of American high school students to choose among four labels for their family's social class: upper class, middle class, working class, lower class. Forty-seven percent of the respondents whose fathers were "unskilled laborers," 59 percent of those whose fathers had "mid-level jobs working with tools," 48 percent of those from "low" income families, and 52 percent of those whose mothers had no education beyond grade school all identified themselves as middle-class. Bailey concludes that the general postwar culture was "a culture *defined* as middle class."[2] In a 1961 article, the sociologist Robert H. Bohlke argued that "values" and "virtues" were the defining characteristics of the middle class, and relegated statistics on income to his footnotes.[3] Regardless of their socioeconomic conditions, it seems, postwar individuals felt pressed to "pass" as middle class, an identity that was cast more as a matter of surfaces and appearances than structures or depth.

This tension is at the center of the iconic 1955 postwar text, Sloan Wilson's novel *The Man in the Gray Flannel Suit*. In the context of a general postwar transition from scarcity to abundance, the gray flannel suit itself both masked and revealed the paradoxes of a growing middle class. This exterior uniform allowed the postwar "middle" to be perceived—and to perceive itself—as normal, as unified, as uniform. The suit itself, or the "white collar" of the shirt beneath it, was a tautological mark: wearing a suit meant being middle-class; being middle-class meant wearing a suit. But a closer look at the culture surrounding this midcentury uniform reveals that this variety of "normality" was only suit-deep—not only for those Americans still in the process of moving into the middle class, but also for those who might be expected to embody it most perfectly. American middle class identity was becoming a performance, fashioned out of consumer surfaces.

"GI Dilemma": From Zoot Suit to Postwar Uniform

Although still somewhat marginalized by historians, fashion, as Lois Banner notes, is "an integral part of the culture of any period." Simultaneously constituting art, material culture, design, and consumer culture, fashion "provides bodies with meaning and identity and makes them social," the fashion historian Christine Boydell writes.[4] Fashion can be distinctive, but it can also be a homogenizing force, collecting us into groups, blurring distinctions. As a material culture remnant, the gray flannel suit has been seen as a mark of conformity, a bit of inconspicuous consumption in a postwar consumerist culture. Ironically enough, at the time, its very drab sameness drew considerable attention. In the 1951 sci-fi classic *The Day the Earth Stood Still*, for example, an alien visitor named Klaatu, simply by donning a gray flannel suit, is able to pass as a mild-mannered business-man for the rest of the film. The first line of the sociological study *White Collar*, by C. Wright Mills, published the same year, echoes such sci-fi paranoia by casting fashion as a kind of disguise, masking another sort of invasion: "The white-collar people slipped quietly into modern soci-ety."[5] In both cases, the clothing identifies—or misidentifies—its wearer as respectable and middle-class. Before World War II, the fashion historian Anne Hollander argues, there still existed "huge visible divisions between the classes" in apparel, but the postwar suit helped disguise those differ-ences, and it allowed suburbanites—importantly, *white* suburbanites—to "assimilate" one another into a kind of "middle-classlessness."[6] In the de-cades following the end of the war, the suit functioned as a sign, symbol, and symptom of struggles over postwar middle-class identity. Effectively masking the starkest of differences, the gray flannel suit helped its wearers to "pass" for normal.

A few weeks after V-J Day, a *New York Times* feature titled "New Plum-age for the Male Animal" set up postwar men's fashion as an explicit dilemma. The accompanying drawing shows a panicky, uniformed GI trapped between two mirrors showing competing images of himself, the first in a conservative dark suit, the second in a flamboyant polka-dot and checkered ensemble with broad-brimmed hat. The caption reads, "GI di-lemma—Blue serge or all the colors of a rainbow?" The article, by Edith Efron, cites some fashion designers' predictions: "In the shiny new post-war world, . . . men are going to want things different . . . Color!" Other designers, however, "hot for the status quo, . . . can't think of anything nattier than a nice gray suit with a dark blue tie." Efron interviewed men on the street to discover a firm consensus response: "It all depends on what everyone else is wearing." Ex-serviceman Merrill Mitchell, the editor of the ad industry publication *Men's Modes,* concluded, "I'm an average man, I think, and I sure wouldn't want to dress up in a lot of colors."[7]

He was right. Postwar men chose the somber business suit over more flamboyant alternatives. This gray-flannel surface, inconspicuous and unmarked, hegemonic and status quo—constituted a move toward the middle, not the margins. Two years earlier, the excesses of the "zoot suit" had made the headlines. Where the zoot suit had mocked the middle class, the gray flannel suit embraced it. Since wearing a zoot suit had been cast as un-American, donning a gray flannel suit became the postwar man's patriotic duty.

The term "zoot," likely a play on the word "suit," meant "something done or worn in an exaggerated style."[8] In the early 1940s, facing harsh repression in the contest over opportunities and acceptance, more and more black and Chicano men began to don the zoot suit as a form of cultural resistance, to set themselves apart from both "mainstream" Anglo culture and their often assimilationist parents. The *pachuco* style was characterized by flamboyant, brightly colored, and long-cut jackets, baggy pants, and broad-brimmed hats. This costume mocked and confronted Anglo society, suggesting an ethnic pride that was unmistakable and highly visible (fig. 18).

The historian Edward Escobar notes the precedent set in 1938, when the Los Angeles Police Department declared a "war on crime" and began intensively patrolling specifically black and Latino areas of the city (a practice that continued throughout the war), effectively linking race and crime together in police policy for the first time.[9] In a climate of strong anti-Latino sentiment, the War Production Board banned zoot suit production in March 1942. Cloth rationing made the suit "contraband," and its wearers could therefore be marked as unpatriotic and un-American.[10]

Escalating racial conflicts between police and young zoot-suiters in the wake of the infamous 1942 "Sleepy Lagoon" murder case, along with sensational and alarmist press coverage, culminated in a full-scale race riot in Los Angeles in June 1943. For eight days, scores of white U.S. servicemen—sometimes accompanied by civilians and police—roamed the streets and attacked and beat zoot-suiters, often stripping them and leaving them naked and bleeding. As the riots intensified, attackers entered homes, theaters, bars, and restaurants, eventually targeting any Chicano or African American youth, whether wearing a zoot suit or not. The L.A.P.D. allowed the beatings, then moved in and made their arrests. In all, some six hundred Mexican-Americans were arrested for "disturbing the peace," along with a "handful" of servicemen.[11] In the midst of the riots the City Council passed a resolution to ban the wearing of a zoot suit within the city limits.[12]

The Los Angeles Zoot Suit Riots have become an important touchstone for revisionist histories of the racial/ethnic and youth subcultures that co-

FIGURE 18. "A Los Angeles police officer pretends to clip the 'Argentine' hair-style of a young pachuco zoot-suiter." From Cosgrove, "The Zoot Suit and Style Warfare." By permission of Oxford University Press.

alesced during World War II and continued in the postwar period. The zoot suit itself had been a target, but it also became a lasting symbol of self-possession and membership in a "brotherhood." Ralph Ellison's title character in *Invisible Man* (1952) discovers this collective identity when he dons a zoot suit: "[It] was as though by dressing and walking in a certain way I had enlisted in a fraternity in which I was recognized at a glance—not by features, but by clothes, by uniform, by gait."[13] The zoot suit transformed the dress suit from something mundane into something unique, dramatic, and outrageous. The zoot subculture would also have links to the radicalizing social movements of the 1950s, 1960s, and 1970s: long before they became activists, Malcolm X wore a zoot suit, and Caesar Chávez was an L.A. *pachuco*.[14]

The zoot suit mocked the respectability that a "straight" suit was imagined to confer, but it also amplified the potency of fashion as a site for power relations. The zoot-suiters wore their garments as a visible manifestation not only of class position, but also of ethnic or racial identity, political belief, and a gendered claim to power. In this way, the spectacular zoot suit brought the gray flannel suit into relief as the mild-mannered uniform of the conservative, domesticated, "American" middle-class. It also helped establish men's fashion as a site for continued social rebellion.[15]

Inconspicuous Consumption: "Keeping Down with the Joneses"

Well before the war's end, the suit was an explicit topic for public conversation. Fashion editors and the menswear trade were bracing themselves for the demobilization of millions of men who would be eager to swap their uniforms for civilian clothes. In July 1945, Oscar E. Schoeffler, the fashion editor of *Esquire* and *Apparel Arts* magazines, told a gathering of the International Association of Clothing Designers to anticipate "mass fashions" in order to aid the industry in retaining its wartime volume. His forecast included a new uniformity of body: "Broadening of shoulders and slimming of waists in Army training will have an effect upon the men's fashion silhouette," he noted, and returning veterans will demand clothes "as comfortable and utilitarian as those supplied by the military."[16]

The cover of the *New Yorker* issue of June 16, 1945 (fig. 19) emphasized this irony with a tongue-in-cheek cartoon illustration of a paper-doll World War II soldier surrounded by his various postwar apparel choices: dark and pinstriped business suits, golf togs, smoking jacket, tuxedo, and topcoats. Notably, this doll's original, permanent clothes are not tasteful white skivvies, but his army uniform. This image effectively linked the returning GI to the postwar white-collar businessman by inviting the viewer—mentally, at least—to place the clothing of one over the other. Under all the new postwar fashions, then, this smiling American male would always be a soldier. The artist's use of the paper-doll format parodied what must have seemed to be an amusing sameness in the millions of American men shifting en masse from military to civilian life, and from one uniform to another. "The uniform of the day," thinks Tom Rath, protagonist of *The Man in the Gray Flannel Suit*; "Somebody must have put out an order."[17]

Psychologically, there may have been some comfort in perpetuating the uniformity of dress that had characterized wartime, but the evidence suggests that returning GIs were eager to shed their tired uniforms for civilian clothes.[18] In fact, the immediate postwar years of 1945 and 1946 saw a national suit shortage, affecting even President Truman himself.[19] One sheriff

FIGURE 19. Cover illustration by Alajalov. *The New Yorker*, 16 June 1945. Constantin Alajalov, © Condé Nast Publications.

in Rockford, Illinois, unable to find a summer suit in his size, pinned his badge on a pickle-barrel and, "clad only in his barrel, straw hat, tie and shoes," marched down to the CPA office to talk about the shortage.[20] By October 1945 some retailers were refusing to sell suits to anyone not wearing a service emblem.[21] Six months later white shirts were still in short supply, and President Truman still "could give no assurances when shirts or two-pants suits might be generally available."[22] One journalist reported that "the crying need is for suits, and suits are the immediate and biggest concern of the Civilian Production Administration."[23]

Although the end of World War II brought suits into public discourse, the men's business suit certainly predates the period. A form of the suit appears at least as early as the late seventeenth century, when what fashion historians call the "great masculine renunciation" resulted in a movement away from ornament and display and toward conservative, clerical simplicity.[24] By the middle of the nineteenth century, the business suit as we now recognize it—the broad-shouldered, straight-lined, three-piece ensemble—was well in vogue, often topped by a bowler hat by the turn of the century. According to Anne Hollander, "male lounge suits" finally came into their own between 1910 and 1930, "as esthetic echoes of the machine age."[25] Even the suspicion over the uniformity of men in suits is not new. A 1909 trade magazine, for example, singled out the bowler hat as "an abomination to the individualist."[26] What, then, was new about the post–World War II suit?

Even for apparel that inherently has a very limited degree of style flexibility, postwar suits show surprising similarity in cut, style, and color. Compared with the softer-cut suits of the 1930s and 1940s and the wider ties, lapels, and pants of the late 1960s and early 1970s, postwar suits were more severe and subdued, with a streamlined, military stiffness that was more confined, controlled, columnar. Extremely straight-edged hankies rise like stiff military bars over the breast pocket. Nothing swings loose, nothing is tufted. Such crisp verticality set the gray flannel suit apart from more rounded, differentiated, or loose-fitting business apparel of other periods. Suits of the 1950s have little if any ornamentation. Hollander champions the sexiness and utter modernity of the business suit, but even she bemoans a "return to unmodern circumstances" in the post–World War II years, when "male fashion became more intensely sober, rigid and deliberately reticent."[27]

Postwar suits in and of themselves are unremarkable—but then that was the point. It was desirable to look like everyone else, to blend in, to be inconspicuous.[28] According to a sly 1948 *Fortune* magazine essay, "The Business Suit," the somber postwar version reflected a "lust for *security*" as opposed to a lust for money, and was intended to exhibit "membership [in] a *respectable* class; for this reason it [was] uniform."[29] These middle-class attributes—security and respectability—were stitched into the suit itself, so that it would somehow demonstrate both. The same *Fortune* article listed the characteristics of the "one category of business suit" that was always "wholly acceptable": "The S.E. [Standard Executive] or N.A.M. [National Association of Manufacturers] is most commonly a neutral-colored, double-breasted affair, remarkable neither for trimness nor for premeditated illness of fit. It is usually worn with a soft shirt and a necktie either deadly sober or dully bright." The writer concludes, unequivocally, that this suit is "the safest garb," which "may be, profoundly, why so many people wear it. Uniforms still matter."[30] The homogenous features of the postwar suit—the qualities that made it "uniform"—also made it safe.

Men in particular craved apparel that would satisfy their need to communicate "conformity" and "conservatism," according to the authors of a 1958 article titled "Can You Sell Conformity?" in the marketing journal *Tide*. Describing the findings of a *Chicago Tribune* study of buyer motivations, the *Tide* piece notes that men dress well out of a "fear of ridicule" for being slovenly, and a fear "of being embarrassed in a social situation." Men dress "not to create an image or to strive for a goal as much as they dress to avoid being wrong." A 1957 *Ladies' Home Journal* cartoon bears out this claim, even as it highlights the gendered power struggles over the bounds of class and taste. An exasperated wife looks on as her husband tries to choose between two equally garish ties to complement his violently striped sportcoat; the caption reads, "Well, *I'll* tell you something that won't go with that jacket—ME!"[31] According to the market research, some 1950s advertisers capitalized on this "fear motivation," while others tried to convince "psychological suburbanites" that they were really "frustrated, continental bon vivant[s]." *Real* men-in-suits, according to *Tide*, "recoil" from newness and have a "vehement antipathy to daring and attention-getting apparel." "A fancy Ivy League" suit, the author argues, would be as much of a threat as a shabby one, since both would fail to be inconspicuous.[32]

The jacket of *The Man in the Gray Flannel Suit* shows a slim, suited man, striking what looks like a military "at ease" stance. With shoulders squared, feet apart, and hands clasped behind him, this dark-gray figure is a clever combination of legibility and illegibility (fig. 20). The copy on the dust jacket of the first edition emphasized that the gray flannel suit was a direct descendant of the World War II uniform, and that this transition was in fact the "theme" of the novel: "These men are all over America wearing gray flannel. A few short years back, they were wearing uniforms of olive drab. The central theme of this novel is the struggle of a man to adapt himself from the relative security of O.D. [olive drab] to the insecurity of gray flannel."[33] Ironically, wartime is seen as a time of "relative security," while the postwar world is marked by "insecurity." The turn to gray flannel—a

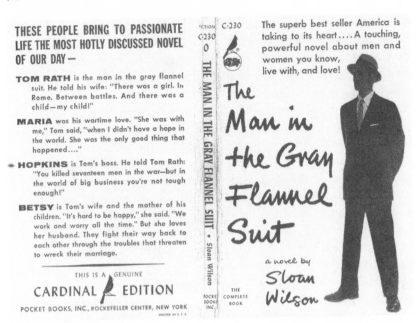

FIGURE 20. Cover of *The Man in the Gray Flannel Suit* by Sloan Wilson. Copyright © 1955 by Sloan Wilson. Reprinted with the permission of Simon & Schuster, Inc. All rights reserved.

re-turn to drab—was a contradictory move. The 1956 paperback edition implies that readers of the 1950s already knew this hero's story: "The superb best seller America is taking to its heart. . . . A touching, powerful novel about men and women you know, live with, and love!"

The Man in the Gray Flannel Suit was extremely popular. Critics praised it, especially for its realism: "This is a good novel—neat, smooth, and reportorially exact in its account of the pressures, problems and tribal customs of the men in gray flannel suits."[34] The novel was a Literary Guild choice even before it landed in book and department stores, and a big-budget Twentieth Century–Fox motion picture two years after its debut.[35] Sloan Wilson had tapped into the issues of his day, and by suggesting "The Man in the Gray Flannel Suit" as a title, his wife, Elise Pickhardt Wilson, provided a powerful metaphor at a pivotal moment.[36]

The shadow of World War II dominates this text, though it was published over a decade after the war's end. The novel features a back-and-forth between veteran Tom Rath's tribulations in his new job and flashbacks to his service as an army paratrooper in the war. Living with his wife and two children in a Connecticut suburb, Tom Rath one day "glance[s] down" and is shocked to discover that "[he] too [is] wearing a gray flannel suit" (283). Like other middle-level office workers, he has automatically donned gray flannel to go to work, denoting his membership in a tribe. Tom Rath's new public relations job in a cutthroat broadcasting corporation unearths his disturbing memories of the war, and his wartime secrets literally come back to haunt him: he killed seventeen men, he accidentally killed his best friend with a grenade, and in his most hopeless hour, he began a passionate affair and fathered a child with a young woman in Italy. Wilson links Rath's postwar anxieties directly to his wartime ones: his own dishonesty playing the corporate "yes-man," for example, reminds him that he has also been lying every day to his wife about his earlier affair. The very nihilism that helped him survive combat, he realizes, is what helps him adapt to the humiliations and immoralities of big business.

Rath pretends to be "adjusted," but the war is always just a flashback away, triggered by a passerby's leather jacket, the familiar face of an elevator operator, or the captivity of a train ride to work—a little too similar to his airlifts as a paratrooper. The experience of war has created a deep fear that still permeates Tom's world—a fear of death (evidenced by the obsessions with "life insurance"), a fear of losing his wife, a fear of losing his class position, of losing his job—or worse, the fear of *keeping* his job and being swallowed into the corporation. "It hadn't been necessary for a man to be very bright to be a soldier; all he had to do was to remember a few basic rules," Tom recalls (74). What, he wonders, were the rules in a postwar context?

In one climactic scene, Tom realizes that he mustn't expect to know himself or to find meaning in his work—he must just "keep his gray flannel suit pressed," as if it were a costume in a performance: "They ought to begin wars with a course in basic training and end them with a course in basic forgetting. . . . for now is the time to raise legitimate children, and make money, and dress properly, and be kind to one's wife, and admire one's boss, and learn not to worry—I'm just a man in a gray flannel suit. I must keep my suit neatly pressed like anyone else, for I am a very respectable young man" (101). In a postwar context, then, the "rules" were simply to pass for normal: to remember one's lines, to raise children, to work hard, dress well, and try not to think about who one was under one's gray flannel uniform.

The Man in the Gray Flannel Suit, in telling the story of the dangers of Tom Rath's dishonesty, warns against trading depth for surface. The novel's resolution only comes about when Tom unifies his past with his present, and takes the "honest" approach both at home and at work. With the help of his clear-sighted wife, Betsey (who criticizes his cynical approach to his job), and the moral vision of working-class elevator operator Caesar Gardella (who—having served with Tom in the war—reminds him to do the right thing for the woman and child he left behind in Italy), Tom eventually recovers his integrity. He levels with both his wife and his boss, and in the end is able to enjoy the things he thought incompatible: honesty and financial reward, integrity and corporate employment.

Like so many others, Tom Rath had gone from the uniformed positions on "slate-gray troopships" to the uniformity of gray flannel suits and the "opaque-glass-brick-partitioned world" of the corporation, searching for comfort again in "routine" (23). He finds the postwar world of the gray flannel suit nearly as dangerously threatening as the war had been. For postwar men who were *newly* or marginally middle-class, however—especially previously poor or working-class whites, African Americans and other minorities, and first- or second-generation immigrants—the suit, like the military uniform that had preceded it, retained its democratizing potential: it helped to signify a move into the middle class, a move toward the mainstream. Was this new middle class of alienated organization men the postwar male's version of "the problem with no name," or was it more of a name with no problem?[37] Prominent social critics played their own part in the construction of a problematic "new middle class." And the suburban dwellers whom William Whyte found "keeping *down* with the Joneses" had a sense of what was at stake: fashioning the "middle" required the downplaying of lingering class distinctions.

"Surface Uniformities": The Sociological Critique

Two of the most prominent observers of the generalities of postwar men in suits were C. Wright Mills, a Columbia University sociologist, and William H. Whyte, a Princeton-trained sociologist who was assistant managing editor at *Fortune*.[38] In his 1951 study *White Collar: The American Middle Classes*, Mills not only employed the sartorial "white collar" (first coined by Upton Sinclair) to define his subject, he claimed that these workers in particular constituted the "new middle class," and, further, that this new middle class was "symptom and symbol of modern society as a whole" (xx). Whyte's popular 1956 text *The Organization Man* took a more anthropological approach to the corporate employee, studying him in school, at work, and cavorting in his natural habitat of "suburbia." Whyte was also anxious about his subject, concluding that corporations and social institutions should emphasize individualist thinking in order to keep the new "Social Ethic" of "group-mindedness" in check (435).

Writing from their respective positions at Columbia and *Fortune*, Mills and Whyte were the white-collar organization men they wrote about. Mills placed "professors" in his categorization of white-collar workers, and some of his most impassioned writing falls within his critique of the incorporation of the intellectual: "The political intellectual is, increasingly, an employee living off the communication machineries which are based on the very opposite of what he would like to stand for" (129, 159). Whyte thanks his managing editor at *Fortune* in his acknowledgments page, "and not merely because I am a good organization man," he adds. Such positionality lent an urgency to their texts: they knew whereof they spoke. But it also led them to generalize from where they stood.[39]

Both authors confess a lack of clarity about their subjects. Mills admits the group may be diverse, but argues that it could be distinguished by what it was not—neither an "entrepreneur class" nor "manual laborers." Mills understands the middle class only in relation to others. Even the structure of his text reveals this, as he begins with a section on the "Old Middle Classes" in order for his "New Middle Class" to become perceptible. He is not sure who is middle, but he knows they are neither propertied entrepreneurs nor unionized workers. Although Mills refers to white-collar men and women regularly, and acknowledges the presence of women in the "white-collar pyramids"—with seven pages devoted to the "Office Girl"—his conception remains largely male. The whiteness of these "new" middle classes and of the "organization men" is so much a part of the definition that the two critics barely acknowledge it. Such realities as the new segregation in suburbia, created by racially restricted lending and housing policies, are mentioned only in passing as "segregation problems" by Whyte (325). The hiring of only "native-born" workers for white-collar jobs, which Mills calls "status by descent" (74)—is mentioned just once or twice in these studies, which run to four and five hundred pages. Instead, it is the suit—what Mills calls white-collared "street clothes"—that becomes the visible symptom which enables them to define and diagnose the disorders of the "new middle classes."[40]

Whyte states early on that he has a subject, but is unsure how to tackle it: "This book is about the organization man. If the term is vague, it is because I can think of no other way to describe the people I am talking about" (3). His suburban interviewees show similar confusion in trying to describe the distinctions between themselves as residents of the solidly middle-class Chicago suburb of Park Forest and their neighbors in the lower-priced adjacent development of Eastgate: "No one can bring himself to say 'working-class people'; the phrases are more likely to be 'people who work with their hands more than their heads,' 'artisans,' or, at worst, 'blue collar'" (340). Whyte acknowledges that Park Forest residents have "pretensions of classlessness" that "strain" under the proximity of working-class "newcomers," yet he continues to collect together "suburbanites" as a class himself. The vagaries of the postwar middle class were thus perplexing even to those who claimed to be experts.

Generally, Whyte's work is descriptive; he is, as one critic noted, an "industrious investigator."[41] What disturbs Whyte most is the "Social Ethic" replacing the Protestant Ethic: he fears for the individual in the face of corporations that ask men to hand over their souls, and he fears for individuality in organization families where men, women, and children became ensnared in "webs" of friendship and "tyranny of the majority" in the suburbs (6, 365, 439). Purporting to write specifically about men who *belong* to the organizations they work for, Whyte regularly collapses them together as "suburbanites" in general, the "middle class," or the "main stream" (309, 12, 3) By the end, he is studying bridge parties, church-going, and child-rearing.

And how does the suit figure into these texts? For Mills, exterior appearance becomes one of the few ways he is able to collect these workers together and conceptualize them as a class. In his appendixes, Mills relies on a Bureau of Labor Statistics paper on the "Problem of Definition" to define white-collar workers: "The Labor Economics Staff of the Bureau of Labor Statistics uses, along with 'fixed payment by the day, week, or month,' two other criteria which I found helpful: 'A well-groomed appearance' and 'the wearing of street clothes at work'" (359). In a postwar context, then, he relies on surfaces—cleanliness and fashion—to demarcate class.

The Organization Man was published only a year after Wilson's *Man in the Gray Flannel Suit*, and by the same publisher. Perhaps because of this, Whyte pointedly refuses to discuss the suit as significant. In fact, he protests too much:

> I am not . . . addressing myself to the surface uniformities of U.S. life. There will be no strictures in this book against "Mass Man" . . . against ranch wagons, or television sets, or gray flannel suits. They are irrelevant to the main problem, and furthermore, there's no harm in them. . . . Unless one believes poverty ennobling, it is difficult to see the three-button suit as more of a strait jacket than overalls, or the ranch-type house than old law tenements.

> And how important, really, are these uniformities to the central issue of individualism? . . . The man who drives a Buick Special and lives in a ranch-type house can assert himself as effectively and courageously against his particular society as the bohemian against his particular society. He usually does not, it is true, but if he does, the surface uniformities can serve quite well as protective coloration. (11–12)

Here Whyte clearly links exterior appearances (suits, overalls, ranch houses, tenements) to class identities. Yet his invocation of the "gray flannel suits" shows that the suit was by this point the subject of what seemed to him tiresome debate. Whyte's argument is that the suit could function as a kind of camouflage; since "surface uniformities" are "disarming," he suggests, clever organization men can dress one way, and act another. More precisely, they can *look* like conformists but *act* like individuals. Faulty logic operates in Whyte's description of the suit as "irrelevant" and "harmless" followed by his advice to use the suit as "protective coloration" in order to act more deviant. If the suit can operate as a disguise, then it is no longer harmless.

Whyte proposes that the Organization Man can "turn the future away from the dehumanized collective" by studying his sardonic final chapter, "How to Cheat on Personality Tests." This chapter, along with his concluding discussions of facades and the "mutual deception" of trying to be normal, reveals that normality as a homogenizing concept could be produced and critiqued simultaneously. Whyte closes with the wry promise that "in all of us there is a streak of normalcy" (441, 456). In his view, the resistance to conformity lay in what he himself had achieved: an awareness, or self-consciousness about one's own conformity.

Whyte's analysis of the suffering of "the deviant" and the paradoxical combination of control and warmth from "the group" illuminate the contradictions of a culture in which being middle class could be both a mark of security—the comfort of "fitting in"—and a mark of conformity—the anomie of being indistinguishable from all the rest. His notions of "keeping *down* with the Joneses," "inconspicuous consumption" and "belongingness" were philosophies that united the postwar middle class, yet all of these practices were about surfaces, rather than interiors.

A 1956 Bureau of Labor Statistics essay titled "White-Collar Employment and Income" divided laborers into two groups: "office" workers and "factory" workers.[42] This simplified conceptualization of class divided workers by their places of work and by the colors of their collars.[43] With the moral and intellectual authority of the postwar "expert," both Mills and Whyte had also helped to locate white collar corporate workers in the middle and to cast them as a class. In this way, the sociological critique functioned to normalize middle-class identity.[44]

In 1951 Mills argued that "in America, unlike Europe, the fate of white-collar types is not yet clear" (xi). But it would be. In 1955 Wilson's meta-phor of "the man in the gray flannel suit" helped further define the white-collar "type," and in 1956 *The Organization Man* had charted his fate. As early as 1957, however, parodies such Frank Tashlin's farce *Will Success Spoil Rock Hunter?* (Twentieth Century–Fox) were already turning this white-collar office worker into a comic figure.[45] While the sociological cri-tique had helped to imagine a postwar middle class, the irony attached to the gray flannel suit almost from the beginning would begin to reimagine it—through the fashion of the sensitive, alienated, individualistic "rebel."

Rebel without a Tie: Establishing "The Establishment"

For the zoot-suiters of the 1940s, the suit had been a site for the ar-ticulation of style, individuality, and resistance to the homogeneity and respectability of the middle class. The Zoot Suit Riots showed that the zoot suit could lead to the literal imprisonment of the young men rebel-lious enough to wear it. By the mid-to-late 1950s, the gray flannel suit came to connote entrapment, but this time it was the securely middle-class gray-flannel workers who were "imprisoned in brotherhood" at the corporation (Whyte 404). Unlike the zoot suit, with its exaggerations and put-ons, sartorial rebellion would now be about taking it off. For many middle-class whites, the gray flannel suit's association with normal-ity began to connote a conformity that felt dangerous to the integrity of the "individual." Tellingly, white male rebels would choose to reject the gray flannel suit precisely as many women and people of color were at last gaining access to its privileges. As Fred Miller Robinson has suggested, the "fear that people will look like one another" is "fundamentally" an alarm over "the blurring of class boundaries . . . [or] the sartorial assimilation of all classes."[46]

Elise Pickhardt Wilson's role in suggesting the title for her husband's best-selling novel *The Man in the Gray Flannel Suit* brings to mind the gender dynamics at play in making the suit a metaphor for middle-class identity. The focus on the "gray flannel suit" or "white collar" or "organiza-tion *men*" following World War II had subtly gendered the definition of middle-class status. Yet, as the novel's publisher suggested, if ambivalence over the business suit and all it represented was a "theme," it was one often more visible to the wives of these men than to the men themselves. In 1958 Madeleine Carroll Heiskell, a former British actress who was married to the publisher of *Life* magazine, gave a speech reprinted in the advertising trade journal *Tide*, titled "The Wife of the Man in the Grey Flannel Suit." Through her title, she revealed that the gray flannel suit had become symbolic, a reference point for her advice about gender roles and the perilous tension between white-collar work and white-collar marriage: "Marriage is *being with each other*, Grey Flannel Suit, or no," she argued. In her conclusion, Heiskell recommended that "to make a marriage work in our difficult times—wives should ideally try and limit their activities to that time of day when their husbands, too, are occupied."[47] Subtly equating women's domestic labor with men's wage labor, Mrs. Heiskell (as she was identified by *Tide*), implied that women, too, should be able to confine their work to business hours, "flannel suit or no."

Although women were excluded from the suit-centered anxieties of the late 1940s, they were of course subject to the forces of fashion, shaped by and encased in sexualized uniforms of normative femininity: rubber girdles and bullet bras, especially, as well as crinolines, circle skirts, pumps, and tightly-fitted shirt and sweaters.[48] By the late 1950s, however, women were no longer beyond the reach of gray flannel. An April 1957 *Ladies' Home Journal* issue contained a fashion spread titled, suggestively, "A Suit of Importance." Featuring gray flannel work suits for women, the copy notes that "a gray flannel suit [is the] basis of a spring wardrobe." The editors recommend that women "wear clear yellows with gray flannel" with "cork beige for casual accents."[49] The discourses on the new middle classes may have been gendered male, but the symbolic value of the gray flannel suit had made it a sign of "importance" powerful enough to be grafted onto any body.

For African American men whose humanity itself was being denied under Jim Crow, putting on the suit could be both necessary and strategic: a powerful public pronouncement of manhood. Cornel West has noted the symbolic value of the suit for black male political leaders in the 1950s and '60s: "The black dress suits with white shirts worn by Malcolm X and Martin Luther King Jr. signified the seriousness of their deep commitment to black freedom. . . . Malcolm and Martin called for the realization that black people are somebodies with which America has to reckon."[50] And yet, as E. Franklin Frazier's classic, if controversial, 1957 study *Black Bourgeoisie* claimed, middle-class status never applied to "more than 5 percent

of African-Americans before the Civil Rights era."[51] These exterior assertions of bourgeois status were made, then, in the absence of real access to
middle-class income, housing, or white-collar work.

In its 1950s fashion advertising, *Ebony* magazine illuminated these tensions, targeting its "mainstream" black readership with a promise of visibility, power, and influence at a time when the vast majority of black Americans were disenfranchised, denied basic civil rights, and largely shut out of
the middle class. But along with style, status, and sex appeals, *Ebony* ads
used price appeals, celebrity endorsements, and iconography that relayed
particular messages about black masculine power: the promise of being
"somebodies." *Ebony's* October 1957 issue included a feature on "Men's
Fall Fashions" in which, at first, dashing models sport casual wear that emphasizes "vibrant colors," "skillful use of color and texture," and a "fire-en-
gine red oxford cloth shirt."[52] In the subsequent section, however, models
portray the black male businessman with more sobriety: "Busy executives
will wear gray flannel this fall"; "For that young executive look, popular
three-button suit with flap pockets and center vent is just the thing." While
the suit seems the same, subtle differences emerge between *Ebony's* ads
and the emulation, class, or comfort appeals in similar ads targeting white
consumers. One ad's copy describes the Princeton suit's "strong, masculine
look . . . [in] all wool fancy flannel," and images show black men leaning against cars, boarding planes, or walking in urban settings, appealing
frankly to a fantasy of public power, wealth, mobility, and status. Another
"young executive" photo features lion statues in the background, doubly
emphasizing the masculine power the suit will confer, while a Botany 500
ad uses celebrity endorsements from prestigious African American public figures such as jazz musician Mercer Ellington. With images of suited
men posing before impressive desks and office buildings, checking their
watches, or relaxing on the golf course, the advertisements clearly link success with wardrobe and encourage a psychology of emulation: "Thousands
of other successful, well-dressed men agree. . . ," or "dress right—you can't
afford not to."[53] Fashion features and advertisements in the center of *Ebony*
offered the suit as a kind of ticket to manliness and success. Yet a prepon-
derance of "FREE Suit!" solicitations in the back pages of these mid-to-late
1950s *Ebony* issues suggests that, unlike Mercer Ellington, many African
American men simply could not afford to "dress right."

While black men were essentially excluded from the "normality" of
middle-class status, the suit could help them "pass" for normal. But the
suit was hard to come by for populations either prevented by segregationist

FIGURE 21. "Free Suit" solicitation, Stone-Field Corp., *Ebony*, Oct. 1958.

norms from shopping for them, or still unable to afford them. "Free suit" advertisements, promising the outfits to anyone willing to sell made-to-measure suits door-to-door, presumably appealed to readers unable to afford a fine suit but interested in the socioeconomic status that supposedly accompanied one: "Men! Send for This Money-Making Outfit FREE!" reads one (fig. 21). This "outfit" was a "money-making" one for women, too: "Add to Your Profits with Tailored Suits for Ladies. . . . Many husbands sell suits to men, their wives sell suits and skirts to women—and the profits roll in!" Here the suit is offered as a potentially equalizing force: "Every man prefers better-fitting, better-looking made-to-measure clothes," the advertisement proclaims, and it promises that "it's amazingly easy to take measures, and you don't need any experience to take orders."[54] Such ads suggest the continued importance of the suit as a uniform, but the continuing realities of white racism and segregation most likely made door-to-door sales a necessary alternative for people of color. Because of the physical intimacy necessary to tailor made-to-measure clothing, this system was the only means by which many African American professionals could shop for suits.

In the early postwar years, the suit helped mask troubling upper/lower distinctions to help produce a more homogenized middle-class identity. In the late 1950s the suit remained a necessary mark of inclusion, humanity, and respectability for some businesswomen and men of color. This reality contrasted sharply with an emergent rebellion against the suit on the part of young middle-class white men—those whom Barbara Ehrenreich calls the "Gray Flannel Dissidents."[55] The very uniformity that had made the gray flannel suit appealing now made it a site for critique of what was by then understood to be a conformist collection of "status seekers."[56]

In what seems a complete reversal of signification, by the end of this era the freedom *not* to don a suit would come to signify one as solidly middle class, and the suit would become a marker of something else: being dangerously conformist, a part of the "establishment." According to the *Oxford English Dictionary*, the first use of the phrase "the Establishment" as it came to be used in the counterculture movements of the 1960s actually dates to 1955. One *OED* source from 1957 describes "the Establishment" as a term taken to signify "those elements in society and politics which are self-satisfied and opposed to all radical change."[57]

When figures such as Marlon Brando, James Dean, or the Beat poets rebelled in the mid-1950s against a middle-class value system, the suit was frequently the first thing to go.[58] Through such larger-than-life "rebel" figures of the 1950s, Americans learned that nonconformity must be as outwardly visible as conformity. As the fashion historian Farid Chenoune notes, "Almost overnight, [Brando and Dean] forged a new fashion trinity—jeans, T-shirt, black leather jacket. Dark and heretical, this trinity emerged from fashion's waste lands, a world devoid of suit, shirt, tie and other trappings of white-collar society."[59] The wardrobe changes of James Dean's character, Jim Stark, in the 1955 film *Rebel without a Cause* illustrate the process: in the opening scene, the "drunk and disorderly" youth is wearing a rumpled suit and tie; as he becomes more of a "rebel" he dons a red jacket; by the film's conclusion, he has stripped down to only a white T- shirt and jeans. This "uniform" of rebellion was itself replicable, and it was a style reproduced by teens and their idols and carried on into the 1960s, from Bob Dylan emulating James Dean's "existential slouch" on the cover of his 1963 album *The Freewheelin' Bob Dylan* to Fonzie's 1970s *Happy Days* get-up and beyond.[60] These were rebellions against the middle class from within the middle class. The director, Nick Ray, and his writers pointedly set *Rebel without a Cause* in an "upper-middle-class California context," rather than a working-class or inner-city setting as other "juvenile delinquency" films had done.[61] The promotional poster for *Rebel* emphasized this fact, showing the "delinquents" played by James Dean and Natalie Wood embracing beneath the caption, " . . . and they both come from 'good' families!'"[62] Rock rebel Elvis Presley was obsessed with James Dean, and, according to Nick Ray, saw the movie at least "a dozen times . . . and remembered every one of Jimmy's lines."[63]

Numerous 1950s films also reveal this emerging discomfort with the implications of the suit. A central theme in Alfred Hitchcock's *Rear Window* (1954), for example, is the ongoing effort of marriage-minded socialite Lisa Fremont (played by Grace Kelly) to convince her rough-edged, free-spirited traveling photojournalist boyfriend, L.B. Jefferies (Jimmy Stewart), to settle down. At one point, Lisa playfully suggests how comfortably L.B. could slip into a New York magazine job, and how "handsome" he would look in a "nice, dark blue, flannel suit." Lisa's projection of the suit onto L.B.'s helplessly wheelchair-bound and pajama-clad body emphasizes the suit as a mark of entrapment. Lisa's fantasizing gaze is highly ironic, as she literally seems to be *dressing* Stewart with her eyes. For her, the suit is linked to sexual desirability and handsomeness. But for the freedom-loving L.B., the suit means domestication, marriage, being tied down. Like the other gray-flannel "dissidents," L.B.'s fear was that the uniformity of the suit would threaten his identity, his integrity, and his individuality.

In June 1953, *Fortune* magazine ran what would become a classic photograph showing a throng of commuters crowding off the train platform in the new Chicago suburb of Park Forest.[64] Nearly one hundred men—and a few women—inch along the platform toward the camera, descending the stairs at the front of the frame. They present a curious combination of uniformity and specificity. Nearly every man wears a somber topcoat and hat, and a white shirt and tie. Nearly every man whose arms are visible clutches a newspaper, and nearly all their faces seem tight, nervous, or tired. It was the classic image of the "organization men," the "white collar" workers of the urban centers, retiring to their suburban ranch houses at the end of a day.

And yet the longer one "looks," the more differences emerge. No two hats are *precisely* alike: brim up, brim down, curled brim, wide brim; thin ribbon, wide ribbon, very wide ribbon; worn straight, worn askance, worn high on the head, worn low over the eyes. Even the gray topcoats differ in pattern, material, and width of lapel. And the men's bodies, at first so homogenous, begin to distinguish themselves: narrow shoulders here, round face there; dark features, hollowed cheeks, deep-set eyes; a thin, older-looking man walks stiffly up front; a lummox of a man looms above others in the back. This photograph is emblematic of the way the homogenizing force of "normality" obscured the subtleties and contradictions of the postwar middle class. Seeing oneself as part the middle class meant seeing oneself as "normal," yet it also inevitably meant seeing oneself as part of a mass, a collective—and, potentially, therefore, as a conformist.

By the early 1960s, some sociologists were suggesting that a key component of the postwar middle class was its coherence. Robert E. L. Faris, for example, saw the middle class as "organized" while the working class was "adrift." The middle class, he found, joined clubs, while the working class remained "unaffiliated."[65] Further paradoxes inhere in this: conformity was part of the process of becoming middle class, yet individualism was its dominant ideology. Mass-produced consumer goods brought one into middle-class life, yet their cookie-cutter sameness threatened to undermine one's uniqueness. "Success" made one middle class, yet one could never stop striving for it because "in an economy of abundance," as another sociologist explained, "to 'stand still' in terms of income is in reality to 'fall.'"[66] A final tension lay in the twin desires to identify as middle class and to promote the myth of America as a classless society. To resolve these and other contradictions, some chose to conform, but with irony. Others began to normalize "alienation" as the middle-class American condition. Meanwhile, the middle class began to incorporate classlessness as its central ideology. With this move, the "normalization" of the American middle class helped to accomplish its status as unmarked: being middle class meant that class didn't matter.

None of the attempts to fashion the postwar middle class could ever fully overcome its instability as a subject. While in the 1940s the zoot suit had been characterized by its dashing excess, the turn to the somber suit as a democratizing postwar uniform quickly proved too confining. By the early 1960s it would become a target for parody even within "the organization." In 1962 one tongue-in-cheek corporate publication, called *The Consultants' Coloring Book*, presented a nearly nude white businessman, clad only in hat, tie, boxers, shoes, and socks, with instructions to add clothing in various shades of gray (fig. 22).

By the early 1960s, the suspicions voiced in *The Man in the Gray Flannel Suit* had been fully borne out. If middle-class identity had been about surfaces, such parodies as the *Consultants' Coloring Book* confirmed this to be the case: there was simply no *there* there. Cast for the first decades following World War II as the uniform of the middle class, by the early 1960s, the gray flannel suit—like "normality" itself—had become a put-on, a performance, a great gray projection always more appearance than reality.

This Is A Consultant.

He Is A Professional.

Color His Hat Professional Grey,

His Tie Sincere Grey,

His Garters Confident Grey.

Clothes Maketh The Man.

FIGURE 22. "This Is a Consultant," cartoon from *The Consultant's Coloring Book,* 1962.

4

From Queer To Eternity
Normalizing Heterosexuality in Fact and Fiction

The decades following World War II in the United States cannot be fully characterized by sexual "containment" nor by "sex panic,"[1] not by sexual obsession nor by sexual excess, but rather by deeply contradictory attitudes and practices that were neither fully progressive nor repressive. World War II created a massive social upheaval that had a major impact on U.S. sexual life. The dislocations of war loosened sexual mores and sanctioned a broader range of sexual expression, but the mechanisms of war also produced a culture of sexual oppression, repression, and violence. The postwar period was thus characterized by a kind of sexual tension: a broader understanding of sexual *behaviors* was met with a narrower sense of sexual *identities*: homo and hetero.[2] Although such transitions were part of a longer-term historical process, the war constituted a watershed. The sexual tensions of postwar culture reflected the changes wrought by decades of depression and war. For enlisted men and women volunteers, the war created homosocial environments in which many gay men and lesbians were able to form same-sex romantic and sexual attachments as well as a new and lasting sense of community.[3] For other men and women at home and abroad, the unsettled war years created new opportunities for sexual expression and experimentation.

The sexual behaviors and experiences of midcentury Americans were captured, charted, and graphed in the Kinsey Reports, the two landmark studies of human sexual behavior published in 1948 and 1953.[4] Both Kin-

90

sey's critics and his champions accepted the studies as scientific snapshots of American sexual life, and both books were consumed by an American public hungry enough for sex facts to make them best sellers. Rather than accept Kinsey's "continuum model" of human sexuality, however, postwar readers moved toward a binary understanding of sexual identity: human sexuality seemed either "normal" or "queer." Kinsey himself felt the terms "normal" and "abnormal" were inadequate, inappropriate labels to describe the complexity of human sexual behavior. But despite his best intentions, the Kinsey Reports had actually helped to produce this binary understanding of sexuality to some degree, by constructing a scientifically quantified "norm" and casting "normal sex as majority sex."[5]

James Jones's 1951 novel *From Here to Eternity* is a revealingly transitional text in terms of the historical and discursive shift to a homo/hetero binary.[6] A blockbuster novel made into a major motion picture in 1953, *From Here to Eternity* reflects both the freeing of sexual behaviors facilitated by the dislocation of war and the fixing of sexual identities that was part of a postwar impulse to "return to normal." Although the work of one writer cannot be representative, it is telling that Jones's personal experiences in the military and his own preoccupations with sex created in him a desperate urge to write—to tell some uncensored "truths" about men and women, sex and violence, and the army. Both the characters and the author explore sexual boundaries in this transitional text, but by the end of the story, as at the end of the war, the boundaries are less porous than they were in the beginning.

In pursuit of sexual "normality," postwar Americans would consult the models, advice, expertise, stories, and orthodoxies found in postwar "fact" and "fiction." Convergences in the fields of psychiatry, psychology, mental health, and sexology produced a voluminous new *scientia sexualis*, while postwar literature—newly available in cheap, paperback form, and concerned with "sexual realism"—was being consumed on a new scale.[7] In this chapter I chart the corroboration between postwar science and postwar literature in attaching heterosexuality to normality.

Sexing the Facts: Psychiatry, Statistics, Linguistics

With the influence of Freud and the rise of the field of "mental hygiene," psychiatry in the early twentieth century began to transform itself from somewhat remote investigations of the "insane" to an equally arduous task: the diagnosis of the "normal." Jonathan Ned Katz describes Freud's "incantation of the normal": "Throughout his essays Freud proclaims the 'normal' sexual intercourse of 'normal' men and 'normal' women as the 'normal' object, the 'normal' aim, and the 'normal' end of these 'normal' individuals' 'normal' sexual development. . . . While rebel Freud often devastatingly questions the idea of normal sexuality, conformist Freud was normal sexuality's prime mover."[8] It was in this context that World War II psychiatrists institutionalized a process of defining and policing both the homosexual and the sexually "normal" person as personality types. After unexpectedly high numbers of psychiatric casualties returned from World War I, experts were determined to screen out the mentally "unfit" for service ahead of time. Psychiatry extended and expanded its authority in this role. Homosexuals had never been systematically excluded from military service, but in the months before the United States entered World War II psychiatrists began developing screening procedures specifically designed to "discover and disqualify" homosexuals.[9] According to Michael C. C. Adams, 32 percent of the rejections were made for "psychological reasons," but these could be based on as few as four standard questions, such as "'How do you feel?' 'Do you like the Army?' and worst of all, 'Do you like girls?'" Only the United States, Adams notes, rejected men "for an alleged leaning in that direction."[10] In 1942, revisions of "previously vague psychiatric screening procedures" not only defined the homosexual; they also specifically identified the sexually "normal" person. While the homosexual would be "unsuitable for military service," the "sexually normal" person, who possessed a "conventional attitude toward sexual problems," was an acceptable citizen-soldier. As Allan Bérubé writes: "[Psychiatrists'] success in shifting the military's attention from the sexual act to the individual had far-reaching consequences. It forced military officials to develop an expanding administrative apparatus for managing homosexual personnel that relied on diagnosis, hospitalization, surveillance, interrogation, discharge, administrative appeal, and mass indoctrination."[11] Although the military had rejected "only 4,000 to 5,000 individuals" as homosexual out of nearly 18 million screened during the war years, by the end of the war approximately 10,000 more had been "condemned" by the military of occasional homosexual offenses.[12]

Psychiatry would continue to be a fountainhead of postwar discourse on sexual normality. By the late 1940s an emergent Cold War preoccupation with conformity resulted in "fearful scapegoating" of anyone deviating from an increasingly fixed understanding of "normal" sexuality. With the 1946 establishment of the National Institute of Mental Health, psychiatry moved into the "mainstream" of American medicine and "enormously expanded its claims and its clientele."[13] From the late 1940s to the mid-1950s, the category of "normality" was more and more narrowly conceived in the binarized, diagnostic language of mental health, but the concept was increasingly being applied in realms well beyond the medical or psychiatric.

Historians have documented that the onset of the Cold War in the late 1940s brought with it a sex panic, and more active persecution of a perceived "homosexual menace."[14] To be "queer" in these contexts was not only "abnormal," it was a perversion, pathologized and criminalized. Between 1947 and 1955, twenty-one states enacted sex psychopath laws—a series of statutes that cast criminal sexual conduct in psychological terms, as the consequence of mental disorder, and set up an alternative disciplinary system in which so-called sexual psychopaths could be indefinitely committed to psychiatric institutions, rather than serving sentences in penal institutions, for their offenses. Under such postwar conditions, lesbians and gay men "stood out more than they had during the war as 'queers' and 'sex deviates,'" and were persecuted—not for violent sexual crimes, but for "nonviolent offenses" such as consensual sodomy, public indecency, patronizing gay bars, touching in public, or cross-dressing.[15] Nevertheless, in 1952 the American Psychiatric Association, building on the "standardized nomenclature" developed by the army in 1945, established homosexuality as a pathology by listing it in its first *Diagnostic and Statistical Manual of Mental Disorders*.[16] This intense marginalizing of homosexuality helped to produce a newly rigid brand of heterosexuality as its Other. Being "not-gay" was no longer enough; one had to be "straight." This postwar sexual normality was gendered, hetero, monogamous, reproductive, lawful, and idyllic. Such a "perfectly average" postwar sexual identity was, like its pathologized Other, a fantasy. But it carried enough power that its alignment of gender with sexuality reshaped American sexual cultures and subcultures.[17]

The division of sexual identities into the homo/hetero binary coincides with the constructing of orthodoxies and the drawing of boundaries that are a sign of normality at work. Yet here again, as in other moments in this story, the politics of "normality" are complex in their effects, since the emergence of this binary with its homogenizing politics also coincided with the coalescence, organization, and politicization of gay and lesbian individuals and communities. As historians have convincingly argued, World War II pushed both women and men, whether in the armed forces

or on the home front, out of "familial—and familiar—environments,"
freeing queer erotics from the structural restraints that had marginalized
and isolated them. By the late 1940s, an urban gay subculture had taken
shape.[18] And in 1951, the founding of the first national gay-rights group,
the Mattachine Society, would mark the beginning of what John D'Emilio
calls an "unbroken history" of gay and lesbian organizing that continues
to unfold.[19]

Terminology for sexual behaviors and identities was also shifting during
the first half of the twentieth century, reflecting a sex/gender system in
flux. In his book *Gay New York*, the historian of sexuality George Chauncey
shows *heterosexuality* and *homosexuality* to be historically specific social categories and identities, and he discovers the strict heterosexual/homosexual
binary to be a "stunningly recent" historical creation. Between the 1930s
and 1950s, the "now-conventional division of men into 'homosexuals' and
'heterosexuals' based on the sex of their sex partners" emerged, replacing
earlier categorizations of men into "fairies" and "normal men" based on
what Chauncey terms their "imaginary gender status." Chauncey not only
analyzes the gay male subculture in early twentieth century New York, but
also reveals how the "'normal' world constituted itself . . . by creating the
gay world as a stigmatized other."[20]

The early decades of the twentieth century were marked by a gender
system in which men were labeled "queer" only if they "assum[ed] the
sexual and other cultural roles ascribed to women." Any man who re-
sponded to "the fairy's solicitations," as George Chauncey writes, was not
considered "abnormal" as long as he followed "masculine gender conventions." As early as the 1920s, American men who identified themselves by
their homosexual interests (rather than any "womanlike gender status")
usually called themselves *queer*. Essentially synonymous with *homosexual*,
Chauncey writes, *queer* also "presupposed the statistical normalcy—and
normative character—of men's sexual interest in women; tellingly, queers
referred to their counterparts as 'normal men' (or 'straight men') rather
than as 'heterosexuals.'"[21]

The history of heterosexuality moves from its first usage by sexologists
in the late nineteenth century, to its gendering via the rise of psychiatry, to its eventual incorporation as a way of "marking normality" by the
mid-twentieth century.[22] Before this "invention" of heterosexuality, Jonathan Katz writes, "the abnormal and the homosexual were posed as riddle,
the normal and heterosexual were assumed." By the mid-1930s, the term

heterosexuality—defined as "a manifestation of sexual passion of one of the opposite sex; normal sexuality"—began to enter public discourse.[23] Once the term came into circulation, a "new heterosexual ideal" had been "stabilized, publicized, and normalized."[24]

During the war years, as Allan Bérubé notes, *queer* and *normal* were the "most common words used by both gay people and the general public" to describe sexual identity.[25] Significantly, the first documented use of "straight" to signify "heterosexual" dates from 1941, and as Katz adds with some amusement, the term seems to have been coined by those to whom it did not apply: "The 'not homosexual,' a new creature, defined by what he or she isn't, . . . emerged among the cast of erotic characters on the twentieth-century stage. . . . Now, the sex variants are doing the defining—categorizing is a game that two preferences can play."[26] In the immediate postwar years, the queer/normal binary narrowed further and was lent an air of scientific legitimacy with the popularization of the labels *homosexual* and *heterosexual.* Kinsey's 1948 and 1953 studies of sexual behavior would soon demonstrate that alongside the midcentury baby boom, Americans were also engaging in same-sex activities, though not necessarily identifying as homosexual.

The word *queer* had certainly become a slur by 1951, when Jones's *From Here to Eternity* was published. In his text, Jones uses the term in a derogatory way, collapsing distinctions that Chauncey's subjects had been "so careful to draw" in labeling themselves.[27] Contemporary theorists such as Michael Warner, Judith Halberstam, and Alexander Doty have reappropriated the word *queer* as "a term with some ambiguity, a term that . . . describe[s] a wide range of impulses and cultural expressions." This more contemporary use of the term "includ[es] space for describing bisexual, transsexual and straight queerness." As Doty notes, "queer erotics are already part of culture's erotic center," and "basically heterocentrist texts can contain queer elements, and basically heterosexual, straight-identifying people can experience queer moments."[28] While I use the term *queer* from the contemporary context of "queer theory," it is important to remember that Jones employed the same word in a much different spirit—that of a World War II army lexicon that also included terms like *nigger* for blacks, *wop* for Italians, *hebe* for Jews, and *snatch* or *pussy* for women. A contemporary understanding of the concept *queer* nevertheless functions well for discussing the sexual themes of *From Here to Eternity*, as it is a "basically heterocentrist" text with "queer elements," and one in which "basically heterosexual" characters experience "queer moments." Furthermore, as

Michael Warner argues, the shift from "gay" to "queer" self-identification offers "a more thorough resistance to regimes of the normal."[29]

From Here to Eternity brings into play many of the contradictory sexual discourses and practices of its time. Rather than behaviors being separate from the pressures of identity,[30] sexual behaviors were *becoming* sexual identity, *sex* was becoming *sexuality*: "Theres [*sic*] a difference" as one of Jones's characters puts it, "between being queer and thinking you're queer" (558). Jones's articulation of these shifts is visible on multiple levels. First, the historical background of the novel and the lived experience out of which he composed it turned on the social and sexual upheavals of World War II, since the war "created something of a nationwide coming out experience."[31] Second, the novel itself contains "queer" characters and allows homosexuality a space for articulation, debate, and discussion. Jones imagines a variety of gay characters: the confident, effeminate, intellectual Hal; the burly, quiet, and persecuted Tommy; the bullying, tortured, tragic Bloom; and—arguably—the loveable, murdered sidekick Angelo Maggio and the "outsider" hero Prewitt. They all meet different ends, but live with a common sense of fear: are all endangered. Finally, these characters move, across the course of the novel, from a world of sexual "play" to one of sexual orthodoxies, where the punishment for unorthodox activity is imprisonment or death.

Jones's characters dialogue about the meanings of *queer*. They also, in their behaviors, move from a period of relative freedom, unhindered by binaries of identity, through individual and military "queer investigations" that terrorize them into choosing sides. By the end of the novel, male heterosexuality has become menacing, and homosocial attachments have become connotative, displaced. The rules have been clarified, and the men have learned to express their attachments toward other men exclusively through violence. While Jones wished to use his text to talk about sex, to subvert the romantic plot conventions of novels, and to expose the facades of middle-class respectability, he essentially leaves heterosexuality itself intact. Homosexuality has been invoked in order to recast heterosexuality against it—as its opposite, and as the "normal" condition. The result of these lines, drawn by the military and by the men themselves, is a more concretized politics of sexual difference. In Jones's novel—as with postwar sexual science—two patterns converge: heterosexuality is normalized and homosexuality is marginalized. In the film version of *From Here to Eternity*, this process was made complete.

Queer Content: "I can spot them a mile away"

Postwar literature became a place to negotiate the meanings of World War II, either via a new genre of "World War II novels," or through particular narratives, subtexts, or subplots in a range of literary forms.[32] Many post–World War II novels and stories, in marked contrast to the fiction following World War I, "confirmed, explored and exploited the American soldier's experiences with homosexuality." Among these were James Michener's *Tales of the South Pacific*, Norman Mailer's *The Naked and the Dead*, Gore Vidal's *The City and the Pillar*, and Allen Drury's *Advise and Consent*, as well as Jones's *From Here to Eternity*.[33] While Jones considered himself a sexual realist, in this respect his novels seem to have been more like other novels of their time and genre than different from them, and Jones himself more emblematic than exceptional. A critical and popular success, *Eternity* was a Book-of-the-Month-Club alternate selection (because of its "frankness" they decided not to make it a main selection), it won a National Book Award in 1952, and it made Jones rich—according to *Newsweek*, "the most successful novelist in American literary history." Columbia bought the film rights in March 1951.[34]

From Here to Eternity is surprisingly explicit in its engagement with homosexuality, though scholars have not addressed this element of the novel with any depth. Himself a veteran of the war, Jones was self-conscious in his attempt to use his fiction to depict both military life and sexual life with a new kind of explicitness and honesty. Pointedly including gay characters in the novel, he asserted that he wanted to write about "queers. . . [because] nobody had really written about them right."[35] This chapter argues, however, that Jones's novel—like the World War II–era military itself—worked to normalize a particular *kind* of desire. Jones evokes, but then excises, homosexual or "queer" desire and erects a public, predatory, violent male heterosexuality in its place.[36] *From Here to Eternity* thus reflects and participates in a cultural drift toward a more polarized understanding of sexuality—a homo/hetero binary in which queerness is positioned as the other side of a "normality" more forcefully cast as heterosexual.

At eight hundred pages and with numerous secondary plots, *From Here to Eternity* is not easily summarized.[37] The novel interweaves the sexual adventures and the violent internal conflicts of the peacetime army's "G Company," stationed in Schofield Barracks, Hawaii, in the months prior to the attack on Pearl Harbor. The text opens with one Robert E. Lee Prewitt, an undereducated, poor-white Kentucky coal-miner's son who has fumbled his way into the army because "a man has got to have some place" (14). Angry after being unjustly passed over for a promotion in the Bugle Corps, Prewitt volunteers for "straight duty" in G Company. Strong-willed and individualistic, Prewitt refuses to join the boxing team of his company's captain, Dana "Dynamite" Holmes, and the resulting "treatment" he must endure is only the first in an escalating series of punishments for his independence. The story of Prewitt's eventual martyrdom is interwoven with a subplot about his love affair with a white prostitute called Lorene (whose real name is Alma). Despite Prewitt's deep love for the army, it eventually—literally—kills him. Having gone AWOL after murdering a sadistic stockade sergeant, Prewitt is shot by MPs during his desperate attempt to return to his barracks after the Japanese attack on Pearl Harbor.[38]

While Prewitt is introduced first, Jones places equal emphasis on a second major character, Staff Sergeant Milton Warden, a gruff, hardened man-in-charge. Warden too is an individualist, though more in thought than action. Disdainful of the bureaucracies and humiliations of the army, and ambivalent about his own role in it, he remedies his own boredom and disillusionment by beginning a passionate affair with Karen Holmes, the equally bored and disillusioned wife of his superior, Captain "Dynamite" Holmes. (In the film, it is Warden and Karen who roll in the surf in the classic scene on the beach.) Their romance is thwarted by the combination of her ambition and his intransigence: he is "married to the army."

The rest of the men in G Company form a classic World War II "multiethnic platoon": an Italian from Brooklyn (Maggio), a bullying Jewish boxer named Bloom, an American Indian called "Chief" Choate, and a Southern mess sergeant, Maylon Stark, among others. The men of G Company spend most of their time bonding, fighting, gambling, drinking, "queer rolling" (in this context, engaging in a game of sexual "play" with gay men in Waikiki bars, in exchange for money or free drinks). and, as often as possible, hitting the brothels. A number of subplots develop: Prewitt has a brief affair with Alma's roommate Georgette; Maggio is cruelly beaten to death while in the stockades; Warden discovers Karen's past affair with Stark; Bloom, suspecting himself to be gay, commits suicide. Such grim events intensify the larger sense of doom that overshadows the novel, both for the characters, who know that war is imminent, and for Jones's readers, who, remembering Pearl Harbor, read with ever-increasing anxiety over the fate of G Company.

A broad range of male characters, identities, and masculinities inhabit Jones's prewar Hawaii. As Beth Bailey and David Farber argue, Hawaii was "a strange place . . . at the margin of American life. . . . But sometimes it is at the margins that the messy definitions and complicated interactions are pushed to extremes and made visible; far-reaching changes sometimes germinate in marginal places."[39] Though the hetero romance plots are certainly present, it is the male friendships that dominate the novel, making the deep homosocial attachments of "soljers" the text's most central topic. These attachments result in both queer dynamics among/between men and also a shared male culture of subjugation of women. As Jones's mouthpiece Prewitt remarks, "homosexuality is the direct result of chastity in women" (368). For Jones, queerness and the sexuality of women are linked, and both have roots in this prewar community of the army. While the attitudes toward women are left unquestioned, homosexual attachments are clearly cast as a problem in the text.

Meeting Dr. Kinsey's percentages almost exactly, 10 percent of the novel—eighty out of eight hundred pages—deals explicitly with "queers" or homosexuality. Jones himself was aware of Kinsey's studies of human sexuality, as most Americans would have been in the early 1950s, but he seemed to feel that the real truth about human sexuality was revealed in novels, and only obscured by science. Discussing his second novel, *Some Came Running*, in a 1955 letter, Jones wrote: "All I can tell you about it now is that its principally about Sex—what book isnt? Except Kinsey's, of course."[40] Jones's candid treatment of homosexual themes and characters in *Eternity* is all the more surprising because these topics are utterly censored from the film version. Jones's postwar readers may not have been prepared to approach these topics, and most contemporary biographies and criticism of Jones fail to discuss the homosexual content of the novel in any way.[41] A more plausible explanation, then, is that Jones managed to incorporate queerness with one hand, and then erase it with the other, leaving his readers, like his characters, in a forgetting frame of mind.

Homosexuality is made an explicit issue by the second page of the novel. The opening scene has Prewitt preparing to transfer to a "straight duty" post in G Company from a cushy position in the Bugle Corps. The transfer is a matter of pride, because, as he says, the chief bugler, Houston, chose "his young punk First Bugler over [me]" (10). As George Chauncey notes, the word *punk* denoted "a physically slighter youth who let himself be used sexually by an older and more powerful man."[42] After Prewitt mentions this event, his friend Red considers, just for a moment, whether this "Queer Houston" (52) might ever have tried to make Prewitt an "angelina" as well: "Chief Bugler Houston's tastes in young men were common knowledge and Red wondered if he could have made a pass at Prew. But it could not be that; Prewitt would have half-killed him, Chief

Warrant Officer or no." Although the novelist has raised the subject of homosexuality, the hero must be "straight." Red quickly switches the subject to Prewitt's *hetero*sexuality—through the question of what will become of Prewitt's "wahine" (the Hawaiian word for woman or girl) when Prewitt transfers: "'Thats good,' Red said bitterly, 'made up her own mind. Where is her mind? In her head, or down between her legs?'" "Watch your goddam mouth," Prewitt responds, "'Since when is my private life any of your business anyway? For your information, its between her legs and thats the way I like it, See?' You liar, he thought" (12). Jones establishes here the differences between Prewitt's interior and exterior identities ("You liar, he thought"), suggesting that Prewitt succumbs to the macho pressures to speak of women as sexual objects, but thinks of women in more romantic terms—terms that are disallowed in this military environment.

Jones goes on to describe a world where GIs pay for sex with white women and take local, "ethnic" women as concubines, but must be paid (in the form of drinks and/or cash) to spend time with "queers." The military's sexual marketplace is institutionalized, built upon the idea that "soljers" need these outlets.[43]

Early on, the men of G Company attempt to interact with "queer" characters without their own sexual identity coming into question. "Queer rolling" and "queer hunting" make up the majority of the homosexual adventures of the platoon. But the moral of the story ends up being that such interactions with queers constitute a *risk* to their heterosexuality. The cabdriver giving Prewitt and Maggio a ride to Waikiki says, "Lissen let me give you joes a tip. . . . You steer clear of them queers. You keep runnin around with them long enough and youll be queer too. Thats what they want. . . . I hate the bastards. I'd kill every one I seen" (357). But as they exit the cab, Maggio laughs, "If I hadnt of heard that guy talk so, I'd swear that driver was a queer. I can spot them a mile away" (359). In this moment, Jones tries to undercut the cabbie's homophobia with the GIs' ridicule, but the logic of the cabdriver's lines persists in his narrative.

The central thirty-page scene that follows this cab ride (significantly, it falls at the end of the section called "The Women") has first-timer Prewitt joining the more seasoned Maggio on a "queer chase." Jones here introduces his major homosexual characters: a wealthy, erudite French teacher named Hal, with whom Maggio has developed a regular relationship, and Hal's friend Tommy, a burly writer of romance stories, who will be Prewitt's "date." (If Jones was aiming for realism, he surely sets into motion some powerful clichés of homosexuality here.) The four meet at a Waikiki bar, where Jones attempts to tease out the meanings of homosexuality from the point of view of his gay characters as well as that of the "straight" soldiers who come to call. In the bar, when Prew pointedly uses the term "queer" in conversation, Hal flinches:

> "I don't need any direction," Prew said. "I make up my own mind. About everything. Including queers."
> Across the table Maggio shook his head warningly and scowled. . . .
> Hal was sighing heavily. "That is a harsh word to use. But then we are used to that. And of course, you are all slightly ill at ease now, your first time meeting us and all." (361)

Although the sexual situation is perfectly queer here, Jones constructs a homo/hetero binary by keeping Prewitt's sexuality unambiguous, and by having Hal speak collectively, dividing himself from the soldiers: "we" and "you," "us" and them.

The foursome move on to Hal's luxurious house, drinking champagne cocktails and talking—about homosexuality, differences in gay identity, and about who's queer and who isn't, and why. Tommy and Prewitt have a long discussion about art and writing. Hal and Prewitt argue over the causes of homosexuality: "decadence" in society, according to Hal; "chastity in women," according to Prewitt (368). In the past, Maggio says, he had dealt with "queers" by "just let[ing] them talk," but Prewitt actively engages the men at every step. Tension builds as Prewitt and Maggio get drunker, and Prewitt becomes more and more hostile toward Hal and Tommy. He doubts their claims to "freedom," questions Hal's self-identity as a "rebel," and accuses them of what he sees as the "hate" behind all homosexual relationships. For Prewitt, the tension is high because the date is nearing its close: "If they would only let us drink up their shade, he thought, and then leave us alone, not exact their pound of flesh" (372–74). By the end of the evening, Prewitt has successfully "messed it up" for Maggio, by suggesting that he is "kept," and questioning the price he has been paying for "queer rolling." Maggio explodes in defensiveness:

> "I'm free," Angelo yelled. . . . "I'm free as a fucking bird. . . ."
> "Quiet down," Hal said sharply. . . .
> "Gothell," Angelo said. . . .
> "I think its time you went to bed . . . ," Hal said sadly. "And slept it off."
> "Sure," Angelo said. "Sing for your supper."
> "Thats not a very nice thing to say to me," Hal said.
> "Sorry, old boy. I can't help it. Its the truth, aint it?"
> "Yes," Hal said. "But one doesnt always have to mention the truth, does one?" (372)

The "truth" of this scene is not mentioned, or mentionable, but is implied: the "price" Maggio has been paying has been sexual. After this exchange, Maggio runs off into the night, is picked up by the MPs, fights with them, and is eventually sent to the stockades for "*Drunk & Disorderly, . . . Resisting Arrest, Insubordination, Disobeying a Direct Order, Striking a Non-Commissioned Officer . . . , and Conduct Unbecoming to A Soldier*" (389). Maggio protects Prewitt from discovery by the MPs, and Prewitt protects himself from having to "sing for his supper," even extorting forty dollars from Hal in the process.

A "queer investigation" by the city police soon follows, and the men of G Company find themselves hauled in to be interviewed by army and FBI officials, These scenes in the novel are direct and critical references to the antigay witch hunts and purges that took place throughout the war. "A single rumor that someone was gay," Allan Bérubé writes, "could spread like wildfire and lead to a full-scale purge, filling the stockades with suspected 'queers' who were held for interrogation."[44] Suspected or convicted GIs were locked into segregated jails, called "queer stockades," "queer brigs," or "pink cells," in which they were publicly humiliated. While some prisoners "camped it up" in the queer stockades, others were made victims of sadistic physical and sexual abuse by guards.[45] Jones has the appealing character Maggio eventually die of such injuries inflicted by the baton-wielding stockade sergeant Fatso Judson. In Jones's "queer investigation," no one is caught except Tommy, whom the officials have brought in to identify soldiers. Prewitt thinks the pitiable Tommy "makes a very poor monster," and he ridicules the army's efforts: "Hell, if they threw all the queens and queer-chasers in Honolulu into jail, the city'd go broke . . . and the Army'd have to declare a holiday" (398). Jones casts the gay characters as relatively harmless, and makes the true villain the army, which tortures, incarcerates, and murders its own best adherents.

Jones's representation of the character Isaac Bloom, however, is much more troubling. Bloom is drawn with a combination of deep anti-Semitism and homophobia. He is established as a despicable character—the men of G Company hate him. Early on, even the good-natured Maggio snaps when Bloom tries to use the same language with him that others use: "Listen," he said in a contorted voice, "I'm particular who calls me Wop" (136). Bloom is a bully, a boxer for the company team who constantly assumes people are persecuting him for being Jewish: "For Christ's sake, shut up!" Julius Sussman yells at Bloom in the midst of a poker game, "You make me wish I'm not a Jew" (138). After losing in a fistfight with Prewitt,

Bloom sinks into a torment of deep self-loathing: "It did not make any difference that he had made corporal . . . had won the Regimental middle-weight division . . . he was still Isaac Nathan Bloom. And Isaac Nathan Bloom was still a Jew." He slowly "faced the rest of it. He didn't have what it took" (542–43). In a melodramatic scene lasting several pages, Bloom finally retrieves his rifle from his locker, "place[s] the muzzle in his mouth," and thinks the final thought that will make him pull the trigger: "You're a queer, Bloom thought bitterly, a monster. Lets face it all, while we're fac-ing. You did it, and you liked it, and that makes you a queer. And every-body knows you are a queer. You dont deserve to live. His hand released the safety" (547). Bloom's death tangles together homosexual anxiety and a violent, self-destructive masculinity in a not-so-subtle image of gun-in-mouth. Bloom's suicide, occurring as it does in the close, isolated space of the deserted barracks, seems representative of what will become the trope of the closeted gay character's suicide.[46] In the subsequent experimental section, however, Jones explores Bloom's thoughts *after* he has pulled the trigger. The sequence of his thoughts reveals both a gesture of affection from Jones, and a curious *return to heterosexuality* for Bloom: "I didn't mean it! he tried to yell. I take it back! . . . He had always wanted to com-mit an irrevocable act, and he had finally done it, only to find out it was the wrong one. . . . There were so many steaks to be eaten, so many whores to be laid, so much beer to be drunk. Dont forget the steaks and whores and beer, boys, he wanted to yell, dont ever forget that. What a silly thing to do, he thought. . . . Bloom died" (548). This shift is telling. Bloom's death constitutes the final step in excising the homosexual, as it shuts down any further explicit invocation of queerness in the novel.[47]

Complicating the question of queerness in *From Here to Eternity* is the reality of the homosocial environment: the same-sex attachments of the army brotherhood.[48] The persistent tension of men in close quarters pro-duces undeniably "queer" moments. For example, the members of Barrack Two love to play something called "The Game," transparent in its amalga-mation of homoeroticism and violence:

> In the evening after chow the mattress from an empty bunk would be hung on the chain mess grid across the center window in the back wall with strings of knotted shoelaces. Then one man, usually the smallest unless there was a volunteer, would stand with his back against the mattress and the rest would line up at the far end of the aisle . . . and, one at a time, run at the man against the mattress and hit him in the belly with their shoulders like a fullback . . . except that with the mattress behind him there was no place to fall back to and it was up to the belly muscles to protect themselves. . . .

> It was a hard game. But then they were hard men . . . they were the tough-
> est of the tough, they were the cream. If the man at the mattress could stay
> up there clear through the entire line, he had won the game. As the prize he
> got a free run at every man in the line. (603–4)

The practice of standing in line to slam the smallest man into a mattress—
essentially a clothed gang-bang—is all the more loaded given its close juxtaposition to the suicide of Bloom.

If homosexuality is a surprisingly open topic in *From Here to Eternity*,
then, it is also a fraught one. Despite his efforts at realism, Jones's depictions of gay characters and the fear and loathing expressed toward "queers"
by other characters constitute some of the most cruelly offensive moments
of this novel. Jones is critical of the army's "queer investigations," which
criminalized both "queer" men and the "straight" men who play at "queer
rolling." Prewitt complicates everything by asking too many questions and
making people think too much about the issue. As he tries to comprehend
the reason for Bloom's suicide, for example, Angelo Maggio proposes that
"he was afraid he had gone queer." Prewitt counters, "Hell, Bloom was no
queer. . . . If I ever saw a not-queer, it was Bloom." "I know it," Angelo
replies. "There's a difference . . . between being queer and thinking you're
queer" (558). Here, in the last explicit mention of queerness in the novel,
Jones asserts that a line between "queer" and "not-queer" exists, but that
this line is more visible to others than to the self. If "thinking you're queer"
was a common conflict in wartime Hawaii, "being queer" was something
altogether different. As Maggio's remark also implies, in this time and
place, the suicide of a *real* "queer" would have made perfect sense.

The Heterosexual Menace: Excising the Homosexual

In *From Here to Eternity*, a "homosexual menace"[49] is merely imagined,
while the "menace" of a violent predatory heterosexuality, gendered male,
and sanctioned by the army, poses the real threat. The text is filled with
outward, public displays of aggressive male heterosexuality. These scenes
function both to diffuse the tensions of close, same-sex environments and
to define acceptable sexual behavior among men. This menacing heterosexuality works to ensure its own normalization by drowning out the fledg-
ling alternatives present in the text, among them interracial attachments,
love without sex, and same-sex affections. Such representations also helped
make the novel popular. As one reviewer tellingly admitted, "The book's
extreme naturalism gives it a special importance at this time, when much

of our serious fiction has turned introspective and somewhat effeminate in quest of psychological rather than social relationships."[50]

Though a certain macho Americana can be traced from the pin-up culture of World War II well into the *Playboy* "bachelor culture" of the early 1960s, the immediate postwar popular culture was saturated with images of violent male heterosexuality.[51] The dark, gory noir crime novels of the 1940s—famously showcasing a violent, misogynist and homophobic male heterosexuality—found a willing readership among GIs, and they maintained that readership for at least the first decade after the war's end. This trend extended to films as well, as evidenced by the "film noir" of the late '40s and the Cold War westerns and World War II films that shaped the next generation. The escalation of the Cold War and the ever-present threats of communism, the bomb and other dangerous technologies kept Americans in a "shadow of war" throughout the postwar decades. Such conditions bred fear and loathing, and they fueled continued militarization: it was a "postwar without peace."[52] A generation of writers had been exposed to violent conflict first-hand, and that violence became one more of the experiences from which to spin stories, particularly stories like Jones's, which explored the boundaries of male desire and violence, sex and death.

From Here to Eternity was a literary phenomenon—enormously popular, stylistically risky, and boldly critical of the U.S. Army. Jones's hyper-masculine, sociological approach was appreciated both by a massive readership and by the literary establishment that selected the novel for the National Book Award for fiction in 1952 over its two competitors, *The Caine Mutiny* and *The Catcher in the Rye*. Reviewers in the 1950s saw Jones's text as neorealist. It was a gendered neorealism, in the tradition of Hemingway, Fitzgerald, and Faulkner, and it was seen as an antidote to a new "psychological" turn. His realism reveals more than Jones likely intended about the state of the times, the culture, the ideologies of the fifties. Readers and critics enjoyed the book's "pungent dialogue," and praised the "integrity" and "punch" of Jones's writing, "as exciting as a sock on the nose."[53]

The novel seemed to speak with the voice of "soljers"—the "real" Americans, the "straight joe[s]" who constitute what Jones calls "common ordinary verynormal" men (138, 603). Jones too felt that the profanity in his novel got him closer to the real, the truth, and he struggled with his editor, Burroughs Mitchell, over it: "I am willing to cut considerable of it; but . . . if you take it all out . . . the whole thing is going to sound like a historical novel of the *Amber* ilk which cunningly hints at everything but

never has the guts to say anything. . . . I dont care if anybody thinks I'm
a dirty writer. Maybe I am. After all, I've only my American background
and training to pattern after."[54] Jones saw himself in a realist tradition that
was "American"; he thought he had more "guts" to represent reality than
the female author of the very popular romance novel *Forever Amber*, which
was set in Restoration England. Jones, Mitchell, and Jones's lawyer Horace
Manges worked together to revise only the parts of the book that could
land them in obscenity court. Explicit sexual references had to be cut,
including a reference to gay male pornography (though references to heterosexual male pornography remain): "[A] large part of [the love scene between Prew and Lorene] had to be cut. All the part on the . . . 'Unguentine
Galley' [on the relief provided by sex]. . . . all mention of 'one-way, two-
way, and three-way girls.' The scene with the queer Hal, the part of his
pornographic picture sitting on the desk had to be cut out completely."
The book's profanity was also toned down, particularly sexually connotative words. As Jones recounted, "Manges had a 'score sheet' he had kept
while reading, and there were 259 fucks, 92 shits, and 5 pricks. He did
not count pisses for some reason. . . . Mitch and [Manges] cut the fucks
down again to around 106 and some shits. Manges wanted, Mitch wrote
me, to cut the fucks to 25 or 6, but Mitch balked there because they had
promised me to print the fucks in unprecedented scale." Jones concluded
this letter with more resignation about these changes to his manuscript:
"I was disappointed of course, but then this is a practical problem, not
an artistic one. . . . I want to be printed."[55] Interestingly, including "fucks
in unprecedented scale" is what Jones felt would allow him to retain his
integrity as a realist; the other cuts simply helped him dodge the censors
and "be printed."

From Here to Eternity is largely about sexual desire, especially the army's
cultivation of a particular version of male heterosexuality. In the midst of
a tension between wartime sociosexual upheavals and increasing military
discipline and control of sexual identity, this novel became a site for the
articulation and exploration of normal and abnormal desires, sexual and
violent. Constantly, the realms are narratively commingled—the sex has
violent consequences, the violence has sexual overtones.[56] In one striking
example, Jones describes the peacetime soldiers, on leave for the weekend,
heading into Waikiki brothels en masse:

> They came up the lightless stairs of the New Congress Hotel. . . . and . . . car-
> ried with them . . . all the unmentionable, unspeakable, pride destroy-
> ing heart shakiness and throat thickness and breath chokiness of men

about to mount women. . . . the same attributes displayed so shame-
lessly by all the male dogs on the Post as they chased . . . after reluctant
bitches. . . . [N]ow . . . disembodied breasts and bellies and long thighs, all
of a completely unearthly loveliness, swam through their minds. (216)

By turning the clock back to 1941 for this 1951 novel, Jones chose to re-
write history—retroactively encoding a narrative of American masculinity,
individuality, and sexual power that preceded the war. This move helped
remedy his postwar middle class readers' emerging sense of gray-flannel
anxiety by constructing a substitute: a cadre of "Gentlemen Rankers / Out
on a spree" who are "*Damned* from here to Eternity."[57] These men have
"enlisted" in a culture of predatory masculine heterosexuality merely by
signing up.

By setting his novel in Hawaii, Jones selected a location long marked
as both an exoticized paradise and a colonized space, and one occupied
by the U.S. military.[58] By the early 1950s, when the novel was published,
Hawaii had already begun to recover its prewar "tropical allure." The film
version helped bring "aloha shirts" back into vogue, and this Tiki-chic affection for "Polynesia" intensified through the late 1950s, accompanied by
an "increasing drumbeat for statehood," which was granted in 1959.[59] But
in Jones's narrative, this was a prewar army with plenty of leisure time; they
were stationed in Hawaii, an alien locale to most, where men vastly out-
numbered women; and so his soldiers are living with the double tension of
a crowded, homosocial environment, on the brink of war.

The heterosexual menace goes beyond male domination of women and
into issues of colonialism: white domination of ethnic Other, outsider
domination of insider, military domination of the civilian population,
and the prostitution and concubinage that the military either encouraged
or institutionalized, in Hawaii and elsewhere.[60] An early example of this
menacing and colonizing male heterosexuality occurs when Prewitt visits
his "wahine," a young Nisei girl named Violet, after he's transferred from
the Bugle Corps, essentially to bed her once more and then tell her that
he is moving on. But Prewitt cannot decide what he wants from Violet:
he may want to hold onto his "good shackjob" even though he's changing
locations. Jones's description of Prewitt entering his Violet's "shack" of a
home, and later having sex with her in a back room after having been given
dinner by her embarrassed and impoverished elderly parents, suggests the
continual sexual and economic exploitation of an already suffering population. Jones normalizes Prewitt's behavior, however, by turning the encounter into a scene about Prewitt's individualism.

When Violet half-sarcastically suggests marriage as an alternative to separation, Prewitt snaps:

"Married!" Prew was dumbfounded. The picture of Dhom, the G Company duty sergeant, bald and massive and harassed, crossed his eyes, trailed by his fat sloppy Filipino wife and seven half-caste brats; no wonder Dhom was a bully, condemned to spend his life in foreign service like an exile because he had a Filipino wife. . . . "Why in hell would I marry you?" he shot down at her. "Have a raft of snot-nosed nigger brats? Be a goddam squawman and work in the goddam pineapple fields the rest of my life?" (93–94)

Prewitt rejects marriage here, not as a middle-class institution (it could never be middle-class with this racial Other), but as retrograde motion: "Why the hell do you think I got in the Army?" he continues. He could have stayed in Kentucky to "sweat my heart and pride out in a goddam coalmine all my life and have a raft of snot-nosed brats who look like niggers in the coaldirt, like my father, and his father" (94). Prewitt himself was one of those "brats who look[ed] like niggers," so his repetition of this fear that he is displacing onto the Other, Violet, is rather a fear of something in himself—the lower-class "marks" of poverty, work, and region which could literally erase whiteness and its privileges. For Prewitt (unlike Dhom), interracial marriage is not an option: this relationship is, like his tour in Hawaii, exotic but temporary, and he finds it absurd that Violet would imagine it to be anything other than a sexual exchange.

Jones casts Violet's reaction to Prewitt's outburst as stoic: "She lay back in her chair letting it sweep over her, helpless . . . letting the force hit her, yielding instead of fighting it, with a patience born of centuries of stooped backs and dried apple faces" (95). While Violet is written in collective and racialized terms, Prewitt's individualism is foregrounded. While Prewitt acts and speaks, Violet is passive and "helpless." The novel is emphatically not *about* the lives of the usually nonwhite people on the receiving end of this charged, masculinized, heterosexual "occupation": they are simply the bodies upon which the male drama is staged.

At times, this "male oppression" projects itself onto the very landscape. The army's inhabiting of the base becomes a (hetero)sexualized conquest of a feminized Hawaii. Early on, Jones constructs Hawaii as a female landscape—but more than gendered, this landscape is eroticized, ready to be "taken" by these new inhabitants: "The deep V of Kolekole Pass . . . was like a whore's evening dress" (18). Jones has the seasons themselves correspond to the land's desire: "There was never any cold to suffer in the winter in Hawaii. . . . nor any sudden awakening to the warmth and quickened thighs of spring's young April. . . . But in early March the times between the rains got shorter. . . . Until at last the whole earth and everybody on it, like a honeymooning bride, begged for thirst again" (99–100). At one point, Captain "Dynamite" Holmes quips, meaningfully, that Colonel Delbert "believes in taking advantage of the locale in which he's stationed" (326). Through this construction of Hawaii, Jones symbolically absolves his male characters of responsibility for the sexual oppression of the locals: the island itself is the "whore," waiting to be "tak[en] advantage" of—in fact, she is "begg[ing]" for it.

If the military's "Why We Fight" propaganda encouraged soldiers to think of themselves preserving the privilege of making love to white women, the peacetime army assured its men of sexual reward on a regular, if temporary, basis, by sanctioning brothels.[61] Prewitt finally parts with Violet "because once a week just aint enough" (94). Throughout the text, Jones describes a general environment where men constantly look for sex, talk about women in violently sexualized terms, fantasize over pornographic images, and finally stand in line at whorehouses. Jones describes these realities bluntly, and in the bureaucratic language of military supply and demand: "Mrs. Kipfer's had just got in a shipment of four new beaves to help take care of the influx of draftees" (706).

Significantly, the "best" brothels are filled with white prostitutes, and at certain moments in the text, Jones openly describes the racialized elements of the military's sex trade, as with the high-ranking officers who have a "partiality to Kanaka [Native Hawaiian] maids" (38). In another scene "Dynamite" Holmes is honored to attend one of Colonel Delbert's "stags," where a brigadier general named Sam Slater is also present. Colonel Delbert arrives with "six women," and remarks to the General, "More excitin' that way. Eh? And these, sir, 're all dark. Two Japanese, one Chinese, two Chinese-Hawaiians, and one pure nigger—or damn' near pure: Th' say th' are no pure Hawaiians any more." Delbert, after displaying the fine liquor and steaks also being served, "spread his arms and said facetiously, 'Gen'r'l Slater, we . . . welcome you to th' haven of th' male oppressed" (327). This "male oppression" is the entrapment of the heterosexual in a homosocial environment, the separation of men from "their" women. And although the reader knows that Captain Holmes has "stag" parties of his own, this scene reveals that even the colonels and generals express their sexuality in this more public sphere; at all levels, it is an identity performed in the company of other men.

Countless other throw-away lines in *From Here to Eternity* easily expose this theme of the fine line between male desire and male fury; for example: "Prew felt a murderous rage crack and burst in him like an orgasm"

(519). On his way home to shower for a date with his commanding officer's wife, Milt Warden "stopped on the stairs and raised his arm and put his nose to his armpit happily and inhaled the mineral-salts male smell of himself, feeling his chest expanding infinitely with maleness, feeling from inside himself the hard columnar beauty of his thighs and the slim thickly muscled beauty of his waist and loins; he was Milt Warden and he was meeting Karen Holmes in town tonight" (299). Of course, Warden then suddenly remembers that the company mess sergeant has also bedded Karen Holmes, and, picturing this man's face, immediately "straightened up with his nostrils sickened and smashed his fist against the wall, punching stiff-wristed, solid-forearmed as a fighter punches, at the place where Maylon Stark's husky battered face was amorphously hanging" (299). Warden's sensual view of his own body as "hard . . . columnar . . . thickly muscled," beyond its phallic symbolism, recalls descriptions of the "columnar" postwar gray flannel suit, but here, the male self-love of the prewar military contrasts with the male anxiety and self-consciousness that would emerge in Sloan Wilson's postwar text of corporate masculinity five years later (see chapter 3). And the physical violence Warden exhibits seconds later is no accident: it is *part* of his manliness, the "male smell of himself."

Jones's representations of male heterosexuality were also likely less reflective than prescriptive. While he himself was stationed in Hawaii, Jones wrote bragging letters to his brother about his active sexual life, but later confessed they were all lies: "All those women I used to write to you about sleeping with I didn't. I took care of myself instead. No very pleasant or heroic picture, is it?" Frank MacShane writes that "[Jones] would go into the whorehouses to drink and dance with the girls. . . . but if they suggested making love, he would make excuses and eventually leave. Afterward, . . . sharing a taxi with some other soldiers, they would boast of their conquests." According to MacShane, Jones wrote in one letter of a soldier who exclaimed, "Uniforms! Uniforms! All he can see or smell is uniforms, a pounding, roaring sea of uniforms, and here and there . . . a snobbish, egotistic officer with his lovely wife." In search of relief, Jones's imagined soldier goes to a whorehouse, where "all he found was the blaring of a 'juke box,' the raucous laughter of the whores, fifteen minutes in a tiny barren room with a whore with sagging breasts and tiny bulging belly, and he is lost and disillusioned. He does the only thing he knows to erase the stench: he goes out on a drunk, and then goes back."[62] Despite his urge to represent sexuality more realistically, Jones's novel was likely as exaggerated and romanticized as his letters and boasts.

After the attack on Pearl Harbor, the deaths of Maggio and Prewitt, and the stateside return of Lorene/Alma and Karen, Staff Sergeant Milt Warden and Mess Sergeant Maylon Stark become bosom buddies (since they share the intimacy of having bedded the same woman). In the novel's final scene, they head off to Choy's Bar looking for a good time. There a waitress, Rose, is described, in an omniscient voice, as erotic, exotic prey: "with her Chinese eyes and Portagoose nose and mouth and the startling eye-arrestingly beautiful waggling waggling take-a-hold-of-me bottom that seemed to be distinctively peculiar to Portagoose-Chinese girls" (697). Warden starts a bar-fight by pinching Rose's "beautiful bottom," which had been "trembling enticingly with each step." When Rose fights back, trying to slap or claw Warden for this violation, he holds her hands; and then "rose from the stool on his left leg, pushing it between her legs," so that "the struggling cursing girl was off balance and powerless." He says, "Take it easy, baby. . . . I wont hurt you. You're a woman after my own heart, but dont get me all excited. I'm liable to lay you right here on the floor." With that, the "real" fighting can begin between Warden, Stark, and Rose's artilleryman "boyfriend" and his buddies. Warden gives Rose "a little shove that plumped her against the back wall out of his way, as if she were something that had served its purpose," and gets on with the boys-only brawl he and Stark had apparently been seeking all along (802).

With a few edits, this scene even makes it into the film version. But the slapstick humor that it is supposed to elicit is troubling: this kind of sexual threat was seen as *play*, as boys being boys, but it is overdetermined that it will conclude with violence. After the fight, Warden and Stark retire to their favorite high-priced brothel to enjoy two whores and four steaks. The echo of the dead "queer" Bloom's dying wish is clear: "Dont forget the steaks and whores and beer, boys" (548). After the prewar tests of the stockade, "queer rolling," and hetero heartbreak, the novel ends with the firm reestablishment of the menacing variety of heterosexuality that will supposedly get these men through a war.

Film Version: Controlling the Narrative

In 1953 Alfred Kinsey's *Sexual Behavior in the Human Female* was published, completing his efforts to replace the normal/abnormal binary with a continuum model of human sexuality. The movie version of *From Here to Eternity* premiered that same year, but pushed forcefully in another direction. As Jones's novel was translated from words to pictures, further institutional pressures would be brought to bear, and queerness moved from presence to absence. The homosexual themes and heterosexual critiques Jones explored in the novel become a stabilized, whitewashed heterosexuality for a film-going audience. The result was an uncomplicating of desire.

One mark of the popularity and currency of Jones's novel was how quickly the film rights were bought. Jones, after a failed attempt at writing the film treatment from his own text, largely removed himself from the production of the big-budget Hollywood film. He treated it only as a source of income;[63] he felt that the novel would outlast any filmed version. On this point, it seems, he was wrong. The movie, which opened in the summer of 1953, was extremely popular: in New York, the Capitol Theater remained open around the clock to satisfy the demand for seats, "closing only in the early morning to allow the janitors to clean the floors."[64] The film, starring Burt Lancaster as Milt Warden, Montgomery Clift as Prewitt, Frank Sinatra as Maggio, Deborah Kerr as Karen Holmes, and Donna Reed as Lorene/Alma, gained a record-setting thirteen Academy Award nominations, and won six, including Best Picture, Best Director, and Best Screenplay (fig. 23).[65] The famous make-out scene (fig. 24) in which Burt Lancaster (Milt Warden) and Deborah Kerr (Karen Holmes) roll in the Hawaiian surf was so popular it has become iconic, reproduced in countless montages, recirculated in everything from campy parodies to music videos.[66] Tellingly, this scene was not in the novel.

FIGURE 23. Cast members Sinatra and Clift, producer Mortimer Adler, and author James Jones on the set of *From Here to Eternity*. From *Films in Review*, Oct. 1953.

FIGURE 24. Film still, *From Here to Eternity:* Male bodies are more fully eroticized than women's bodies in the film. Even in this famous shot from the beach scene, Burt Lancaster's body is featured, while Deborah Kerr's is obscured. *From Here to Eternity* © 1953, renewed 1981 Columbia Pictures Industries, Inc. All rights reserved. Courtesy of Columbia Pictures.

In the postwar context, the freedom to complicate normative sexual identities was far narrower onscreen than in print. If the book had to be changed to avoid being banned under obscenity laws, the film had to face the Hollywood Production Code, which was still in effect, although it was being tested.[67] While the novel's explicit depiction of homosexuality worked to illustrate the boundaries of male heterosexuality, a complication arose when the film had to erase such depictions. In the absence of queer content, the filmmakers chose to foreground the heterosexual romantic plots.[68] The effect was to solidify the normality of heterosexuality even further, and this time for a mass viewing audience.

The film version of *From Here to Eternity* is vastly different from the novel. It picks up effectively where the novel leaves off, with heteronormativity intact, and homosexuality erased. This time, all the postwar sexual tensions arise from mildly improper heterosexual pairings. The production was threatened by legal and censorship problems that had to be carefully navigated by the director and producers from the beginning.[69] The first step was to work from a transformed screenplay written by Daniel Taradash, which cut all homosexual content, focused on the two romantic plots and connected them more closely, and attempted to preserve the effect of the stockade scenes while toning them down enough to receive the cooperation of the U.S. Army to film on location at the Schofield Barracks in Hawaii.[70] The changes that resulted are striking.

There are no references to homosexuality in the film: no Hal or Tommy, no "queer investigation," and no Bloom. Instead the focus has shifted to Milt Warden (Burt Lancaster) rather than Prewitt (Montgomery Clift). To gain the army's cooperation, sadistic mistreatment by the stockade guards does not go unpunished in the film, nor does Captain "Dynamite" Holmes's corruption: he is fired in disgrace after an army inquiry. No American planes are shot down by friendly fire during the bombing of Pearl Harbor, although one is in the novel. There is no playing of "The Game," and there are no references to the use and abuse of local wahines, silencing both homosexual and interracial desire. The brothels are represented, but in subtle, coded terms, so that they seem more like dance halls or meeting houses. Karen is married in the film, but, importantly, childless.

Despite these changes, *From Here to Eternity* was one of the most successful and influential American films of the 1950s.[71] If viewers recall anything about Hollywood's version of the tale beyond the infamous scene on the beach, it is often the tender, dramatic performances of Montgomery Clift as Prewitt or Frank Sinatra as Maggio. Jones, after meeting Montgomery Clift at a party, wrote to the director, Fred Zinnemann, that he wanted Clift for the role of Prewitt. After he was cast, Clift occasionally came to Indiana to visit Jones, and Jones himself confessed that he thought "Monty [Clift] actually took the picture right away from everyone."[72]

According to Jones's biographer Frank MacShane, Jones made a famous comment about his friendship with Montgomery Clift: "I would have had an affair with Monty Clift, but he never asked me."[73] Although Clift was certainly "closeted" about his sexuality, Jones knew that Clift was gay, and fought to have him play Prewitt. The director, Fred Zinnemann, also lobbied for Clift to play the role, against the objections of Harry Cohn, who, according to Zinnemann, felt that it was an "idiotic suggestion"; in Cohn's view "Clift was wrong for the part of Prewitt . . . He was no soldier and no boxer and probably a homosexual." Zinnemann, however, felt that "this story was not about a fellow who didn't want to box: it was about the human spirit refusing to be broken, about a man who resists all sorts of pressure from an institution he loves, who becomes an outsider. . . . It was quite clear to me, if difficult to explain, what Clift would make of that character."[74] This outsider status was something that Clift seems to have conveyed with deep authenticity.

Thus the casting of Montgomery Clift in the lead role, and his portrayal of Prewitt, may have reinscribed queerness into the film in subtle ways, using what George Chauncey calls "connotative rather than denotative codes that foiled the efforts of censors."[75] Clift worked hard to preserve the nuances of the novel. MacShane reports, "Montgomery Clift took his role very seriously, and talked to Jones at length about Prewitt. He rehearsed every scene privately in advance, and carried a dog-eared copy of the novel with him, sometimes suggesting changes in dialogue that would better reflect Prewitt's character."[76] Such details raise intriguing questions about whether gay viewers and actors may have seen the film differently. Cloaked representations and interpretations make homosexual "accents" difficult to perceive: they depend upon an audience familiar enough with the novel and sophisticated enough—or even "queer" enough—to see them.

Some of the film's "queer moments" are quite perceptible from a contemporary point of view, however. There are striking "beefcake" moments when male bodies—particularly Clift's and Lancaster's—are erotically portrayed, even more so than women's bodies (see fig. 24). There is the fact that the major emotional center of the film (and, in truth, the book) is the love between Prewitt (Clift) and Maggio (Sinatra) (fig. 25). The sadistic torture suffered by Maggio in the stockade scenes is sexualized through the symbolic use of the stockade sergeant's baton. Finally, the hetero couplings in the film are foiled: Karen (Deborah Kerr) and Warden (Lancaster) end their affair because Warden is "married to the Army." Without hesitation, Prewitt (Clift) leaves Alma (Reed) to return to his barracks after the bombing of Pearl Harbor, and is shot en route. The final scene of the film (like that of the novel) shows the two women leaving Hawaii alone, while Warden strikes up a new friendship with mess sergeant Maylon Stark. Yet despite these queer distinctions, in the broadest terms, the book and the film cooperated. Whether or not the queerness of the novel was successfully displaced onto the character of Prewitt through Clift's portrayal, the fact that Prewitt/Clift dies in both the novel and the film means that the queerness is excised once again. If the novel employed queerness largely to excise it and endorse a certain brand of male heterosexuality, the film's foregrounding of heterosexual romance accomplished the same ends, and more effectively. The film and the popular memory of

Figure 25. Film still, *From Here to Eternity:* Prewitt (Clift) and Maggio (Sinatra) reconnect on Prewitt's first day at G-Company. Maggio's line: "I'd feel for you, pal, but from my position, I can't quite reach you." *From Here to Eternity* © 1953, renewed 1981 Columbia Pictures Industries, Inc. All rights reserved. Courtesy of Columbia Pictures.

"that scene on the beach" continue to feed the nostalgia for the 1950s as the decade of heteronormativity.

A 1956 scholarly article on *From Here to Eternity* claimed that Jones "penetrat[ed] to the very center of the most important cultural, political, and philosophical questions of [the] day."[77] Yet the erasure of Jones's "queer" content by both Hollywood and literary criticism perpetuates a simplistic dystopian reading of the 1950s as the decade of consensus and repression, rather than as a period of complex transition, one that saw both the persecution of homosexuals and the coalescing of a community with the establishment of the first national gay and lesbian organizations.[78] Jones's blockbuster novel, even as it tried to complicate dominant ideas, gives us access to those ideas, and it constitutes a record of its cultural moment. Within the text, the historical movement toward a homo/hetero split was made visible. The story of the novel becoming a film reveals a broader process of normalization at work. In the cultural recirculation of

From Here to Eternity, what lingers is that scene on the beach: that passionate, heterosexual kiss. By replacing the ambiguities of the novel with this celluloid fantasy, the filmmakers helped link romantic heterosexuality to "normality" in a way that has endured.

Sexual historians have argued that a binary conception of sexuality was well in place before the onset of World War II, but a closer look at the themes in *From Here to Eternity* suggests that such constructions were still under way a decade later.[79] Early in the novel, both central characters, like Prewitt, and more minor characters, such as Maggio and Bloom, discuss and participate in the gray areas of sexual behavior and sexual identity in the homosocial military environments of prewar Hawaii. But by the end of the novel, Jones's characters have articulated rigid boundaries, the army has institutionalized them, and the novel's "queer" characters have been banished to the margins. In synch with a postwar science of sexual "facts," Jones's "realistic" fiction thus reflected and helped to constitute a cultural shift from "queer" to "normality" in postwar understandings of sexuality.

5

Picture Windows and *Peyton Place*
Exposing Normality in Postwar Communities

In the 1956 blockbuster novel *Peyton Place*, the town itself becomes the central character: "Talk, talk, talk," says the young protagonist Allison MacKenzie, impatiently. "Peyton Place is famous for its talk. Talk about everybody" (350). Peyton Place speaks in voices, it judges, it watches, it keeps track: "From the day Allison was born, [her grandmother] Elizabeth Standish lived with fear. She was afraid that she had not played her part well enough, that sooner or later someone would find out. . . . In her worst nightmares she heard the voices of Peyton Place."[1] Generalized, collectivized, and internalized, the town of Peyton Place forces its residents to "play [their] parts," and to "live with fear." In this way, *Peyton Place* represented the culture of normality that had taken hold in midcentury American communities: practices of surveillance and performance, self-scrutiny and the scrutinizing of others. Both the townsfolk and the town en masse engage in these practices. They were behaviors that the author, Grace Metalious, despised, but they resonated deeply with her readers.

Surveillance and performance were central normalizing practices of postwar communities. As the quotations above suggest, surveillance allows for a multidirectional web of discipline, one that becomes most successful when it becomes internalized, when one *feels* observed whether or not one is in fact being observed. Michel Foucault has described "surveillance" as a supremely effective disciplining behavior: "The system of surveillance . . . involves very little expense. There is no need for arms, physical violence, material constraints. Just a gaze. An inspecting gaze, a gaze which each individual under its weight will end by interiorising to

118

the point that he is his own overseer, each individual thus exercising his surveillance over, and against, himself."[2] "Interiorizing" the gaze leads to a kind of voluntary self-disciplining, but it also leads to another practice, "performance": a posturing, pretense of self, a projection through the veil of what one suspects others wish to see.

This chapter focuses in on two geographies in which these normalizing practices played out: first, the "imagined community" of suburbia, the ground on which one-third of Americans lived by 1960; and second, the imaginary community of Peyton Place, setting for the era's all-time best seller. While the history of the postwar suburb has been well documented, its demographic and geographic shifts take on new meaning in light of the normalizing practices they fostered. And while *Peyton Place* is well remembered as a postwar potboiler, few have taken seriously its far-reaching cultural critique of what one reviewer called the "false fronts and bourgeois pretensions" of American life. As Metalious demystified small-town life, critics of the suburbs began to trace what the social critic John Keats would later call the cracks in their picture windows, so that in both suburbia and Peyton Place, the homogenizing practices of "normal" midcentury communities were not just portrayed, they were exposed.

Picture Windows: The Culture of Surveillance in Suburbia

The collective impulse for a "return to normal" after World War II was met by both a national housing shortage and a continuing baby boom. The GI Bill and FHA loans were designed to remedy the crisis, by promoting and funding homeownership for millions of returning veterans and their families. Suburban "development housing" sprang up nationwide to meet the demand, so that postwar families were effectively offered "community" as a commodity. As John Keats describes them in his satirical 1962 work *The Crack in the Picture Window*, suburban developments easily recalled the wartime military in their regimentation: "Where there had been one bright sample house rising bravely from a sea of mud, there were now hundreds of houses, just as neat and small as the sampler. Squads and platoons of these little boxes marched in close order beside what seemed to be red-clay canals. Each house was surrounded by a patch of bilious sod, and two rusty dwarf cedars struggled for life beside each identical doorstep."[3] This commodity was far from perfect, and it was not offered to all, yet families flocked to suburbia, often "for the children's sake," and put down roots.[4] The postwar "return to normal" the suburbs helped to embody was, in fact, not a "return" at all. It was the wholesale invention of a community that had never existed. In this way, suburban communities, filled with what would come to be called "nuclear" families, can be seen as a final, central puzzle-piece in the picture of "normality" as a postwar pursuit. All at once, suburban spaces worked to incorporate all of the elements I have discussed in the previous chapters: postwar suburbia purportedly contained "normal" bodies; it cultivated a nationalistic "American character"; it promoted the normality of being "middle-class"; it mandated reproductive heterosexuality and sanctioned neo-Victorian gender segregation. Eventually functioning as synecdoche for midcentury American life itself, suburbia became an imagined community, a "perfectly average" postwar location that was neither perfect nor average.

But what could be more normal than a car, 2.5 kids, and a house in the suburbs? Benedict Anderson notes that "regardless of the actual inequality and exploitation that may prevail in each, the nation is always conceived as a deep horizontal comradeship."[5] This homogeneity of the suburbs was produced in spite of—in fact, *because* of—the radically unequal living experiences of actual U.S. citizens. The first decades following the U.S. entrance into World War II saw two major and related internal population shifts: millions of African Americans moved from the rural south to the urban centers of the North, while millions of white Americans moved from urban and rural locations to newly fabricated, startlingly homogenous housing developments close to, but not part of, America's cities (fig. 26). Midcentury suburban and urban development was thus built on three major tensions: race, class, and disparate visions of a postwar community. As the great American opportunity, suburbs were easy to hold out, but hard to reach.

Between 1940 and 1970, some five million African Americans from southern states trekked to northern and western cities, while hundreds of thousands more moved from the rural to the urban South. In a few short decades, this movement dramatically altered the racial balance in most American cities.[6] While popular memory of the postwar years locates black oppression in the Jim Crow South, the whiteness of postwar suburbs dispels any illusions about the midcentury North. Historians have charted explosions in white-collar and service industries that helped create an era of affluence; indeed, the sustained growth of the economy after 1945 was "the great fact of American social life."[7] But FHA lending practices ensured that the suburbs would remain overwhelmingly white and middle-class.

FIGURE 26. "Park Forest, Illinois, Aerial Views," Bernard Klein, photographer, Aug. 1955. Postwar aerial photography of sprawling suburban developments, increasingly easy to produce, was its own kind of surveillance. Such long-distance views had homogenizing/normalizing effects as well, implying the interiors were as uniform as the exteriors. Courtesy of Park Forest Historical Society.

Race had been a factor in bank lending policies for decades, but with the GI Bill the government helped to institutionalize discriminatory lending. During the postwar housing shortage, the FHA used redlining (refusing housing loans to neighborhoods containing black residents) and greenlining (marking all-white neighborhoods as financially stable for lending) for the "development of harmonious, attractive neighborhoods." Such policies in the late 1940s excluded not only blacks, but also single white women, the white working- and lower-class elderly, and minority men and women of all classes, including the elderly.[8] Because of redlining, the presence of any people of color could lead entire neighborhoods—such as Boston's South End and Los Angeles's Boyle Heights—to be defined as "slums" in urban housing and policy discourse. Between 1934 and 1962, the federal government underwrote $120 billion in new housing; less than 2 percent went to non-whites.[9] Furthermore, by making loans available to white GIs and their families, national lending policy helped to construct "whiteness" as a monolithic race category, and to normalize it. At the beginning of the century European ethnics had been believed to be different races; now, in these segregated neighborhoods, they could be homogenized into white Americans. As the legal scholar John A. Powell notes, "In the past *white* [had] meant being a citizen and being a Christian; it now meant living in the suburbs."[10]

Discriminatory housing practices such as redlining and the use of "deed covenants" kept blacks and other supposed risks out of the postwar land-rush of suburban homeownership in ways that have had lasting economic and political effects.[11] The Federal Housing Acts of 1949 and 1954, followed by the 1956 Federal-Aid Highway Act, helped to make class and racial segregation public policy by the early 1960s.[12] Some blacks did move to suburbs in the years after World War II, usually to older, working-class areas or to new black subdivisions just beyond city boundaries. Andrew Weise has shown that the strengthening civil rights movement emboldened some black families to "transgress" the racial boundaries and move into mostly white suburban communities. These movements would increase by the early 1960s, with the passage of civil rights legislation. Other minority groups, such as Chinese Americans, were also moving into suburban communities with increasing frequency throughout the 1950s. Their movement, as Cindy Cheng shows, required a "negotiation" of America's racialized Cold War democracy, as their assimilation into "white" suburban spaces could intensify, rather than mollify, continued black/white race and space tensions. Yet by 1970, despite such efforts, close to 95 percent of all suburbanites were still white.[13]

In the 1940s and 1950s, most migrating blacks had moved to large cities, where another new "community" was unfolding: the single-class, often single-race inner-city housing developments—governmental units, low-income housing, and eventually, full-scale urban renewal programs. Adding geographic segregation to already-existing divisions in race, class, and opportunity, postwar urban housing deepened the cleavages in the American postwar community, and created new sets of problems for African American families. According to the reports of the Governor's Select Commission on Civil Disorder (also known as the Hughes Commission) in New Jersey, and the National Advisory Commission on Civil Disorders (also known as the Kerner Commission), inadequate housing was a top complaint, second only to police brutality, expressed by Newark and Detroit residents following the 1967 riots.[14]

Although the newness of suburban communities left them seemingly unburdened by a corrupt national past, "normal" life in the whitened American suburbs was clearly linked to an "Other" life in these new majority-nonwhite urban developments. Though the two types of developments shared many ties—government funding, shoddy construction, and uniformity among them—their primary bond was a tension: Which location represented America? While an increasingly multiethnic and pluralistic society was manifest after World War II, by 1960 suburbia had been established as the image for the national community. "Like rural Winesburg and industrial Middletown in another era," Richard and Katherine Gordon wrote in *The Split-Level Trap* (1960), "the mobile Suburban town represents the thoughts and feelings of the majority of Americans."[15] White, suburban communities had replicated themselves, in popular culture and in fact, to become the new geography of the "norm."

As with the Great Northern Migration, the class and character of American geography changed quickly and markedly with the parallel phenomenon of suburbanization. This was a policy encouraged by "the promise of fast profits for the developer, the eagerness and affluence of the home-buyer, the general suspicion of planning, and the mortgage policies of . . . government agencies."[16] Between 1950 and 1960 more than 13 million homes were built in the United States—and 11 million of these were in suburbs. The suburbs grew six times faster than cities: the volume of housing starts reached a record 1.65 million in 1955 and leveled off at over 1.5 million for the rest of the decade. Almost overnight, a new kind of community had come into being. Suburbs were designed as family spaces, as reproductive spaces, spawning a remarkable 84 percent of the nation's population increase during the 1950s. By 1960 some 60 million people, one-third of the total population, lived in suburban neighborhoods. The suburbs housed more Americans than any other geography.[17]

According to *Better Homes and Gardens* and Housing and Home Finance Agency surveys from 1950, two kinds of families bought houses in 1949 and 1950: roughly half were veterans of World War II with young children, who had run out of space in their apartments. The other half were "older families" who moved from previously owned houses for more space, more quiet, or because of a change in job. This higher-income group purchased "more expensive homes on larger lots." Together, these two populations had fueled suburban growth, although most of them "were forced to compromise their goals because of price and location." Significantly, a large percentage of these new suburban homeowners were not buying their dream homes, but were settling for less space, smaller lots, and less privacy than they wanted.[18]

Surveillance was a way of life enabled and encouraged by suburban geographies, but it was not new. Wartime and later Cold War civil defense programs had required self-scrutiny as well as spying on one's neighbors; atomic-age films and duck-and-cover drills had promoted a "stay in your homes" isolationism and the fantasy of domestic safety in an atomic age. These practices gave fresh resonance to the idea of the "nuclear" family.[19] Suburban homes housed these families, and, by their very design, functioned to sustain this culture of surveillance. By 1950, nine out of ten new houses were ranch-style homes. By 1970, four out of five new homes were either ranch homes or split-levels. Developers placed these homes in uncomfortably close proximity, thrusting families under each other's noses with adjoining driveways and fenceless, treeless front and back lawns. Features such as window walls, single-story design, yards, and carports were explicitly designed to integrate the ranch house more fully with the outside world, creating "unity with nature," although this nature was a "tamed" environment of "perfect lawn[s] without weeds or dandelions."[20]

Adding to this proximity and exposure, suburban architecture regularly incorporated what came to be called the "picture window," a key metaphor (and tool) in building a postwar culture of surveillance. John Keats's title metaphor in *The Crack in the Picture Window* hinges on this feature and its ocular function: "Through their picture window, a vast and empty eye . . . they could see their view—a house like theirs across a muddy street, its vacant picture eye staring into theirs."[21] Picture windows are meant both for looking out and for looking in; William Whyte wrote that "the picture [outside] the picture window is what is going on *inside*—or what is going on inside other people's picture windows."[22] They were displays, opening the house up to the street: "'Feel free to look in,' the picture window announces, 'we have nothing to hide.'"[23] In his work of literary reportage, Keats ridicules the picture-window-watchers who inhabit in his fictional suburb of Rolling Knolls: "Everyone knew the Spleens shouted at each other and beat their child, just as everyone thought Buster and Gladys Fecund were probably a trifle common because they had all those children. . . . And everyone was disgusted with the Wilds. Adam didn't water his lawn when everyone else did, and he didn't keep it well cut, [and] that back yard of his. . . . But Adam's really unforgivable sin, in the eyes of every woman on the block, was getting that automatic dryer for Eve" (56). The eye gazing out the picture windows in Rolling Knolls was knowing, yet passive; critical, but also covetous. This practice of watching and being watched helped seal normality as the new goal for which to strive in the suburbs.

Television effectively extended the eye of the "picture window" across the nation. In the first fifteen years after World War II, television fully saturated American communities. While in 1946 only 0.02 percent of American households had a television, by 1955 the figure had jumped to 65 percent, and by 1960, nearly 90 percent of American homes contained at least one television set, with the average person watching approximately five hours per day.[24] Consumer culture was of course tied to this new mass medium, as "expenditures for advertising between 1950 and 1959 rose at a faster rate than did the gross national product."[25] When Keats describes the arrival of television to Rolling Knolls, he emphasizes the collectivity of the experience, and its power to "bewitch" the community:

> From seven p.m. on, in those days, there was not a light to be seen in Rolling Knolls. Every house . . . was dark . . . but within every shuttered living room there gleamed a feeble phosphorescence, a tiny picture flickering in that glow. Over the bewitched community there swelled a common sound. Sometimes it was a fanfare, introducing a commercial. Sometimes it was the thin, jubilant cry of the studio audience in New York wildly cheering a contestant who had just announced he came from Detroit, Michigan. Sometimes it was the dumb-de-dumb-dumb musical signature of a period crime piece. But whatever the sound, it was a common sound, rising above the darkened houses, for everyone watched the same shows. (Keats 79)

The powerful presence of this new national medium after World War II, paired with the increased circulation of large-format, color-saturated magazines and the growing field of photojournalism, made mass communication increasingly visual. Simultaneously, as Lynn Spigel shows, the primary site for spectator amusements moved from the public space of the theater to the private space of the home.[26]

The most powerful normalizing function of television in the postwar decades was its ability to construct and project a mass-mediated version of "typical" American spaces, and their accompanying aesthetics, dialogues, relationships, bodies, and commodities. As Nancy Armstrong argues, "the most powerful household is the one we carry around in our heads," as it has shown us "what normal behavior is supposed to be."[27] Americans on opposite ends of the continent could *see* what normality looked like by focusing on the interiors of televised households. Certain postwar sitcoms, such as *I Love Lucy* (CBS, 1951–57), *The George Burns and Gracie Allen Show* (CBS, 1950–58), and *The Adventures of Ozzie And Harriet* (ABC, 1952–1966), blurred the boundaries between reality and fiction by casting real-life couples or families to "live their lives" on-screen.[28] Characters such as Cuban bandleader Ricky and his kooky midwestern housewife Lucy (married both onscreen and off) helped to smooth over race and class tensions for the "real" Americans watching on the picture windows of their television sets. On January 19, 1953, more than twice as many Americans "watched" Lucy have Baby Ricky than watched Ike's second inaugural the following day.[29] The intimacy and authenticity of the casting helped invest early television images with a special resonance, a hyperrealism.

Television's picture window helped to construct notions of the nation itself. The projection of domestic life on television was a "primary means of reconstituting and resocializing the American family after World War II," according to the television and film historian Mary Beth Haralovich. Perfect American living rooms, with "deep-focus photography exhibiting tasteful furnishings, tidy rooms, appliances, and gender-specific functional spaces: dens and workrooms for men, the 'family space' of the kitchen for women"—projected themselves into American living rooms, constructing an increasingly consistent picture of what "normal" homes looked like.[30] Even though significant differences existed (shows like *The Goldbergs* or *The Honeymooners*, for example, represented working-class, multiethnic, or urban families), the longest-running programs (*Ozzie and Harriet*, *The Donna Reed Show*, *Leave it to Beaver*, *Father Knows Best*) were those that presented homogeneity. Moreover, the careful placement of "ethnic" characters in wildly popular sitcoms such as *I Love Lucy* made difference comic, made it American, and sealed it with a kiss. The image of domestic life on television ameliorated the tensions of real-life suburbia. The sitcom's very plot—calm, problem, resolution—enacted a return to normal over and over again.[31]

If life in the suburbs came to epitomize a return to normality after World War II, however, what is forgotten is the critique that they engendered. Right from the start, observers saw the planned developments in Levittown and Park Forest, Illinois, as "potential disasters." Sociologists in particular linked the cookie-cutter developments to a "creeping consumer conformity." The unplanned and uncontrolled phenomenon of mushrooming suburban neighborhoods seemed a new form of "residential monotony."[32] In 1954, for example, Sidonie Gruenberg, a writer and child development expert, published an article titled "Homogenized Children of the New Suburbia" in the *New York Times*, which warned that "mass-produced, standardized housing breeds mass-produced, standardized inhabitants, too."[33] Paired with droll illustrations by Roy Doty showing rubber-stamp nuclear families imprinted on a suburban sprawl (fig. 27), the article proposed that, in contrast to the "old suburbs" that had developed into "real *communities*," the "new suburbs," which had been "constructed on mass-production principles," had by their very design engendered a "pressure to conform" that was "intense, and stultifying." The demographic sameness of the environment, Gruenberg warned, could warp children's worldviews and leave mothers feeling "frustrated and discontented."[34] The suburban "dream house" threatened to be a "split level trap" for many, financially and spiritually.[35]

Powerful critiques of "normal" American life had of course been made much earlier, and more vehemently, by those outside its parameters.[36] But by the mid-1950s, a deep and sustained critique of normality in the suburbs was finally being launched by its own inhabitants. In 1955 Sloan

Figure 27. "Homogenized Children of the New Suburbia," illustration by Roy Doty, *New York Times,* 19 Sept. 1954. Caption: "New Suburban families are in danger of becoming as alike as the houses they live in." Reprinted by permission of Roy Doty.

Wilson, a Connecticut WASP, published *The Man in the Gray Flannel Suit* (see chapter 3). In 1956 William Whyte's *Organization Man* included pointed critique alongside detailed maps of fishbowl-like suburban social networks. In 1957, John Keats, a WASP from Maryland, published *The Crack in the Picture Window*.[37] By this point, Cold War rhetoric was clear in Keats's dismay over the conformism of suburban spaces: "It is true that the dwelling shapes the dweller. When all dwellings are the same shape, all dwellers are squeezed into the same shape. Thus, Mary Drone in Rolling Hills was living much closer in every way to 1984 than to 1934, for she dwelt in a vast, communistic, female barracks. This communism, like any other, was made possible by the destruction of the individual."[38]

The complaints Keats launches in *Crack in the Picture Window*, like William Whyte's, Sloan Wilson's and others, were frequently misogynist, blaming the "matriarchy" of suburbia for its ills.[39] At other times, his critiques were a kind of elitist cosmopolitanism—suburbia simply offended these writers' sensibilities. Keats used a fictional couple, John and Mary Drone, to lampoon what he saw as the dangers of suburban development. "The physically monotonous development of mass homes is a leveling influence in itself," Keats wrote, "breeding swarms of neuter drones."[40] The central problem he saw, beyond the shoddy construction and anti-individualism and ennui, was that these "developments" failed to function communities in any meaningful sense: "There is no park in Rolling Knolls or near it. There is no school or churchyard, no community center. Mary has no car. The shopping center is two miles away; the bus stop, one mile away. Mary will therefore take her children out to play on the tiny lawn just like everyone else." Meanwhile, John Drone "didn't see the reasons" for Mary's boredom and irritation "because, for one thing, he didn't live in the house. He left in the morning, came home at night for supper and bed, lounged around over the weekends, and remained completely oblivious of the nature of Mary's days."[41] In the absence of a "true" community, Keats argued, inhabitants of the suburbs mistook their neighbors for friends, engaged in conspicuous consumption, and slid ever closer to conformity.

A final explosive exposé of suburban life appeared in 1960. *The Split-Level Trap*, coauthored by Richard E. Gordon (a psychiatrist), his wife, Katherine K. Gordon (a social psychologist), and *Time* editor Max Gunther, was a sordid survey of eight family case-histories supposedly emblematic of those "most commonly handled in a psychiatric practice" in suburban Englewood Cliffs, New Jersey. The teasers on the paperback cover called it "A Kinsey Report on Suburbia" and asked, "Are We Commuting to Disaster?" After spending the first parts of the study outlining terrifying but purportedly "typical" psychosocial disorders in the geography they like to call "Disturbia," the authors offer expert advice and "proven techniques" for how to manage the "emotional problems" of high-pressure living. Condemning the "typical American" for his very normality—his "shiny mass-produced house and car," as well "his manners and mores,"—*The Split-Level Trap* concludes that "he represents the great sad joke of our time. Having amassed a wealth that used to be the subject of fairy tales, he often finds that he isn't happy after all."[42]

Together, the suburban critiques produced from the mid-1950s through the early 1960s found the homogeneity of suburban communities to be a kind of entrapment. "We're not peas in a pod," a mother with two children in a Midwestern suburb protested to one interviewer. "I thought it would be like that, especially because incomes are nearly the same. But it's amazing how different and varied people are. . . . I never really knew what people were like until I came here."[43] But because whiteness, reproductive heterosexuality, middle-class status, and masculine American "character" were so explicitly embedded into suburban living, these postwar geographies were seen to epitomize the postwar pursuit of normality. When the suburbs became target for critique, it was a signal that normality itself was beginning to unravel.

Watching and Being Watched in *Peyton Place*

When a working-class New Hampshire housewife named Grace Metalious produced her first novel in 1956, she located her tale in the immediate historic past and in the geographic margins. Set in a quintessential small New England town, with action spanning the 1930s through World War II, *Peyton Place* focused on the lives of three major female characters. But its most central character, recognized by the editors who suggested the title, was Peyton Place itself. The forces of a surveillance and performance converge in *Peyton Place*, but they are not celebrated. Rather, Metalious used her lush and provocative novel to reveal what the original *New York Times* review called the "false fronts and bourgeois pretensions of allegedly respectable communities."[44] The reviewer for the *New York World Telegram* was more explicit: "Earthy, crude, and Falstaffian, [Grace Metalious] swaggers down Main Street, figuratively peering through keyholes, ripping the roofs off bedrooms, and kicking in windows, the better to report on her fellow citizens."[45] Within eighteen months, this novel would become the

best seller of the era, in part because of the powerful critique it launched
of the oppressively disciplining gaze of postwar communities. "*I* live in
Peyton Place," was a regular refrain of Metalious's readers.[46]

In an age when the average novel sold two thousand copies, *Peyton Place*
sold sixty thousand within the first ten days of its official release on September 24, 1956. After seventeen months, and "in spite of chilly reviews,"
one out of every twenty-nine Americans had purchased the book (some
estimate that far more, perhaps as many as one in six, *read* the novel).[47]
Metalious had sold all film and television rights to the story for $250,000,
but the film version went on to earn $11 million and nine academy award
nominations for Twentieth Century–Fox.[48] By January 1958, *Peyton Place*
had sold more copies than *Gone with the Wind*. And well before the very
dissimilar television serial debuted in September 1964, *Peyton Place* had
sold 300,000 copies in hardcover, and over 8 million copies in paperback.
Grace Metalious's novel had rapidly surpassed all previous best sellers to
become, in its day, the best-selling novel of the twentieth century.[49]

The phenomenal success of *Peyton Place,* in spite of local and national
attempts to ban it, suggests the power of its audience's response.[50] But
something further is revealed in the leap readers made between reading a
novel and then imagining the novel was about *them*: "My town was a real
Peyton Place," or "Whose town wasn't a Peyton Place?" This town came
to represent every town, and its themes came to represent broader American cultural/historical problems. Such a response confirms that the novel's
popularity came as much from a sense of *identification* as from a sense of
titillation.[51]

Peyton Place is a long novel, with a huge cast of characters, and the action
spans a nearly a decade, with many subplots. The central narrative threads
primarily interweave the stories of three women: the sexy "widow" entrepreneur Constance MacKenzie, her adolescent aspiring-writer daughter,
Allison MacKenzie, and Allison's impoverished friend Selena Cross. When
the book opens, Allison is a sensitive, naïve, pre-pubescent; by the end
she has moved to New York, started a writing career, and lost her virginity
and much of her idealism. Constance begins as a sexually repressed single
mother, trying to hide her daughter's illegitimacy. By the end of the novel,
Constance has been sexually "released" by the handsome new Greek school
principal, Tom Makris, "come clean" about her past, and married him.
Selena begins as the victim of physical abuse and eventually rape by her
stepfather, which results in a pregnancy. She receives an illegal abortion by
the town's kind, upstanding doctor, and she murders her stepfather when

he returns to assault her again. Selena is sent to trial for murder, but after the doctor testifies, the town exonerates her. In the end, she makes the feminist move of leaving behind her weak-willed boyfriend, and the middle-class move of taking over the management of Constance's dress shop.

In contrast to all the midcentury critics of suburbia, Grace Metalious offered a different angle. First, her text was not misogynist, but rather focused in on the lives and trials of women, whom she casts as more tragically victimized by a culture of "keeping up appearances." Second, *Peyton Place* was not about the boredom of conformity or the ennui of status-seeking, but rather the hypocrisy, cant, and moral culpability of a entire community built on pretense.

Moments of surveillance—of watching, being watched, and *feeling* watched—are central elements of *Peyton Place*. The eye of the town is always present, functioning as an internalized critic and judge, establishing itself as an audience, and demanding a convincing "performance." Metalious employs surveillance not only as a theme, but as a narrative device that allows her to introduce her cast of characters by having one character "see" another, and then talk about that character for the benefit of the reader. Although this is not an uncommon narrative technique, Metalious uses it pointedly, to emphasize her theme of watching, and being watched. For example, in the introductory scene, a group of old men sit on the "wooden benches which seem to be part of every municipal building in America's small towns," sizing up the town's citizens as they pass by, in a kind of literary gossip:

> "There goes Kenny Stearns," said one man unnecessarily, for everyone had seen—and knew—Kenny.
> "Sober as a judge, right now."
> "That won't last long."
> The men laughed. . . .
> " . . . Ain't nobody in Peyton Place can make things grow like Kenny. He's got one of them whatcha call green thumbs."
> One man snickered. "Too bad Kenny don't have the same good luck with his wife as he has with plants. Mebbe Kenny'd be better off with a green pecker." . . .
> "Ginny Stearns is a tramp and a trollop," said Clayton Frazier, unsmilingly. "There ain't much a feller can do when he's married to a born whore."
> "'Cept drink," said the man who had first spoken. (3–4)

Rarely do observers in Peyton Place say anything positive; the eye that is watching is a critical eye. These men in front of the courthouse continue to sit in judgment of their neighbors throughout the text.

The dissonance between interiors and exteriors, or the "false fronts" in Peyton Place, is the primary theme of the novel, and one that was not lost on readers or reviewers at the time. The practice of "keeping up appearances" continuously creates comic, ironic, and even tragic consequences. As far as the town knows, for example, Allison MacKenzie is the beautiful, virginal daughter of the beautiful, widowed Constance MacKenzie; in actuality Allison is the illegitimate result of Constance's affair with a married man. Selena Cross's stepfather, Lucas, seems acceptable enough, because he stays on his side of the tracks: "They're all alike, those shack-owners. Work for a while, drunk for a longer while, work and then drunk again." . . . "They're all right though. Don't do any harm that I can see. They pay their bills," the townspeople say (30). In reality, Lucas is beating his wife, abusing his children, and molesting his teenaged stepdaughter. And Dr. Matthew Swain appears to be the town's upstanding moral center, but in truth, along with his own list of secrets and regrets, he makes the scandalous decision to perform an illegal abortion for Selena Cross when she becomes pregnant as a result of the rape.

Allison's mother, Constance MacKenzie, has lived in fear of the community's judgment for so long that she begins to project her own sins onto her daughter. For her, it is not Allison's teenage heart which is at risk, but her "decency," which Constance has carefully and secretly constructed through props (like a falsified birth certificate), through her own seamless performance as the pious widow, and with the money her ex-lover left to her and to Allison when he died. Constance has so effectively internalized a sense of being judged that she buckles under her own self-scrutiny. Her wealth, it turns out, cannot secure her reputation. It is the performance that will make or break her, and while she may succeed in the role she has set herself, she cannot fully control the behavior of her daughter. Ultimately, Constance fears the destructive power of talk most of all, because that talk is where her normality is produced:

> A quick picture of her daughter Allison, lying in bed with a man, flashed through her mind, and Constance put a shaking hand against the wall to steady herself.
> Oh, she'll get hurt! was the first thought that filled her.
> Then: Oh, she'll get in trouble!
> And finally, worst of all: SHE'LL GET HERSELF TALKED ABOUT! (50)

In this town, as the journalist Laura Secor observes, "gossip wields a power more binding than the law," although there is both pain and pleasure to be found in the surveillance of the self and others.[52]

Even the sensitive young heroine, Allison MacKenzie, is not above these acts of surveillance as, in one scene, she watches her date, Rodney Harrington, dance with Betty Anderson: "Why is he doing this to me? she wondered sickly. I look nicer than Betty. She looks cheap in that sleazy red dress, and she's wearing gunk on her eyelashes. She's got awfully big breasts for a girl her age, and Kathy said they were real. I don't believe it. . . . I'll bet that dress belonged to Betty's big sister, the one who got in Dutch with that man from White River" (122). Allison's listing of the visual markers that distinguish Betty from herself by extension separates all lower- or working-class girls from all middle-class or "good" girls in postwar U.S. culture: loud dress, make-up, large breasts, and a bad reputation. At this point in the novel, Allison remains unaware of the circumstances of her own birth, but because Metalious makes the reader aware of those circumstances, Allison's judgment of Betty appears both ironic and hypocritical.

Darker scenes in the novel describe the "witnessing" by middle-class voyeurs of the lives of the town's poorest population, the people Peyton Place terms "shack dwellers." Doc Swain, walking by Lucas Cross's tarpaper shack, overhears Lucas beating his wife, Nellie, and is disturbed, but he does not intervene (25–26). In a later, pivotal scene, Allison sits outside the Cross shack, transfixed as her best friend Selena is also attacked by her own stepfather, Lucas:

> Allison knew she should stop looking in the window, but she literally could not move. She had never seen a man strike anyone in her life, and she was held now by a terrible fear. . . .
>
> "You goddamn' sonofabitch," roared Lucas, beside himself. "You goddamn whorin' little slut!"
>
> He grabbed at Selena and when she wrenched away from his grasp, he was left holding the entire front of the girl's blouse. Selena backed away from Lucas, her breasts naked and heaving in the light of the room's unshaded electric bulb, her shoulders still covered ridiculously by the sleeves of the faded cotton blouse.
>
> Why the ends of hers are *brown*, thought Allison foolishly. And she does not wear a brassiere all the time, like she told me! (56–57)

After this moment, Alison tumbles from her perch and flees, never acting on what she has witnessed. On the one hand, Metalious constructs a classic "lowbrow" fiction scene here—the "naked and heaving" breasts, the "unshaded electric bulb," the torn blouse—such details could be taken from countless pulp fiction covers, or from Erskine Caldwell's *Tobacco Road*, as some critics complained. But the important difference is Metalious's positioning of Allison, the middle-class character with whom readers are meant to identify, as a voyeur who is both terrified and somehow thrilled by the spectacle. These scenes reveal the helplessness, fascination, eroticism, and trauma all attached to a middle-class gaze on poor or working-class culture.

When Selena goes to Allison's comfortable, middle-class home for visits, the gaze is inverted: "Selena always stayed to supper on Saturdays, when Constance usually made something simple, like waffles or scrambled eggs with little sausages. To Selena, everything about the MacKenzie house seemed luxurious—and beautiful, something to dream about. She loved the combination of rock maple and flowered chintz in the MacKenzie living room, and she often wondered . . . [how] Allison . . . could be unhappy in surroundings like these, with a wonderful blonde mother, and a pink and white bedroom of her own" (35). Such longing descriptions of the interiors of the MacKenzie household—so perfectly constructed to *seem* normal, respectable, and middle class—function in high contrast to the descriptions of the cabin the Crosses live in. And yet again, Metalious allows her readers to appreciate the irony of Selena falling for Constance's well-polished "performance."

Which comes first, the desire to "perform" out of a sense of being watched, or the obligation to watch, feeling the presence of a "performance"? In one telling scene, Dr. Swain's Catholic nurse, Mary Kelley, ponders the moral consequences of "keeping up appearances" as she faces the ethical dilemma of assisting in Selena Cross's illegal abortion:

> Talk was cheap. It cost nothing to give voice to what you wanted people to think you believed. Mary wondered if medical ethics could be compared to questions of tolerance. When you talked you said that Negroes were as good as anybody. You said that Negroes should never be discriminated against, and that if you ever fell in love with one, you'd marry him proudly. But all the while you were talking, you wondered what you would *really* do if some big, black, handsome nigger came up and asked you for a date. When you talked you declared that if you fell in love with a Protestant who refused to change his religion for you, that you would marry him anyway. . . . You knew you were safe in saying these things, for there hadn't been a nigger living in Peyton Place for over a hundred years, and you didn't date boys who were not Catholics. (153)

Here Metalious unflinchingly reveals the hypocrisy of a culture in which "talk" is the dominant mode of power, but in which it comes "cheap." This talk is separate from "what [they] would *really* do," as well as separate from "ethics," from "questions of tolerance," and from the community's actions. The hypocrisy in Peyton Place encourages a disconnection between what people say and what they think, and it raises serious questions about ethnic and racial difference and religious belief. Metalious pursues this theme throughout the text, often by juxtaposing characters' spoken, external dialogues against their unspoken, interior monologues.

Such "performances" frequently take on gendered significance. As the teenage bad boy Rodney Harrington plots his date's seduction, for example, a humorous dissonance emerges between his interior and exterior motives:

> In addition to the rum, he had six pairs of black market nylon hose in the glove compartment of his car as extra persuasion.
> "Oh, what're these!" cried Helen a few moments later as she held up the stockings.
> Levers to pry your pants off, thought Rodney, but he said: "Pretty nylons for pretty legs." (312–13)

And in the scene where Tom Makris first meets Constance MacKenzie, Metalious highlights the disjunction between Tom's gentlemanly exterior and his predatory thoughts: "'I'm very glad to know you, Mrs. MacKenzie,' said Makris, and he thought, Very glad to know you, baby. I want to know you a lot better, on a bed, for instance, with that blond hair spread out on a pillow" (105). On the surface, Makris is respectful and polite, but internally, he is already plotting his sexual conquest, which does, of course, come to pass. The performance, in this case, brings with it a dangerous tension. The conflict between what both Tom and Constance desire (sex), and what they each feel compelled to do (abstain), results in resentment, anger, and frustration. The scene in which Tom and Constance finally do have sex is a disturbing one, cast by Metalious as simultaneously a rape and a seduction. Tom violently forces Constance to bed, stripping and even slapping her at one point, but in the end the encounter "frees" Constance from her own sexual misery. What they see as their shared responsibility for the brutality of that first night continues to haunt both of them, long after they are married (148–49).

Later employing race as a theme, Metalious also critiques the performative "false fronts" of the town itself. Peyton Place, not unlike postwar America, works to present itself as the bastion of happy, healthy, well-adjusted, moral, churchgoing, middle-class citizens, but Metalious reveals it to be a community characterized by discrimination, abuse, racism, corruption, sexual frustration, subjugation of women, parochialism, hatred, and hypocrisy. When Makris is hired as principal of the high school, the bigoted character of Peyton Place emerges: "'A Greek?' demanded Peyton

Place incredulously. 'For God's sake, isn't it enough that we've got a whole colony of Polacks and Canucks working in the mills without letting the Greeks in?'" (95).[53] The whitened exteriors of Peyton Place are busily hiding its own "darkest" secret: the founding father was a former slave named Samuel Peyton, who escaped to France and married a white woman there; he then returned to the United States during the Civil War and built a castle in rural New Hampshire when Bostonians turned them away. By framing Samuel Peyton as the mysterious villain, Metalious at first seems to imply that his blackness is the sin. But the joke is on her readers: the true shame of Samuel Peyton emerges late in the text, and functions as one of the "morals" of the town's story. From his castle in New Hampshire, the former slave had turned a profit by running guns back down south during the Civil War. So the worst "secret" of is not that he was black, nor that he was married to a white woman, but that he was corrupt: a traitor, or—as the town curmudgeon calls him—a "friggin rebel."[54] By having a Greek outsider bring a moral compass to the town, and having a turncoat ex-slave be the father of the community, Metalious symbolically indicted the longest-standing American communities for their nativist fantasies of cultural superiority.[55]

Metalious's critiques of surveillance and performance are embodied most fully in the midcentury gothic character of Norman Page. As far as Peyton Place is concerned, Alison's aptly named friend Norman Page is the quiet, sensitive, only son of the widow Evelyn Page. In reality, he is his mother's surrogate spouse, the victim of her regular psychosexual manipulation and abuse. Behind closed doors, Evelyn Page has always dominated and injured Norman, giving him enemas at the slightest provocation—"Norman always got a bittersweet sort of pleasure from that" (62)—and doling out regular psychological punishments to test his love for her:

> Norman collapsed on the floor at his mother's feet. He sobbed hysterically . . . but she would not look down at him.
> " . . . I love only you, Mother. I don't love anybody else."
> "Are you sure, Norman? There's nobody else you love?"
> "No, no, no. There is no one else, Mother. Just you." . . .
> "Do you love Mother, Norman?"
> Norman's sobs were dry and painful now, and he hiccuped wretchedly.
> "Oh yes, Mother. I love only you. I love you better than God, even. Say you're not going to leave me." (72)

This scene seems intended to build a portrait of a psychopath. In a second pivotal scene of layered surveillance, Metalious has the adolescent Norman crouch under the porch of his spinster neighbor, Miss Hester, to see what it is that she is always watching next door. (The implication is that Norman has previously watched Miss Hester watching.) With Miss Hester over his head in her porch rocker watching the same scene with her cat on her lap, Norman, through a thick hedge, spies a neighboring couple making love in their back garden. Both attracted and repulsed by the image of the enormously pregnant Mrs. Card, reclining on a lounge chair, being pleasured by her husband, Norman cannot stop watching, yet wants to "vomit." After fleeing, Norman later returns to discover that the elderly Miss Hester has died on her porch, her tomcat still tethered to the side of her rocking chair, yowling. In a fit of horror and panic, Norman strangles the cat to death, crying "Stop it! Stop it! Stop it!" (255). Later in the novel, Norman attempts to escape his mother and his town by enlisting to fight in World War II, but he is soon receives Section Eight discharge, which codes him as either mentally unfit for service or as a homosexual, or both. His mother continues to control his adult life after his return, forcing him to fake a limp (a "normal" injury), to save face in the community.

The Norman Page storyline is, among other things, a classic example of the misogynist "Momism" of the times, as Metalious draws a line from all of Norman's problems back to his overbearing mother.[56] It also invokes another "Norman" and "Norma" of the postwar period—the infamous Norman Bates and his alter-ego/mother, Norma, from Robert Bloch's 1959 novel (and the 1960 Hitchcock film) *Psycho*. Although no one has determined whether Bloch knew of Metalious's Norman Page, he claims that his inspiration was the explosive case of the small-town serial killer Ed Gein, who was arrested in 1957 for a series of gruesome murders and grave-robbings. Though Bloch knew only the general contours of the Gein case (not its horrific details), in a later interview he described the irony of Gein's being from a very small town: "Realizing how much gossip there is in a small town and how neighbors tend to pry into every else's affairs, I wondered just what kind of man, and what circumstances, might be involved in such a crime without anyone suspecting. Working from these questions, I came up with the plot of *Psycho*."[57] In Bloch's anecdote, as with Metalious's Norman Page storyline, the failures of "surveillance" begin to emerge. Ultimately, the Norman Page plot suggests that "normality" was not something that could be determined by a glance through a picture window. From the outside, mild-mannered Norman Page seems normal enough, but for Metalious's readers, who come to know him in more depth, he is anything but. The middle-class culture of surveillance and performance in Peyton Place failed to protect Page, just as it had failed to protect Selena Cross.

Peyton Place thus launched a damning critique of a midcentury culture of "keeping up appearances." The novel's popularity, as well as the discourse surrounding its publication, suggest that postwar readers were ready to hear that critique. In this way, as Ardis Cameron notes, "Grace Metalious not only struck a chord with the modern reading public, she helped to create it."[58] Because of its unprecedented popularity, *Peyton Place* can be seen as both a signal and a cause of a major ground-shift in midcentury attitudes toward normality and its contradictions.[59] Metalious not only blew the lid off small-town New England, she shook the foundations of a culture that had taken hold in small towns, big cities, and the suburbs, too.

Other-Directed: Normality as the New Morality

"Who am I to say what's right and wrong?" remarked one young Pennsylvania woman in response to a 1959 *Look* magazine survey of American moral attitudes. *Look* editor William Attwood summarized the most "essential fact" of the findings: "You no longer refrain from doing something because you couldn't live with yourself—you refrain from doing something because you couldn't live with your neighbors."[60] By the early 1950s observers of postwar communities had in fact begun to express anxiety over what they saw as an increasing slippage between *morality*, which was understood to be internal, and *normality*, which seemed a more external, social, even ocular method by which to measure behavior. The postwar novelist and short-story writer Flannery O'Connor, famous for her use of ocular metaphors, set up disturbing morality plays in most of her stories, highlighting the disjunctions between physical appearances and moral realities. The feminist philosopher Simone de Beauvoir made the morality/normality substitution explicit in the second chapter of her 1949 work *The Second Sex*. Suggesting that *normality* is a concept derived from psychiatry, de Beauvoir noted that the term had gained currency after the war, expanding into realms well beyond the psychoanalytic: "Replacing value with authority, choice with drive, psychoanalysis offers an *Ersatz*, a substitute for morality—the concept of normality."[61] De Beauvoir not only suggested that normality and morality were interchangeable, but blamed psychoanalysis for the confusion, and she insisted that the process subjugated women more than men.

David Riesman's enormously influential 1950 sociological study *The Lonely Crowd* crystallized the terms on which the moral drift of postwar society would be critiqued. According to Riesman, the "lonely crowd" of the American middle class had shifted away from a nineteenth-century morality of "inner-direction," to become "other-directed": they measured themselves in relation to the group and its external rules of conduct. "What is common to all the other-directed people," Riesman wrote, "is that their contemporaries are the source of direction for the individual—either those known to him or those with whom he is indirectly acquainted, through friends and through the mass media."[62] Riesman's conception of other-direction was distinctly gendered, however. Like William Whyte, who would term the phenomenon a new "Social Ethic," Riesman saw suburban consumerism, status-seeking, and concern about "keeping up appearances" as feminized practices.[63]

Even critics of the Kinsey Reports expressed anxiety about what they saw as the substitution of normality for morality in Kinsey's research on sexual behavior. When Kinsey died unexpectedly in 1956, an *America* magazine editorial titled "Normal Isn't as Normal Does," reflected on the event with little remorse: "One of the most controversial figures of our age recently went through the normal process of dying," the article begins. The writer concludes that "the whole bent of Dr. Kinsey's work did incalculable harm by giving countenance and even 'scientific' respectability to an utter misuse of the word 'normal.'" Kinsey's habit of "confusing" the "normal" with the "moral," the writer continues, "takes on a particular virulence in these times. . . . If democracy rests on no more solid basis than a flimsy philosophy of the 'common man,' then any mode of action that is uncommon will be suspected of being undemocratic. Transfer this woolly thinking to the field of morals, and . . . [r]ight and wrong will become a matter to be determined by a counting of noses."[64] The writer's reference to "these times" was an implicit invocation of current Cold War logic, in which democracy was a moral imperative, and moral relativism was the sign of godless communism.

The marked revival of religious life in the postwar decades did not answer the problem of normality as the new morality, because this religiosity, too, appears to have been more about surface than depth. By 1958, 97 percent of American people declared they believed in God, and over 63 percent were officially enrolled in churches.[65] In the cultural war against Communism, Eisenhower convinced Congress to put "In God We Trust" on the currency and "Under God" into the Pledge of Allegiance. Attendance at churches and synagogues soared, movies with biblical themes were box office hits, and religious books were perennial best sellers. But at the same time, many social observers found that postwar religious life was about "churchgoing," but not piety: Lionel Trilling wrote that "religion nowadays has the appearance of what the ideal modern house has been called, a machine for living." It was not that people believed in God more, the MIT philosopher Huston Smith noted, but rather that they "believe[d] in believing in him." The theologian Gibson Winter complained about the church's postwar function as a social club, a place to see and be seen, rather than as a house of worship: "In place of the sacraments, we have the committee meeting. . . . In place of the confession, the bazaar; . . . in place of community, a collection of functions; . . . every church activity seems to lead further in to a maze of superficiality which is stultifying the middle class community."[66] Will Herberg's influential *Protestant, Catholic, Jew* (1960) criticized American "religiousness without religion." Rather than "re-orienting life to God," postwar religiousness was "a way of sociability or belonging."[67] Normality functioned well in a culture that was less about piety or respectability and more about the outward "performances" of self.

Author Grace Metalious had shown that normality itself was a performance and a facade, even—if not especially—in the most charming American communities.[68] By exposing normality as something anyone could project, even as he or she committed countless immoral, illegal, outrageous acts at the same time, Metalious helped to destabilize the category of normality. By representing "moral" characters who are actively sexual, have sex before marriage, give (or receive) abortions, violently defend themselves against abusers, and experience and express desire, the novel also worked to normalize behaviors that had been considered immoral. In this way, Metalious carefully, yet explosively, made *deviance* the norm.

The "cultural work" of Metalious's novel is to be found in the theme of *Peyton Place*, what it came to symbolize, and what led to its survival: the revelation that we are not as we appear, and we have that in common. *Peyton Place*, like the suburban critiques, exposed the tragic hypocrisy of a particular postwar American way of life, and that critique resonated with postwar readers as well as postwar writers. Metalious's targets—the false fronts and hypocrisy of midcentury communities—would continue to be an explicit theme in much of postwar literature, a theme that crossed the lines of race, gender, class, and "brows," and continued the powerful critique of a society focused on surfaces.[69] Eventually, one effect of the repetition of this theme would be *its* normalization into a postmodern philosophy, one in which the performance is the fact, in which the simulation is as real as it gets—so that by 1961, Kurt Vonnegut can write, "We are what we pretend to be, so we must be careful about what we pretend to be."[70]

The blurry boundary between what was morally "right" and what everyone else was doing had been precisely the territory Grace Metalious explored. Despite its well-scrubbed, godly exteriors, the moral compass of Peyton Place fails, and the town operates instead on gossip, hypocrisy, and pretense. Postwar readers, themselves peering voyeuristically into the page of a scandalous book, were positioned between these two worlds—morality and normality—internalizing these characters and spaces to map their own social locations. In the end, both *Peyton Place* and midcentury suburban exposés like *The Crack in the Picture Window* functioned as yet another way for American readers to "survey" one another's communities.

Conclusion
Home, Normal Home

A 1962 *New York Times* article titled "Baffling Search for the 'Normal Man'" concludes with one psychiatrist's complaint that searching for a definition of "normality" was "a little like trying to glue fog to the sky."[1] This metaphor still holds. Normality is difficult to contain because it is constantly moving, shifting, dissipating. Worse, to try to define normality with any precision is to risk reifying its claims to describe. But normality has always had, and continues to have, a particular and traceable history. To show how normality has *functioned* in a specific context allows us to see just how foggy the concept has been, and to assess the cultural and ideological work it has accomplished.

In this study I have worked to show that normality, although it has a much longer history, reemerged into popular discourse and mass consciousness in the first two decades following World War II. At the end of the war, the United States faced a period of readjustment involving the massive demobilization of troops, reintegration of veterans into the workforce, and a collective coping with the emotional, physical, and economic wounds left by the war. Although the term *normality* had been deployed before, it was during the postwar decades that it moved from the discourses of science, statistics, and medicine fully into the spaces of everyday life. During this period, normality went from being a concept for the organization and ordering of esoteric knowledge to being a concept for the organization and ordering of bodies and minds, "characters" and sexualities, classes and communities.

Between 1943 and 1963, normality thus functioned as a powerful epistemological category through which to measure and define American life. Deeply internalizable, it became a "substitute for morality" according to some.[2] Encompassing a range of identity categories while specifying none, normality became a way of talking about heterosexuality, middle-classness, whiteness, able-bodiedness without ever mentioning them.[3] Perpetually alternating between describing an average and prescribing an ideal, normality meant being "perfectly average"—a tension that made it both highly desirable and impossible to achieve. Nevertheless, for a time, postwar Americans—scientists, doctors, sexologists, anthropologists, politicians, academics, novelists, families, and individuals—established normality as a goal for which to strive, as a worthy pursuit.

Ultimately, this project raises the question, What *was* normality? What did normality *look* like, in the postwar decades? A closer look at the "Home, Normal Home" cartoon illustration in a September 1963 *New York Times* essay (see fig. 3) may help to formulate a fair response. A faceless cartoon family of four—husband, wife, daughter, and son—poses beneath a wall plaque inscribed "Home, Normal Home." First, the substitution of the phrase "Home, *Normal* Home" for the classic "Home, *Sweet* Home" on the plaque highlights the shift from a Victorian ethic to a postwar domestic ideology that was more performative. Next, the particulars of the image of a husband, wife, and two children present the subtleties of "what normality looked like" at this time—white, middle-class, attractive, and clean, with reproductive heterosexuality and gender cast as the defining differences.

Considered against the earliest representations of normality discussed here, the 1943 Norm and Norma statues (see fig. 6), the 1963 figures seem consistent in their representation of normality in terms of gender, race, class, and sexuality. Yet while Norm and Norma are decontextualized and showcased for their reproductive potential, the "Home, Normal Home" figures are domesticated and have seemingly completed the task, reproducing themselves in their own cartoonish images. Although the postwar nuclear family has effectively reproduced the social body, the caption, "QUESTION—Cheerfully unambitious, happily in a rut: is this the ideal for which to strive?" makes the postwar critique of normality explicit, questioning its value as a cultural goal. The erasure of the four faces, however, creates the most startling effect.

At first, the blank faces seem to signal a shift in normality from a representable quality to an unrepresentable one, a move from embodiment to disembodiment. But in another sense, the facelessness of this comic vision of normality might have been more intensely representative, because it insisted that the reader fill in the blank, placing his or her own face or family in those empty spaces, to receive the caption's damning question. That normality could be so effectively internalizable at the same moment that it was being critiqued as an enemy of progress illustrates the powerful and paradoxical hold this shifting idea would continue to have over postwar American lives.

To some degree, to look at normality in the postwar decades has been to look at the cultural moment that produced the epistemological category we still live with. Yet it is important to emphasize the distinctions between the normality that emerged after World War II, the normality that preceded that period, and the normality that remains in circulation. The term *normal* arose out of the Enlightenment birth of statistics, which is "remarkably late" in human history, according to Lennard Davis. In his work *Enforcing Normalcy*, Davis notes that the word *statistik* first appeared in 1749, from which the mathematical "normal distribution" of variations from a mean would be charted. The Gaussian, normal, or bell curve became an indispensable tool for mathematics, the sciences, and eventually the social sciences as well. In 1835 the French statistician Adolphe Quetelet formulated the concept of *l'homme moyen*, or the average man, bringing the idea of "normal distribution" to bear on the human form. In this way, as Davis notes, the rise of the category "normal" coincides with the rise of bourgeois hegemony: "The average man, the body of the man in the middle, becomes the exemplar of the middle way of life," and the bourgeoisie is "rationally placed in the mean position in the great order of things."[4] The definition of *normal* as "constituting, conforming to, not deviating or differing from, the common type or standard, regular, usual" was thus firmly in place by the mid-nineteenth century. If the lexicon is reliable, Davis writes, we can date the "coming to consciousness in English of an idea of 'the norm' over the period 1840–1860."[5]

While I have discussed normality's history as a postwar American idea, the way normality has surfaced and functioned in these other times and places begs further investigation. The fact that anthropometry, medical statistics, and the etymology of normality date from the late nineteenth century points to a set of connections worth pursuing. As Davis notes, "The rather amazing fact is that almost all the early statisticians had one thing in common: they were eugenicists."[6] The term *normality* also emerged in the middle of the nineteenth century, directly alongside the rise of medical statistics and social Darwinist ideas about the perfectibility of the human race. According to the *Oxford English Dictionary*, the word *normality* appeared in print as early as 1849, penned by that most abnormal of American writers, Edgar Allan Poe.[7] By the 1890s, discourses on the normal merge with Alexander Graham Bell's early writings on disability, which, as Davis concludes, launched an ongoing process of "enforcing normalcy" as disability's Other.[8]

The number of references in 1950s discourse that point back to the late nineteenth century are also too frequent to ignore: the physique and physical education of Norma, for example, are constantly compared with her "Victorian grandmother" in the publicity surrounding the anthropometric models. In one article, for example, the Dudley A. Sargent models of the "average young man and woman of the Gay [18]90s" are pictured and analyzed as the direct antecedents of Norm and Norma. The Norma Look-Alike Contest harks back to the first newspaper-sponsored photobeauty contests of the late 1800s, or to P. T. Barnum's 1854 brainchild: the first American beauty contest.[9] Even the gray-flannel-suit anxiety is in many ways a recapitulation of debates surrounding the somber-suited, bowler-hatted businessmen of a newly industrialized America. While some continue to look to the 1950s with a strong sense of nostalgia—for the supposed nuclear family, prosperity, religiosity, or clearly defined gender roles—the evidence suggests that Americans in the 1950s were *themselves* backward-looking, nostalgic for the Victorian era, and for many of the same reasons. A more far-reaching historicization of normality might especially pursue these ties to the mid-to-late nineteenth-century period.

In the early decades of the twentieth century, as Julian Carter argues, "normality" was a concept deeply charged with gender, racial, and sexual ideologies.[10] The late nineteenth-century interest in applying science and statistics to the definition of the "average" had given way to the influence of psychology, which saw the consolidation of "normal" as a newly resonant category of "mental hygiene." A brief but consequential linguistic shift also occurred in this interwar period. In his inaugural address, President Warren G. Harding famously called for a "return to normalcy" after World War I: "Our supreme task is the resumption of our onward, normal way. . . . We must strive to normalcy to reach stability."[11] *Normalcy* is both related to and distinct from the post–World War II focus on normality. Etymologically, the two words are essentially interchangeable, though *normality* is preferred by grammarians. But historically, Harding's use of the term at that moment invokes what will become two patterns in its future use: the turn to normality as a regular response to war or other traumas experienced on a national scale, and the strategic use of normality as a political tactic.

While the alignment of normality with the postwar decades may seem unsurprising, what is striking is the critique of normality that emerged in tandem with it. The postwar "return to normality" was embraced by the masses, but never without question. The concept was challenged from the start, by doctors, scholars, novelists, and individuals. Those challenges ranged from the technical quibbles of scientists over the definition of the term, to the skepticism of journalists and cartoonists who questioned the term's utility, to the full-on critique of normality's practices that emerged from the most surprising of locations, from the pulpit to the pages of *Peyton Place*. The postwar period saw the pursuit of normality, but was also a time when the epistemological power of "normality" was being critiqued, questioned, undermined, and challenged. *None* of the thousands of Norma contestants matched her measurements; 80 percent of residents in a 1963 midtown Manhattan mental health study *failed* to exhibit "normality"; few, if any, of the literary characters appearing here seem to qualify. This investigation of the pursuit of "normality," then, moves us beyond simplistic readings of the "complacent" 1950s against the "rebellious" 1960s, forcing a reconsideration the 1950s as generative of self-reflexivity and critique. Furthermore, the coercive, disciplining elements of normality did not disappear in the 1960s. In 1969, the lone reference to be found in the *Readers' Guide to Periodical Literature* under the heading *normality* was an article in *Seventeen* magazine titled "How Can I Tell if I'm Normal?" One place where the logic of normality persisted, then, was with young women and youth culture.

A clearer understanding of the centrality of this homogenizing concept also invites a reconsideration of events that came afterward. To some degree, the various identity movements of the 1960s and 1970s had to have been dependent on "homogenizing" categories that preceded them in order to make sense. How, in other words, would something like a "counterculture" be epistemologically imaginable without the consolidation of something like a culture of "normality" beforehand? Moreover, to some degree, the oppositional quality of identity movements of the 1960 and '70s may even have reified the idea of a "sameness" in the middle, and strengthened the cultural associations between normality and whiteness, middle-classness, heterosexuality, even masculinity.

Normalizing discourse continues to shape us, even up to the moment. After one cross-reference to a 1979 Joyce Carol Oates short story titled "Normal Love," the term *normality* disappears as a *Readers' Guide* category. That is, it disappears until 1995, when, under the label "Social Norm," we are directed to an article entitled "Are You Normal?" in the *Ladies' Home Journal.* "Do You or Don't You Behave Like Everyone Else?" the subhead asks. Similarly, the "Norm and Norma" case I discussed in chapter 1 can seem an amusing relic, until we run across a 2001 *Mademoiselle* piece, "Are Your Bodies Sexually Compatible?"—complete with full-color portraits of a series of young heterosexual couples in tasteful white underwear. The authors give thumbs up to a pair of Aryan specimens named "Morgan and Katie," who have "perfect ratios," but thumbs down to an ethnically mixed couple, since the too-tall Caucasian man towers over his Asian-featured girlfriend. *Mademoiselle's* "ratio rule" for determining sexually compatible bodies begins with the following instructions: "Get a measuring tape and divide your waist measurement by your hip measurement."[12]

Discourses of "normality" also continue to move beyond sexuality and the body to implicate race, class, and nation as well. The terrorist attacks of September 11, 2001, brought the terms *normalcy* and *normality* back into the U.S. mass media with great intensity, as journalists and their readers wrestled with a wish to turn back time, to return to a prelapsarian consciousness before the fall of the twin towers (fig. 28). As in the postwar decades, this was a return to an *imagined* condition, a normality that "had never existed," to borrow Wendy Kozol's phrase. This desire for a "return to normal" after 9/11 was, in one ironic sense, satisfied through the U.S. invasions of Iraq and Afghanistan, a move that reinstated a brand of "normality" that Americans have found quite familiar, and which harks back to the Cold War status quo: the role of the aggressor in an "endless war" against an amorphous enemy. Still, the phrase "return to normal" remains a regular and obfuscating feature in national news stories, whether spotlighting bombings in Baghdad, protests in Georgia, earthquakes in China, or floods in New Orleans. In every case, the term retains its post-traumatic, wishful connotations.

During the 2008 presidential election, "normality" was explicitly invoked again as a political strategy. Labeling herself and her husband "normal Joe Six-pack American[s]," Alaska governor and Republican vice presidential candidate Sarah Palin attempted to align herself with "normality." Calling herself an "everyday, working-class American" running for office against the "Washington elite," Palin revived the Republican ticket

FIGURE 28. , "Getting Back to Normal for Idiots," cartoon by David Sipress, *New Yorker*, 15 Oct. 2001. © David Sipress / Condé Nast Publications.

by seeming to be both an outsider and a representative of the middle.[13] For his part, her running mate, John McCain (a longtime Washington insider), associated himself with "Joe the Plumber," a flash-in-the-pan working-class white Wisconsinite who was also cast as representative of a middle class "norm" after he questioned Barack Obama about his tax policy. No longer a quality to be pursued, normality in these cases is recast as something inherent—something that certain people simply embody. By claiming normality, Palin and McCain were also reencoding it as white, as small-town, as politically conservative, and, in an interesting tension, as male, via these "average Joe" figures.[14] The slipperiness of the category emerged here, again, as "normality" was being aligned with a working-class ethos, by people who labeled themselves as middle class while collecting upper-class paychecks. Whether in the discourse of the news, or out of the mouths of politicians, normality retains its seductive appeal, nostalgic promise, and political capital.

"Normality" passes itself off as a natural, meaningful, universal idea, one that seems always to have existed. It is, however, a concept with a particular and traceable history. Produced and reproduced in the realm of culture as well as by the institutions of science, medicine, and politics, normality has never been complete in its formulation, but rather is caught in an ongoing process of signification. In this sense, this project has much in common with scholarship historicizing other unmarked or homogenizing categories such as whiteness, masculinity, heterosexuality, or middle-classness, all of which have revealed themselves to be similarly unstable, if not wholly imaginary.[15] To isolate this concept as a subject has required that I, too, engage in the "pursuit of normality," and like history, normality does not stand still for its portrait. It is a shifting, fleeting, cloudy thing, sometimes invoked directly, discursively, and at other times implied, encoded, undergirding other discourses and experiences. This project, therefore, tells the story of a struggle: the postwar (re)emergence and uneven trajectory of an idea.

"Normality" remains embedded in all areas of cultural life—statistics, science, psychology, sociology, anthropology, politics, medicine, education—always making meaning, always clarifying the ambiguous with its binary logic: Normal or abnormal? Normal or deviant? A norm or a variable? A normal curve or an anomalous one? The fact that normality must constantly be reinvented or reinscribed reveals its instability, and its instability also makes it slippery subject, one that resists being contained. My approach, then, has been to historicize it. To show the ways in which normality has been subject to history is to denaturalize it, interrupting its presumed universality, timelessness, and meaningfulness, and, potentially, its power.

Notes

Introduction: Situation Normal

1. Sloan Wilson, *The Man in the Gray Flannel Suit* (New York: Simon and Schuster, 1955), 73.

2. Twenty-eight Private Snafu cartoons were produced by Warner Brothers between 1943 and 1946, and have been collected as *The Complete Uncensored Private Snafu* (Image Entertainment, 1999). "SNAFU Jump" was written by Jerry Gray and released by Glenn Miller's Orchestra in 1944. Team SNAFU was attached to the 101st at Bastogne; see William L. O'Neill, *A Democracy at War: America's Fight at Home and Abroad in World War II* (Cambridge: Harvard University Press, 1995), 378; Ralph Mitchell, *101st Airborne Division's Defense of Bastogne* (Bennington, VT: Merriam, 2000), 14.

3. "Normality" is a highly charged term that deserves to be surrounded by quotation marks whenever it is invoked. For the sake of the reader's eye, however, I generally omit them from here on, though they remain in spirit.

4. "Regime of the normal" is Michael Warner's phrase; see *The Trouble with Normal: Sex, Politics, and the Ethics of Queer Life* (New York: Free Press, 1999).

5. Rena Corman, "Close-up of the 'Normal' Wife," *New York Times Magazine*, 8 September 1963, 52–69.

6. I discuss the etymology of the term *normality* more fully in the Conclusion. The major scholarly discussions of "normality" itself are relatively few to date. In addition to Warner, see Lennard Davis, *Enforcing Normalcy: Disability, Deafness, and the Body* (London: Verso, 1995); Mary Louise Adams, *The Trouble with Normal: Postwar Youth and the Making of Heterosexuality* (Toronto: University of Toronto Press, 1997); Mona Gleason, *Normalizing the Ideal: Psychology, Schooling, and the Family in Postwar Canada* (Toronto: University of Toronto Press, 1999); and Julian Carter, *The Heart of Whiteness: Normal Sexuality and Race in America 1880–1940* (Durham, NC: Duke University Press, 2007).

7. The term *keyword* is borrowed from Raymond Williams, *Keywords: A Vocabulary of Culture and Society* (New York: Oxford University Press, 1976).

8. I am indebted to Mary Louise Adams's anecdote about Radclyffe Hall's *The Well of Loneliness* for helping me sort out this distinction between a prewar and a postwar conceptualization of *normal* (Adams, *Trouble with Normal*, 83–84). Adams attributes this shift—from normality as an "innate" quality to normality as "something for which to strive"—to the increasing influence of psychology after the war. But while psychology was certainly influential, it cannot be said to be causal, as other forces were converging around this idea of normality as well: the war itself, quantitative social science, and social policy, for example.

151

9. History is messy, and there are a few exceptions. The very first time *normality* occured in the *Readers' Guide* was in 1932; the entry referenced a 1929 *Science* article titled "When Is Normal Normal?" in which Yale psychologist O. L. Tinklepaugh debates the inherent contradictions of "normal" as a scientific category (*Science*, 19 April 1929, 428). "Normality" also appears in the *Readers' Guide* after 1963, but only three times over the next thirty years, usually referencing advice columns directed at parents or teens. Nevertheless, "normality" remains a potent postwar category, for it is the *proliferation* of discourse that reveals *normality* to be a keyword of that era. Furthermore, most of the postwar articles focus precisely on defining or understanding "normality" itself, as a notion that had come to dominate everyday life.

The trajectory of the *Readers' Guide* entries is also seen in the *International Index of Periodicals*, which collates more academic/scholarly journal articles. The *International Index*, however, reveals a predominance of psychological/sociological discourse. The term *normality* appears first in 1943–46 and proliferates, then peaks in the 1958–60 volume. The years 1943–46 and 1949–52 feature primarily psychiatric reviews, mental hygiene, and similar content, with subheadings such as "Normality, concept of, in clinical psych"; "Normality and psychosomatic illness"; "Normal man""Personality: normal and abnormal."

10. C. Daly King, "The Meaning of Normal," *Yale Journal of Biology and Medicine* 17 (1944–45): 493–94, 497–98, 500.

11. Carl N. Degler, *Affluence and Anxiety: America since 1945* (Glenview, IL: Scott, Foresman, 1975).

12. Lawrence S. Kubie, "What Is Normal?" *Look,* 3 May 1955, 51.

13. Walker Percy, "The Coming Crisis in Psychiatry," *America,* 5 January 1957, 391–93; Walker Percy, "The Coming Crisis in Psychiatry: II," *America,* 12 January 1957, 415–18.

14. By 1965, Dr. Benjamin Spock's *Common Sense Book of Baby and Child Care* (New York: Duell, Sloan and Pierce, 1946) had sold 18.6 million copies in paperback, while *Peyton Place* (New York: Julian Messner, 1956) had sold some 9.6 million. See Alice Payne Hackett, *70 Years of Best Sellers, 1895–1965* (New York: R. R. Bowker, 1967), 40–41. See chapter 5 below for a discussion of *Peyton Place*.

15. Havemann, "Who's Normal?" 78.

16. "Normal Man Pictured as a Contented Bore," *Science Digest,* September 1961, 16; Robert Fontaine, "Normal as a Fox," *Atlantic Monthly,* January 1962, 79.

17. Peggy and Pierre Streit, "Baffling Search for the 'Normal Man,'" *New York Times Magazine,* 3 June 1962, 19.

18. Corman, "Close-up," 60, 69.

19. Foucault, *Discipline and Punish: The Birth of the Prison,* trans. Alan Sheridan (New York: Vintage, 1970).

20. Warren G. Harding, Inaugural Address, 4 March 1921, avalon.law.yale.edu/20th_century/harding.asp.

21. "Identity" and "discourse" are the conceptualizations most frequently employed by Mary Louise Adams; Michael Warner calls normality a "regime"; Lennard Davis refers to its "tyranny." The notion of "epistemological categories" also comes from Mary Poovey, *Making a Social Body,* 3.

22. Poovey, *Making a Social Body,* 3.

23. Thanks to Margo Culley for pointing me to the invaluable work of Lennard J. Davis, whose book *Enforcing Normalcy* contains the first and best genealogy of the concept "normality" that I have found. Thanks to Marta Russell, a writer for www.disweb.org, for an early introduction to the field. The online disability studies archive is available at www.leeds.ac.uk/disability-studies/archiveuk/index.html. See also Russell's work on disability in public discourse, and the social and economic aspects of disablement, including "Madmen?" (November 11, 2001), www.zmag.org/zspace/commentaries/995, as well as her text

Beyond the Ramp: Disability at the End of the Social Contract (Monroe, ME: Common Courage Press, 1998). See also Lennard Davis's *Disability Studies Reader* (New York: Routledge, 1997) and Paul K. Longmore and Lauri Umanski, eds., *The New Disability History: American Perspectives* (New York: New York University Press, 2001).

24. Marta Russell, "Madmen?"; see also Davis, *Enforcing Normalcy,* 48–49.

25. Davis, *Enforcing Normalcy,* 48.

26. Michael Warner and Lauren Berlant define "heteronormativity" this way:

> By heteronormativity we mean the institutions, structures of understanding, and practical orientations that make heterosexualty seem not only coherent—that is, organized as a sexuality—but also privileged. Its coherence is always provisional, and its privilege can take several (sometimes contradictory) forms; unmarked, as the basic idiom of the personal and the social; or marked as a natural state; or projected as an ideal or moral accomplishment. It consists less of norms that could be summarized as a body of doctrine than of a sense of rightness produced in contradictory manifestations—often unconscious, immanent to practice or to institutions. Contexts that have little visible relation to sex practice, such as life narrative and generational identity, can be heteronormative in this sense, while in other contexts forms of sex between men and women might *not* be heteronormative. Heteronormativity is thus a concept distinct from heterosexuality. One of the most conspicuous differences is that it has no parallel, unlike heterosexuality, which organizes homosexuality as its opposite. Because homosexuality can never have the invisible, tacit, society-founding rightness that heterosexuality has, it would not be possible to speak of "homonormativity" in the same sense.

Lauren Berlant and Michael Warner, "Sex in Public," *Critical Inquiry* 24 (Winter 1998): 548n2. See also Gayle Rubin, "Thinking Sex: Notes for a Radical Theory of the Politics of Sexuality," in *Pleasure and Danger: Exploring Female Sexuality,* ed. Carole S. Vance (Boston: Routledge, 1984), 267–319; Adrienne Rich, "Compulsory Heterosexuality and Lesbian Existence," *Signs: Journal of Women in Culture and Society* 5 (1980): 631–60; Michael Warner, "Fear of a Queer Planet," *Social Text* 29 (1991): 3–17; Warner, *Trouble with Normal.*

27. For two examples of scholarship that raises such questions, see George Chauncey, *Gay New York: Gender, Urban Culture, and the Making of the Gay Male World, 1890–1940* (New York: Basic Books, 1995); and John Howard, *Men Like That: A Southern Queer History* (Chicago: University of Chicago Press, 2001).

28. Carter, *Heart of Whiteness,* 23–30.

29. Daniel Horowitz, "Rethinking Betty Friedan and *The Feminine Mystique:* Labor Union Radicalism and Feminism in Cold War America," *American Quarterly* 48 (March 1996): 1–42. See also his book *Betty Friedan and the Making of "The Feminine Mystique": The American Left, the Cold War, and Modern Feminism* (Amherst: University of Massachusetts Press, 2000).

30. James H. Jones, "Dr. Yes," *New Yorker,* 25 August and 1 September 1997, 101; see also Jones's full biography, *Alfred C. Kinsey: A Public/Private Life* (New York: Norton, 1997).

31. For the argument about suburban alienation, see Catherine Jurca, *White Diaspora: The Suburb and the Twentieth-Century American Novel* (Princeton, NJ: Princeton University Press, 2001); see also Degler, *Affluence and Anxiety.*

32. The decision to take my literary evidence from popular/pulp best sellers rather than highbrow or canonical fiction bears some comment. Quite often, literature is studied or celebrated as the site of resistance or as counterculture. Indeed, especially since the 1960s, this quality of social critique has become one of the terms on which "good" or canonical texts are defined. Salinger, Plath, Mailer, Roth, McCarthy, Bellow, Ellison, and Updike, among others, are the celebrated writers of midcentury literature precisely because, among other reasons, they are seen as critics of the ills of that era. In order to study the workings

of "normality," it was necessary to look at best sellers, specifically because of their mass appeal. Whether they are respectable or not, best sellers are crucial texts for answering the questions of cultural studies. As Lennard Davis argues, the novel itself is a "bourgeois" form and a "proliferator of ideology" that is "intricately connected with concepts of the norm": "From the typicality of the central character, to the normalizing devices of plot to bring deviant characters back into the norms of society, to the normalizing coda of endings, the nineteenth- and twentieth-century novel promulgates and disburses notions of normalcy and by extension makes of physical differences ideological differences" (*Enforcing Normalcy,* 49). To trace the power of the postwar ideology of normality, and to understand literature as part of the "homogenizing forces" of culture (as well as a potential site for resistance), I have worked less with the literature that "transcended" the postwar period than with the blockbuster novels that resonated most deeply in their original time.

1. Model Bodies, Normal Curves

1. I am grateful to Jennifer Terry, Alan Swedlund, and Jacqueline Urla for first efforts to excavate the Norm and Norma models, and to Kathy Peiss for originally pointing me to their work. See Alan C. Swedlund and Jacqueline Urla, "The Anthropometry of Barbie: Unsettling Ideals of the Feminine Body in Popular Culture," in *Deviant Bodies: Critical Perspectives on Difference in Science and Popular Culture,* ed. Jennifer Terry and Jacqueline Urla (Bloomington: Indiana University Press, 1995), 277–313. The Dickinson-Belskie reproductive models were displayed at the 1939 New York World's Fair, but the Norm and Norma figures were sculpted later, ca. 1942–43, and were not displayed there. I am indebted to reference archivist Jessica B. Murphy at the Center for the History of Medicine, Harvard Medical School, for her last-minute sleuthing on the question of Norm and Norma's dates of birth. See the Robert Latou Dickinson Papers, Francis A. Countway Library of Medicine, Harvard University, Boston (hereafter cited as Dickinson Papers). See also Harry L. Shapiro, "A Portrait of the American People," *Natural History* 54 (July 1945): 248–55, 251. The models have since been discussed by Christina Cogdell in *Eugenic Design: Streamlining America in the 1930s* (Philadelphia: University of Pennsylvania Press, 2004) and most recently by Julian B. Carter in his introduction to *The Heart of Whiteness: Normal Sexuality and Race in America, 1880–1940* (Durham, NC: Duke University Press, 2007).

2. Dr. Martin Roth and Klaus Vogel, First Foreword, *Der Neue Mensch* [exhibition catalog] (Ostfildern-Ruit: Cantz, 1999). I thank Ruth Scholz for providing the translation of this passage.

3. Mary Jacobus, Evelyn Fox Keller, and Sally Shuttlesworth, introduction to *Body/Politics: Women and the Discourses of Science* (New York: Routledge, 1990), 4. The authors continue, "We cannot speak of the . . . body as if it were an invariant presence throughout history. There is no fixed, experiential base which provides continuity across the centuries."

4. See Stephen Jay Gould, *The Mismeasure of Man* (New York: Norton, 1981), for the prehistory of these tactics. Nicholas Lemann's book *The Big Test: The Secret History of the American Meritocracy* (New York: Farrar, Straus and Giroux, 1999), sheds light on the concomitant development of the ETS and standardized testing, another normalizing practice with its roots in this period. By the 1940s and '50s, "American Literature" and "American Studies" were becoming institutionalized, and anthropological theories and methods that had been applied to investigations of "foreign" cultures were in a sense turned inward, to analyze Americans. See Chapter 2 below for a fuller discussion.

5. Jacqueline Weaver, "Study Finds Similarities in U.S. and Nazi Eugenics Efforts," *Yale Bulletin & Calendar,* 18 February 2000, 1–2, www.yale.edu/opa/v28.n21/story10.html.

6. "Negative eugenics" were practiced in the United States at this time, although certainly on a significantly different scale and scope than under Nazi race policy. The first laws

allowing forced sterilizations were passed in the U.S. in 1907, and by 1944 states with sterilization laws reported a total of more than 40,000 eugenical sterilizations of the "insane or feebleminded." (In contrast, over 400,000 individuals were sterilized by the Nazis.) Despite waning scientific and public support, state-sponsored sterilizations continued long after the end of World War II, totaling approximately 22,000 more in 27 states between 1943 and 1963. See Weaver, "Study Finds Similarities," 1–2. In 2002, Virginia, where some 7,000 individuals considered "genetically inferior" were sterilized between 1924 and 1979, became the first state to apologize for its forced sterilization programs. See "Virginia Apologises for Eugenics Policy," *BBC News*, 3 March 2002, news.bbc.co.uk/hi/english/world/americas/newsid_1965000/1965811.stm.

7. Judith Butler, *Bodies That Matter: On the Discursive Limits of "Sex"* (New York: Routledge, 1993), 16.

8. Shapiro, "A Portrait of the American People," 252. Shapiro also wrote features for *American Weekly*, produced a Science Guide featuring the models for the American Museum of Natural History, and presented Norm and Norma on the television program *Adventure* in 1953 (see further discussion below).

9. Shapiro, "A Portrait of the American People," 251. According to Mrs. George B. Barbour (R. L. Dickinson's daughter), "For Norma and Norman, not only were all obtainable measurements compared, but vast numbers of new ones made." Letter (typescript), Dickinson Papers, box 7, folder 5.

10. Shapiro, "A Portrait of the American People," 252.

11. The "reproductive models" in the Cleveland Health Museum include sculptures of male and female genitalia, also produced from composite measurements conducted or compiled by Dickinson. These models include a series of vulvas, which Dickinson labeled "Normal," "Virgin," "Post-partum," and "Lesbian." They were housed in the basement of the Health Museum when I visited in April 2002, although museum staff have no evidence indicating whether those measurements were also applied in creating Norm and Norma (Thomas M. Bills, e-mail to author, 1 March 2002). In her important work on the "scientific search for homosexual bodies," Jennifer Terry analyzes the meticulous drawings of female genitalia Dickinson produced for a 1941 study of homosexuality (George W. Henry, *Sex Variants: A Study of Homosexual Patterns* [New York: Paul B. Hoeber, 1941]). While Dickinson's sculptured models of genitalia were never, apparently, put on public display, Terry notes that Dickinson did write "several textbooks" featuring "vivid images of male and female genitalia" in the early 1940s. See Jennifer Terry, "Anxious Slippages between 'Us' and 'Them': A Brief History of the Scientific Search for Homosexual Bodies," in *Deviant Bodies*, 167n41. See also Terry's *An American Obsession: Science, Medicine, and Homosexuality in Modern Society* (Chicago: University of Chicago Press, 1999).

12. Thomas M. Bills, telephone interview by author, 24 April 2002.

13. Shapiro, "A Portrait of the American People," 251.

14. "Are You Norma, Typical Woman? Search to Reward Ohio Winners," *Cleveland Plain Dealer* 9 September 1945, 1.

15. Qtd. in Josephine Robertson, "Norma, Not Faint-Hearted, Makes Health Beauty's Ally," *Cleveland Plain Dealer,* 14 September 1945, 2.

16. Josephine Robertson, "Norma's Husband Better Be Good: Outlook Good if Model Girl Weds Wisely," *Cleveland Plain Dealer,* 16 September 1945, 9A.

17. "Discharge Critics Call Marshall," *Cleveland Plain Dealer,* 18 September 1945, 2. This article appears directly opposite the Robinson article, "Perfect Norma Is High School Goal."

18. David A. Gerber, "Heroes and Misfits: The Troubled Social Reintegration of Disabled Veterans in *The Best Years of Our Lives*," *American Quarterly* 46.4 (December 1994): 545–74. See also his edited collection, *Disabled Veterans in History* (Ann Arbor: University

of Michigan Press, 2000), and David Serlin's *Replaceable You: Engineering the Body in Postwar America* (Chicago: University of Chicago Press, 2004).

19. Davis, *Enforcing Normalcy,* 95.

20. Gerber, "Heroes and Misfits," 545, 549.

21. See Lennard Davis's fuller discussion of Frankin D. Roosevelt and John F. Kennedy as presidents whose disabilities were erased (*Enforcing Normalcy,* 91–99).

22. Josephine Robertson, "Nation's Ideal Boy and Girl Come to City—in Sculpture," *Cleveland Plain Dealer,* 6 July 1945, 1. The war headlines also come from this front page.

23. According to the historian James Reed, Dickinson was Margaret Sanger's "most astute critic, sometime rival, and, finally, comrade-at-arms." Qtd. in "Introduction," Dickinson Papers. See also Christina Cogdell, *Eugenic Design,* 196.

24. R. L. Dickinson, November 17 luncheon address, qtd. in "The Dickinson-Belskie Models—Aids to Healthier Sex Education," *Museum News* (Cleveland Health Museum, 1945), 3, Dickinson Papers, box 7, folder 5.

25. Robert L. Dickinson, annual luncheon address, Cleveland Health Museum, 27 November 1945, Dickinson Papers, box 7, folder 5.

26. See G. W. Lasker, "Introduction: The Place of Anthropometry in Human Biology," in *Anthropometry: The Individual and the Population,* ed. S. J. Ulijaszek and C. G. N. Mascie-Taylor (Cambridge: Cambridge University Press, 1994), 2–3.

27. N. G. Norgan, "Anthropometry and Physical Performance," in Ulijaszek and Mascie-Taylor, *Anthropometry,* 141.

28. Urla and Swedund, "The Anthropometry of Barbie," 289–90.

29. Shapiro became spokesperson for the Norm and Norma models in the national press, as discussed above. See Lasker, "Introduction: The Place of Anthropometry," 2–3.

30. Cf. the 1932–35 *Readers' Guide* entry under "normal curve of errors": C. J. Marsh, "Anniversary of the Normal Curve," *Science,* n.s., 77 (16 June 1933): 583.

31. According to Michael C. C. Adams, nearly 30 percent of World War II enlistees and draftees examined by the Selective Service system between 1940 and 1945 were rejected as "mentally or physically unacceptable." See his *The Best War Ever* (Baltimore: Johns Hopkins University Press, 1994), 78. See also Allan Bérubé, *Coming Out Under Fire* (New York: Penguin/Plume, 1990), esp. chap. 1 on the new "Selective Service psychiatry" aimed largely at screening out suspected homosexuals from service in World War II. I will discuss these practices in more detail in chapter 4.

32. Claire C. Gordon and Karl E. Friedl, "Anthropometry in the U.S. Armed Forces," in Ulijaszek and Mascie-Taylor, *Anthropometry,* 178.

33. "Army Makes a Study of Head Shapes," *New York Times,* 3 June 1945, E9.

34. Gordon and Friedl, "Anthropometry in the U.S. Armed Forces," 179.

35. Somatotyping was used in the Harvard Grant Study of Normal Men (see chapter 2).

36. Ron Rosenbaum, "The Great Ivy League Nude Posture Photo Scandal: How Scientists Coaxed America's Best and Brightest Out of Their Clothes," *New York Times,* 15 January 1995, 26.

37. William Herbert Sheldon, with C. Wesley Dupertuis and Eugene McDermott, *Atlas of Men: A Guide for Somatotyping the Adult Male at All Ages* (New York: Harper, 1954), 3.

38. Christina Carroll, "Posture and Photographs," Vassar Encyclopedia, Vassar College, vcencyclopedia.vassar.edu/index.php/Posture_and_Photographs.

39. Sheldon, *Atlas of Men,* 11.

40. Sheldon, *Atlas of Men,* 3. Sheldon's plans for an accompanying volume called "Atlas of Women" collapsed when he was unable to secure access to or publishing rights for the nude photos of women in the wake of growing public skepticism and outright criticism of his project. See Carroll, "Posture and Photographs," and Rosenbaum, "The Great Ivy League."

41. The *New York Medicina* reported that more than 700,000 people saw the Dickinson-Belskie reproductive models at the fair, "an average of 5,000 a day." See "The R. L. Dickinson Sculptural Models Acquired by Cleveland Health Museum," *New York Medicina*, 5 August 1945, Dickinson Papers, box 7, folder 5. Abram Belskie was a "prize student" of sculptor Malvina Hoffman, creator of the "Races of Mankind" series for the Field Museum of Chicago in 1930. See "Introduction," Dickinson Papers; Josephine Robertson, "Health Museum's Sex Work Hailed, New York Physician Praises Frank, Decorous Attitude," *Cleveland Plain Dealer*, 28 November 1945, Dickinson Papers, "Search for Norma 1945" scrapbook, box 7, folder 5.

42. Bruno Gebhard, M.D., "From Cincinnati's Western Museum to Cleveland's Health Museum," *Ohio State Archaeological and Historical Quarterly*, October 1950, 9–14, 12.

43. Cogdell, *Eugenic Design*, 123. See also Laura L. Lovett, *Conceiving the Future: Pronatalism, Reproduction, and the Family in the United States, 1890–1938* (Chapel Hill: University of North Carolina Press, 2007), 142–44, 164–65.

44. See Gebhard, "From Cincinnati's."

45. "Museum History," video installation, Cleveland Health Museum, Cleveland, Ohio, September 2001. In January 2007, the Cleveland Health Museum on Euclid Avenue merged with the Cleveland Museum of Natural History and became HealthSpace Cleveland, so the displays have most certainly changed; Gebhard, "From Cincinnati's," 10–12; See also Cogdell, *Eugenic Design*, 87–89.

46. Cogdell, *Eugenic Design*, 94.

47. Cogdell, *Eugenic Design*, 196.

48. R. L. Dickinson, November 17 luncheon address, Dickinson Papers, box 7, folder 5.

49. "The Dickinson-Belskie Collection—and Facilities for Its Multiple Reproduction," *Medical Times*, September 1945, 23.

50. Minutes (typescript), Cleveland Health Museum, 26 November 1945, Dickinson Papers, box 7, folder 5.

51. See Urla and Swedlund, "Anthropometry of Barbie." I am grateful to Jack Eckert, archivist at the Francis A. Countway Library, Harvard University, for unearthing the *Adventure* episode, and to the American Museum of Natural History for sending me a copy: "The American Look," *Adventure* [television program], featuring Harry L. Shapiro (CBS/AMNH [American Museum of Natural History] Production, 15 November 1953, American Museum of Natural History Film Archives, New York, NY.

52. "Here Are Tips on Measuring Figure for 'Norma' Contest," *Cleveland Plain Dealer*, 10 September 1945, 1, 3.

53. "Gosh, Norma, You're Gaining Already!" editorial cartoon, *Cleveland Plain Dealer*, 16 September 1945, 1. "World Ending So Soon? Poor Norma!" *Cleveland Plain Dealer*, 18 September 1945, 1.

54. *Cleveland Plain Dealer*, 17 September 1945, 3; 13 September 1945, 1; 12 September 1945, 1; 13 September 1945, 3.

55. *Cleveland Plain Dealer* Picture Page, 18 September 1945, 20.

56. "Norma in '45 Styles," *Cleveland Plain Dealer*, 17 September 1945, 3.

57. Dr. Daniel P. Quiring, qtd. in Robertson, "Norma's Husband," 9A.

58. Josephine Robertson, "High Schools Show Norma New Way to Physical Fitness," *Cleveland Plain Dealer*, 18 September 1945, 1.

59. Josephine Robertson, "Theater Cashier, 23, Wins Title of 'Norma,' Besting 3,863 Entries," *Cleveland Plain Dealer*, 23 September 1945, 1, 4. Apparently nothing extraordinary happened to Skidmore after the contest, either: thirty years later, after she had married and become Martha Funk, she returned to the Cleveland Health Museum to pose in her bathing suit for photographs and flaunt her still-Norma-sized figure. Thomas M. Bills,

email correspondence, 1 March 2002; photographs available at the Cleveland Health Museum/HealthSpace Cleveland.

60. Robertson, "Theater Cashier," 1.

61. Robertson, "Theater Cashier," 1.

62. Shapiro, "A Portrait of the American People," 249. Public obsession with the measurements of women's bodies would reach its apotheosis with 1963 Showmen hit "39-21-40 Shape": "For no one else will do / But you / With your '39-21-40 Shape'/ You got me going ape-ity-ape over you." The song, written by Norman Johnson, was recorded in February 1963 on the Minit label as Single #662. The phenomenon continues, of course: in 1993, the ideal was "36-24-36" according to the Violent Femmes on *Add It Up* (Reprise), while in Nelly's 2000 hip hop hit "Ride Wit Me," perhaps for the sake of rhyme, the ideal shape shifts: "Sexy and real slow . . . How could I tell her no? Her measurements were 36-25-34" (from the album *Country Grammar* [Universal Records, 2000]). By 2006, it was back to "36-24-36 (Applebottom Jeans)" by Jin tha MC on *100 Grand Jin* (Crafty Plugz/Catch Music Group/Draft Records, 2006). Props to Ginny Vellani for the Nelly reference, and to her mother, Peggy Boswell, for recalling the Showmen lyric.

63. See Harry L. Shapiro, "The American Figure Figured Out by Science," *American Weekly*, 3 February 1946, 26–27, 27.

64. Shapiro, "The American Figure Figured Out," 27. It is unclear whether this leaf was provided by the sculptor or added by the publishers. According to Thomas Bills, neither statue has ever been displayed in the museum with fig leaves. Also mystifying to the staff of the museum, according to Bills, is the fact that "Normman has a full complement of pubic hair about his monumental penis while Norma is clean shaven." Thomas M. Bills, email correspondence, 1 March 2002.

65. Shapiro, "A Portrait of the American People," 252; emphasis added.

66. Qtd. in Robertson, "Theater Cashier," 1. "4-F" is the military's classification for rejecting a drafted or enlisted individual as physically unfit for service.

67. Josephine Robertson, "High Schools Show," 1–2.

68. Josephine Robertson, "3,700 Send Measurements in Ohio Search for Norma," *Cleveland Plain Dealer*, 20 September 1945, 1.

69. Urla and Swedlund, "Anthropometry of Barbie," 290.

70. Robertson, "High Schools Show," 1.

71. Josephine Robertson, "Norma Wants Her Posture to Be Perfect," *Cleveland Plain Dealer* 13 September 1945, 1, 3.

72. Eleanor Metheny, *Body Dynamics* (New York: McGraw-Hill, 1952), 134, v, 184.

73. See Andrew Dowdy, *The Films of the Fifties* (New York: Morrow, 1973), 193; Marjorie Rosen, *Popcorn Venus: Women, Movies and the American Dream* (New York: Avon, 1973), 282–83.

74. The tensions over masculinity and sexuality are even greater in the novel *Shrinking Man* by Richard Matheson (New York: Doubleday, 1956), who adapted his work for the film.

75. Irving Shulman, *Amboy Dukes* (1947; New York: Bantam, 1965), 11–12. It is worth noting that all paperback versions of *Amboy Dukes* were heavily censored, for raw language, frank sexual content, and violence, and to tone down references to characters' "jewishness." See Joshua Lambert, *American Jewish Fiction* (New York: Jewish Publication Society, 2009), 59–60.

76. Shulman, *Amboy Dukes*, 191–92.

77. Marsha Bentley Hale, "From Plaster to Fiberglass," in "Body Attitudes: Abstract Mannequins," Fashion Windows, www.fashionwindows.com/mannequin _history/ 043body_attitudes.asp. See also Emily and Per Ola d'Aulaire, "Mannequins: Our Fantasy Figures of High Fashion," *Smithsonian*, April 1991, 66–78.

78. See Mary Bellis, "Barbie Dolls," inventors.about.com/library/inventors/ blbarbie-doll.htm. See also M. G. Lord, *Forever Barbie: The Unauthorized Biography of a Real Doll* (New York: Avon, 1995). Barbie sales figures are from Mattel, so they may be exaggerated. See the AP story "It's Splitsville for Barbie and Ken," CNN.com, 12 February 2004, www.cnn.com/2004/US/02/12/offbeat.barbie.breakup.ap.

2. Normalizing the Nation: The Study of American Character

1. See chapter 1, "Model Bodies, Normal Curves," for examples of such publicity. I am grateful to T. J. Boisseau and Kevin Dunn for critical support in the writing of this chapter.

2. See "Getting Back to Normal," *Collier's*, 20 August 1949, 74.

3. Urla and Swedlund, "The Anthropometry of Barbie," 289–90.

4. Philip Gleason, "World War II and the Development of American Studies." *American Quarterly* 36.3 (1984): 343–58.

5. Clark W. Heath et al., *What People Are: A Study of Normal Young Men* (Cambridge: Harvard University Press, 1945); Earnest Hooton, *"Young Man, You Are Normal": Findings from a Study of Students* (New York: Putnam, 1945). Subsequent references to Heath and Hooton are to these editions, and will be cited in-text.

6. E. B. Garside, "Yardstick for Youth," rev. of *Young Man, You Are Normal* by Earnest Hooton, *New York Times Book Review*, 16 September 1945, 7.

7. William T. Grant Foundation, "Foundation History," www.wtgrantfoundation.org/about_us/foundation_history. The Grant Study experienced "intermittent interruptions and mergers with other investigations," one of which occurred between 1945 and 1954. See William Cromie, "UHS Celebrates a Century," *Harvard Gazette*, 19 November 1998, www.news.harvard.edu/gazette/1998/11.19/uhs.html.

8. Henry F. Hubbard, ed., "Research Projects and Methods in Educational Sociology: A Five-Year Study of Healthy and Active Students," *Journal of Educational Sociology* 14.5 (January 1941): 314–16, 315; Heath, *What People Are*, 10.

9. Qtd. in Hubbard, "Research Projects," 315. See also George E. Vaillant, *Aging Well: Surprising Guideposts to a Happier Life from the Landmark Harvard Study of Adult Development* (Boston: Little, Brown, 2002), 17.

10. Qtd. in Hubbard, "Research Projects," 316.

11. Heath, *What People Are*, dust jacket.

12. Heath's definition is actually taken from C. Daly King's "The Meaning of Normal," *Yale Journal of Biology and Medicine* 17 (1944–45): 493–501.

13. C. Daly King, "A Note on the Meaning of Normal," *Science* 1104 (26 July 1945): 88. The concept of "efficiency" of design here echoes the links Christina Cogdell charts between modernist "streamlined" design and eugenicist thinking. See her *Eugenic Design*.

14. Bock, qtd. in Vaillant, *Aging Well*, 327. See also Craig Lambert's cover story, "The Talent for Aging Well," *Harvard Magazine*, March–April 2001, harvardmagazine. com/2001/03/the-talent-for-aging-wel.html.

15. A Harvard physical anthropologist famous for his scholarly and popular press books linking primatology and criminology (including *Up from the Ape*, 1931; *Apes, Men, and Morons*, 1937; *The American Criminal: An Anthropological Study*, 1939; *Twilight of Man*, 1939; *Why Men Behave like Apes and Vice Versa*, 1940; *Man's Poor Relations*, 1942), Earnest Hooton was also a regular voice in more popular newspapers, magazines, and radio, and even the focus of a six-page *Life* magazine feature, "Hooton of Harvard," in August 1939 (60–66). Hooton had been a leading member of the American Eugenics Society since the 1920s. See Nicole Rafter, "Earnest A. Hooton and the Biological Tradition in American Criminology," *Criminology* 42.3 (2004): 735–71.

16. Still immersed in the Grant Study's logic in 2002, Vaillant writes that "the Harvard cohort had been chosen for their capacity to equal or to exceed their natural ability, and most did so. . . . Socioeconomically, the Harvard sample men were mainly drawn from a privileged group but not exclusively so. In 1940 a third of their parents had made more than $15,000 a year, but one father in seven made less than $2,500 ($1.25/hr) annually. (In those days a year at Harvard cost $1,500, and a registered nurse made $2,000 a year.) If one-third of the men's fathers had some professional training, one-half of the men's parents never graduated from college. During college almost half of the men were on scholarship and/or had to work during the academic year" (*Aging Well,* 18–19).

17. The Records of the Grant Study, 1938–1963, are in the archives of the Department of Hygiene, Harvard University, but are sealed until 2040. While the names of the subjects have been changed in all reports on the study to protect their privacy, Kennedy's inclusion seems certain: his time at Harvard—1938–40—coincides with the study (1939–42), and one box of the Grant Study files is specifically labeled "John F. Kennedy's questionnaires and reports, 1940–63." One can deduce, then, that Kennedy was one of the Harvard sophomores selected for the study in 1939—despite, it should be noted, his own well-hidden chronic poor health. See Robert Dallek, "The Medical Ordeals of JFK," *Atlantic Monthly,* December 2002, 49–61. See also Lennard Davis's fuller discussion of the erasure of Kennedy's disabilities in *Enforcing Normalcy,* 91–99.

18. Qtd. in Hubbard, "Research Projects," 315.

19. As George Valliant admitted, defensively, in 2002: "It took thirty years for the Study staff to conclude that physical anthropology was irrelevant to personality. But the Study of Adult Development is almost unique in having both the data and the follow-up to draw such a conclusion" (Vaillant, *Aging Well,* 328).

20. See Jennifer Terry, "Anxious Slippages," 140–41, as well as her full-length study *An American Obsession.*

21. Heath, *What People Are,* 60n8. Of the remaining 20% of the subjects, 14% were classified as having "moderate masculine component" and 6% "weak or very weak." See Hooton, *Young Man,* 82.

22. R.G., rev. of Earnest Hooton, *Young Man, You Are Normal, Psychoanalytic Quarterly* 15 (1946): 121–22.

23. These problems with the "sample" are mentioned once, boldly, by Hooton in his introduction to Part II, "How the Elements Are Mixed in 'Normal' Youths": "The human body is so greatly diversified . . . that only a very large sample offers an adequate representation of most of the distinctive physical variations that must be recognized. The problem is somewhat simplified and restricted when, as in the case of the Grant Study, the physical types under examination belong to a single great race of mankind, the Whites, to a single sex, and a limited age range. It is further narrowed when individuals in obviously bad health are excluded from the series" (*Young Man,* 80–81).

24. "Social class," though never labeled as such, was measured in various ways: by income, father's occupation, and education level.

25. Vaillant, *Aging Well,* 18.

26. Earnest Hooton writes: "The elaborate and searching questionnaires sent out to the men who participated in the Grant Study during their undergraduate days need not be described here, since this is no handbook of sociological method. The important fact is that data on the continuing careers of the Grantees are available for 259 out of the 268 who participated in the study" (*Young Man* 169). Vaillant notes: "Originally data were recorded in ink in huge leather ledgers and analyzed by manual counting. Data were not put onto punch cards until 1965, not onto magnetic tape until 1975, and not into the hard drive of an office desktop computer until 1990. Now, as I write in the year 2000, all of the data of sixty years of study resides in a laptop on my desk at home" (*Aging Well,* 18).

In his own publications on the Grant Study, Vaillant does occasionally quote the subjects themselves.

27. R.G., rev. of *Young Man, You Are Normal*, 121–22.

28. Vaillant, *Aging Well*, 19.

29. Vaillant, *Aging Well*, 18. The qualitative data on these studies is partially made available in Vaillant's popular book-length reports on the Harvard Adult Development Study, *Adaptation to Life* (Cambridge: Harvard University Press, 1977) and *Aging Well* (2002). One striking detail that emerges from a 2000 report (but was absent in 1945) is Vaillant's aside that "only 2 percent of the College sample viewed themselves as homosexual (although two such College men waited until age 65 to tell us)" (*Aging Well*, 46).

30. See The Rockefeller Foundation, *Rockefeller Foundation Annual Report for 1949*, www.rockfound.org/about-us/annual-reports/1940-49/1949.pdf, 128–30. The study was led by Donald W. MacKinnon, and the report notes that "the core of its working philosophy is the conviction that if we wish to promote the well-being of society as a whole we should not seek only to identify sources of failure but should also examine carefully those who have successfully adapted to their surroundings. We should study effective and happy people and try to find out what makes them so" (58). See Chester I. Barnard, "President's Review," *Rockefeller Foundation Annual Report for 1949*, 1–73. For sample media coverage of the study, see "Getting Back to Normal," *Collier's*, 20 August 1949, 74.

31. William Whyte, *Organization Man* (New York: Simon and Schuster, 1956), 216.

32. Dickinson and Belskie's *Birth Atlas* was published in 1940; Sheldon's *Atlas of Man* in 1954; Bassett's *Stereoscopic Atlas of Human Anatomy*, begun in 1945, was printed in 1962. The first edition of the *Diagnostic and Statistical Manual of Mental Disorders* was published in 1952 by the APA, drawn from interwar Census Bureau psychiatric ward statistics, U.S. military classification systems, and surveys of the APA membership. The *International Statistical Classification of Diseases and Related Health Problems* was first published by the newly formed World Health Organization in 1948, and was doubled in size from its prior iterations. In 1959 the U.S. Public Health Service published a modified version for clinical use, titled *International Classification of Diseases Adapted for Hospital Records and Operation Classification*. See Gerald N. Grob, "Origins of DSM-I: A Study in Appearance and Reality," *American Journal of Psychiatry* 148.4 (April 1991): 421–31. See also my discussion of anthropometry and somatotyping in chapter 1.

33. See, for example, George Vaillant's *Adaptation to Life* (1977), *Ego Mechanisms of Defense: A Guide for Clinicians and Researchers* (Washington, DC: American Psychiatric Press, 1992), *Natural History of Alcoholism Revisited* (Cambridge: Harvard University Press, 1983), *Aging Well* (2002), and *Spiritual Evolution: A Scientific Defense of Faith* (New York: Broadway, 2008). See also C. Peterson, M. E. P. Seigman, and G. E. Vaillant, "Pessimistic Explanatory Style Is a Risk Factor for Physical Illness: A Thirty-Five-Year Longitudinal Study," in *Psychosocial Processes and Health: A Reader*, ed. Andrew Steptoe and Jane Wardle (Cambridge: Cambridge University Press, 1994); and Kathleen M. Thies and John F. Travers, *Growth and Development through the Lifespan* (Sudbury, MA: Jones and Bartlett/Quick Look Nursing Series, 2001). According to Craig Lambert, Vaillant's 1977 book, *Adaptation to Life*, "depicted the men at midlife and analyzed their personalities in terms of a hierarchy of defense mechanisms—characteristic ways of handling emotional conflict and stress—that ranged from low-level, immature defenses like blatant denial and passive aggression to mature adaptations such as altruism, humor, and the sublimation of energies into art. Now, in *Aging Well*, [Vaillant] writes that 'it is social aptitude, not intellectual brilliance or parental social class, that leads to successful aging.' Furthermore, the habitual use of these mature coping styles—ways of 'making a lemon into lemonade,' in his words—is, in psychological and social terms, the most powerful predictor of successful aging." See Lambert, "The Talent for Aging Well."

34. The House Un-American Activities Committee convened in 1938, but became a standing committee in 1945. Setting aside the infamous history of this committee, the very notion of "Un-American" activities had to have relied on a sense of what *was* "American."

35. Michael McGiffert, "Selected Writings on American National Character," *American Quarterly* 15.2 (Summer 1963): 271–88; Michael McGiffert, ed., *The Character of Americans: A Book of Readings* (Homewood, IL: Dorsey Press, 1964), vii. My thanks to Randall Knoper for providing me with a copy of this resource.

36. Gleason, "World War II," 355.

37. Qtd. in Gleason, "World War II," 355–56.

38. Schlesinger's presidential address appeared in *American Historical Review* 48 (1943): 225–44.

39. Qtd. in Gleason, "World War II," 353, 356–57.

40. Margaret Mead, *And Keep Your Powder Dry* (New York: Morrow, 1942), 21.

41. Michael Denning, *Cultural Front: The Laboring of American Culture in the Twentieth Century* (London: Verso, 1998), 125.

42. Nikil Singh, "Culture/Wars: Recoding Empire in an Age of Democracy," *American Quarterly* 50.3 (1998): 471–522, 494–95.

43. Reuel Denny, "How Americans See Themselves: Studies of American National Character," *Annals of the American Academy of Political and Social Science* 295 (September 1954): 12–20.

44. Mead, qtd. in Gleason, "World War II," 357n49.

45. Rupert Wilkinson, *The Pursuit of American Character* (New York: Harper and Row, 1988).

46. Leo Marx, "Reflections on American Studies, Minnesota, and the 1950s," *American Studies* 40.2 (Summer 1999): 39–51, 46–47.

47. Gene Wise, "'Paradigm Dramas' in American Studies: A Cultural and Institutional History of the Movement," *American Quarterly* 21 (1979): 293–337, 304.

48. Wise, "Paradigm Dramas," 305; Harry R. Warfel, Ralph Henry Gabriel, and Stanley T. Williams, eds., *The American Mind: Selections from the Literature of the United States* (New York: American Book Company, 1937).

49. See Denning, *Cultural Front*. See also Judith E. Smith, *Visions of Belonging: Family Stories, Popular Culture, and Postwar Democracy, 1940–1960* (New York: Columbia University Press, 2004).

50. W. T. Lhamon, introduction to Constance Rourke, *American Humor: A Study of the National Character* (1931; repr., Tallahassee: Florida State University Press, 1985), xiii.

51. Rourke, *American Humor,* xii–xiii.

52. *New York Times,* 10 October 1940, qtd. in Gleason, "World War II," 348.

53. Michael Holzman, "The Ideological Origins of American Studies at Yale," *American Studies* 40.2 (Summer 1999): 71–99, 86; Kathryn E. Kuhn and Wynne Walker Moskop, "Free Riders or Front Runners? The Role of Social Scientists in the American Studies Movement," *American Studies* 40.2 (Summer 1999): 115–36, 115–16. See also Wise, "Paradigm Dramas."

54. See Paul Lauter, "Reconfiguring Academic Disciplines: The Emergence of American Studies," *American Studies* 40.2 (Summer 1999): 5–21, 32; and Holzman, "The Ideological Origins." See also Robin W. Winks, *Cloak & Gown: Scholars in the Secret War, 1939–61,* 2nd ed. (New Haven: Yale University Press, 1996).

55. This 1949 letter from Dean DeVayne to President Seymour is quoted in Holzman, "The Ideological Origins," 83.

56. Holzman, "The Ideological Origins," 84. Norman Pearson, chair of Yale's American Studies Program, in a 1958 radio broadcast, is quoted in Holzman, "The Ideological Origins," 91.

57. See Nikhil Singh, *Black Is a Country: Race and the Unfinished Struggle for Democracy* (Cambridge: Harvard University Press, 2004).

58. Gleason, "World War II," 352; Lauter, "Reconfiguring Academic Disciplines," 29.

3. Passing for Normal: Fashioning a Postwar Middle Class

1. In addition to the usual suspects, I am grateful to Deborah Carlin, Nick Bromell, Kevin S. Reilly, and Stephanie Bishop for their help with this chapter. "U.S. Family Income Increase in 12 Years," *New York Times,* 21 January 1961, 12. "The Rich Middle Income Class," *Fortune,* May 1954, 97. Otis Dudley Duncan and Beverly Duncan, "Residential Distribution and Occupational Stratification," in *Cities and Society,* ed. Paul K. Hatt and Albert J. Reiss (Glencoe, IL: Free Press, 1957), 283–96. The above are all cited by Robert H. Bohlke in his "Social Mobility, Stratification Inconsistency and Midde Class Delinquency," *Social Problems* 8.4 (Spring 1961): 351–63. Bohlke's interest in delinquency led him to add that family dysfunction could be another stumbling block to achieving true middle class status: "The blue collar worker may become a white collar worker, learn middle class culture and gain social acceptance from the middle class, but his 'successful' transition may require physical, emotional and economic 'expenditures' that produce strain within himself and within the family unit which, in turn, produces deviant behavior. And, one symptom of the tension within the family unit could well be delinquent behavior on the part of the son" (363n61).

2. See Beth Bailey, *From Front Porch to Back Seat: Courtship in Twentieth-Century America* (Baltimore: Johns Hopkins University Press, 1988), 11.

3. Bohlke's article investigates the rise in middle-class delinquency, which he argues is the result of actions by large numbers of "nouveau bourgeois" youth—people who are economically middle-class, but who, he writes, "*have not yet* taken on the middle class values and behavior patterns because their families, despite a dramatic rise in income, have not had to renounce working class values in the cultural context of economic abundance." Bohlke, "Social Mobility," 353–54.

4. See Lois Banner, "Fashion and History [Review]," *Journal of Interdisciplinary History* 13.2 (Autumn 1982): 311–15, 315. Christine Boydell, "Fashioning Identities [Review]," *Journal of Contemporary History* 39.1 (January 2004): 137–46, 145. Scholarly attention to the history and significance of men's fashion is particularly lacking.

5. C. Wright Mills, *White Collar: The American Middle Classes* (New York: Oxford University Press, 1951), ix. All future references are to this edition, and will be cited in the text by page number.

6. Anne Hollander, *Sex and Suits: The Evolution of Modern Dress* (New York: Kodansha, 1994), 153. Gratitude to T. J. Boisseau and Kirk Hoppé for this source. See also Whyte, *Organization Man,* 299. All future references to Whyte will be cited in the text by page number.

7. Edith Efron, "New Plumage for the Male Animal," *New York Times Magazine,* 9 September 1945, 16, 44.

8. Shane White and Graham White, *Stylin': African American Expressive Culture from Its Beginnings to the Zoot Suit* (Ithaca, NY: Cornell University Press, 1998), 254.

9. Edward Escobar, "Zoot-Suiters and Cops: Chicano Youth and the L.A. Police Dept. during WWII," in *The War in American Culture: Society and Consciousness During World War II,* ed. Lewis A. Erenberg and Susan Hirsch (Chicago: Chicago University Press, 1996), 284–309.

10. White and White, *Stylin',* 254.

11. See Stuart Cosgrove, "The Zoot-Suit and Style Warfare," *History Workshop Journal* 18 (Autumn 1984): 77–91, www.edc.org/CCT/lemcen/ u7sf/u7materials/cosgrove.

html; Escobar, "Zoot-Suiters and Cops"; Candida Taylor, "Zoot Suit: Breaking the Cold War's Dress Code," in *Containing America: Cultural Production and Consumption in 1950s America,* ed. Nathan Abrams and Julie Hughes (Birmingham, UK: University of Birmingham Press, 2000), 63–75; George Lipsitz, *Time Passages: Collective Memory And American Popular Culture* (Minneapolis: University of Minnesota Press, 1990); Angela McRobbie, ed., *Zoot Suits and Second Hand Dresses* (Basingstoke, UK: Macmillan, 1989); White and White, *Stylin'.*

12. Anthony Macías, "Bringing Music to the People: Race, Urban Culture, and Municipal Politics in Postwar Los Angeles," *American Quarterly* 56.3 (2004): 693–717, 696. Maruicio Mazón, *The Zoot Suit Riots: The Psychology of Symbolic Annihilation* (Austin: University of Texas Press, 1988), 75.

13. Ralph Ellison, *Invisible Man* (1952; New York: Vintage, 1972), 474.

14. Cosgrove, "The Zoot-Suit," 77–91. Malcolm X, as I mention below, would strategically wear the somber business suit after his conversion.

15. Taylor, "Zoot Suit," 65; Lipsitz, *Time Passages,* 120.

16. "Schoeffler Warns Men's Wear Trades," *New York Times,* 17 July 1945, 16.

17. Sloan Wilson, *The Man in the Gray Flannel Suit* (1955; rpt., New York: Cardinal/ Pocket Books, 1956), 7–8. All future references are to this Cardinal edition and will be cited in the text by page number.

18. "Vets Happy to Discard Uniforms," *New York Times,* 11 November 1945, 39.

19. On a visit to Kansas City in June 1945, Truman tried to order three white shirts from his former haberdashery partner, but was told none were available. When the president's shirt shortage made the press, "three dozen shirts, the correct size . . . arrived from store owners and individuals in St. Joseph, Wichita, and Oklahoma City." See "White Shirts Found for Truman," *New York Times,* 1 July 1945, 10.

20. "Fashion Note," *New York Times,* 8 July 1945, 27.

21. "Veterans Favored in Apparel Pinch," *New York Times,* 29 October 1945, 24, 26; for DePinna clothing advertisement targeting veterans, see *New York Times,* 10 April 1946, 16.

22. "President Offers Shirt, 15 1/2 by 33, to Reporter," *New York Times,* 4 April 1946, 29.

23. Samuel A. Tower, "Outlook Decidedly Foggy for Clothes-Hungry Men, *New York Times,* 28 April 1946, E7. See also John Hudson, "Gleam of Hope," editorial cartoon from the *Erie Dispatch-Herald,* rpt. in *New York Times,* 28 April 1946, E7.

24. See David Kuchta, *The Three-Piece Suit and Modern Masculinity: England, 1550–1850* (Los Angeles: University of California Press, 2002) and Hollander, *Sex and Suits.*

25. Hollander, *Sex and Suits,* 152.

26. Fred Miller Robinson, *The Man in the Bowler Hat* (Chapel Hill and London: University of North Carolina Press, 1993), 26.

27. Hollander, *Sex and Suits,* 166–67.

28. On "inconspicuous consumption," see Kuchta, *Three-Piece Suit,* chap. 7. The term, also invoked in Whyte's *Organization Man,* is derived from economist Thorstein Veblen's concept of *"conspicuous* consumption" in his 1899 *Theory of the Leisure Class.* On "non-fashion" and the suit as a sign of modernity, see Hollander, *Sex and Suits.* Hollander writes that non-fashion "creates its visual projections primarily to illustrate the confirmation of an established custom, and to embody the desire for stable meaning even if custom changes— it is normative," but she maintains that the suit is *not* non-fashion (17).

29. Wilder Hobson [J. K. Galbraith], "The Business Suit: A Short and Possibly Tactless Essay on the Costuming of American Enterprise," *Fortune,* July 1948, 103. Thanks to Kevin S. Reilly for sharing this and other resources.

30. Hobson [Galbraith], "The Business Suit," 104, 126.

31. The cartoon, by Brad Anderson, ran in the April 1957 issue of *Ladies' Home Journal.*

32. "Can You Sell Conformity?" *Tide,* 9 May 1958, 20, 21.

33. Wilson, *Man in the Gray Flannel Suit,* jacket copy, Simon and Schuster first edition, 1955.

34. Orville Prescott, "Books of the Times," rev. of *The Man in the Gray Flannel Suit, New York Times Book Review,* 18 July 1955, 19. See also John McNulty, "Tom Rath, Commuter," rev. of *The Man in the Gray Flannel Suit, New York Times Book Review,* 16 September 1955, 18.

35. *The Man in the Gray Flannel Suit* (film), dir. Nunnally Johnson, with Gregory Peck, Jennifer Jones, and Frederick March (Twentieth Century–Fox, 1956).

36. The penultimate "About the Author" page reveals that "the publisher wishes to add that it was Mrs. Wilson who so ably summarized the theme of her husband's book by suggesting the title" (289). The role of "Mrs. Wilson" here explicitly raises the problem of gender in defining middle-class identity through such masculine surfaces as the gray flannel suit. I discuss this issue further in the "Rebel without a Tie" section below.

37. The expression "the problem with no name" is Betty Friedan's catchphrase for the ennui and frustration of postwar middle-class, suburban women in *The Feminine Mystique* (New York: Dell, 1963). Barbara Ehrenreich makes a similar point in her discussion of the "gray flannel dissidents" as well: "in the fifties 'conformity' became the code word for male discontent—the masculine equivalent of what Betty Friedan would soon describe as 'the problem without a name.'" See Barbara Ehrenreich, *The Hearts of Men: American Dreams and the Flight from Commitment* (New York: Anchor, 1983), 30. In her study *White Diaspora,* Catherine Jurca argues that the literature of the American suburb shows imagined alienation to have been part of white middle-class identity.

38. Whyte and especially Mills were emblematic, if differing, examples of a much larger number of postwar intellectuals. Unlike many others, Mills would stick to his prewar political position, becoming a prophet of the New Left. See Richard Pells, *The Liberal Mind in a Conservative Age: American Intellectuals in the 1940s and 1950s* (Middletown, CT: Wesleyan University Press, 1985), 187–88. David Riesman's 1950 study *The Lonely Crowd,* which I will discuss in chapter 5, was probably the most important and widely read at the time. These authors' names show that the chorus of voices being published on these questions was predominantly male. A study of the full range of influential female social critics and intellectuals who were publishing work during this time—Mary McCarthy, Simone de Beauvoir, Hannah Arendt, and Betty Friedan among them—needs to be undertaken. See Horowitz, *Betty Friedan.* Kevin S. Reilly has unearthed interesting information on the almost entirely female research staff behind much of the social criticism published by *Fortune* magazine; see his "Corporate Stories: *Fortune* Magazine and the Making of a Modern Managerial Culture" (Ph.D. diss., Department of History, University of Massachusetts Amherst, 2004).

39. In *Advertising the American Dream: Making Way for Modernity, 1920–1940* (Berkeley: University of California Press, 1985), Roland Marchand argues that modern ad-men designed their products according to the motivations of themselves and others of their rank, class, and profession. The difference here, ostensibly, is the explosion of sociological research that both C. Wright Mills and William Whyte employ in analyzing the white collar environment. But a similar tendency to extrapolate from their own experiences seems to be at work nonetheless.

40. One reviewer, Horace Kallen, an important prewar intellectual, saw Mills's white-collar worker as "only a unit in an aggregation, mass-man incapable of organic action, seeking refuge from anxiety and futility in a struggle to keep up appearances." See his "The Hollow Men: A Portrayal to Ponder," rev. of *White Collar* by C. Wright Mills, *New York Times Book Review,* 16 September 1951, 4.

41. Orville Prescott, "Books of the Times," rev. of *The Organization Man, New York Times,* 14 December 1950, 27.

42. Jean A. Flexner and Anna-Stina Ericson, "White-Collar Employment and Income: Trends and Current Status of Employment and Income for a Large but Diverse Group of Workers," *Monthly Labor Review* 79.4 (April 1956): 401–9.

43. The use of "collars" to describe labor distinctions has its roots in earlier decades as well. Novelist and social critic Upton Sinclair published the term "white collar" as early as 1919. For another sociological example from the postwar decades, see Mirra Komarovsky with Jane H. Philips, *Blue-Collar Marriage* (1962; New York: Vintage, 1967).

44. By making the dilemmas of the middle class more visible in a pulp paperback formula, works like Vance Packard's *Status Seekers* (1959; New York: Pocket Books, 1964) had by the end of the decade made the sociological critique itself "mainstream." See also Daniel Horowitz's *Vance Packard and American Social Criticism* (Chapel Hill: University of North Carolina Press, 1994).

45. In Frank Tashlin's farce, ad man Rockwell Hunter nearly ends up dead in a frantic attempt to get ahead in the firm with an ad campaign featuring sexy starlet Rita Marlowe. The effeminacy of Tony Randall as Hunter, combined with the comically exaggerated femininity of Jayne Mansfield as Marlowe, has the campy effect of making *both* characters appear to be cross-dressing. In the end, Rock Hunter is rewarded, literally, with a set of keys to the "executive washroom."

46. Fred Miller Robinson, *Man in the Bowler Hat,* 26.

47. Mrs. Andrew Heiskell (née Madeleine Carroll), "The Wife of the Man in the Gray Flannel Suit" [speech at American Association of Advertising Agencies convention], rpt. in *Tide,* 23 May 1958, 38–39.

48. On postwar women's fashion, see Jane Farrell-Beck and Colleen Gau, *Uplift: The Bra in America* (Philadelphia: University of Pennsylvania Press, 2001), and Regina Lee Blaszczyk, ed. *Producing Fashion: Commerce, Culture, and Consumers* (Philadelphia: University of Pennsylvania Press, 2007).

49. "A Suit of Importance" (fashion feature), *Ladies' Home Journal,* April 1957, 82. The effort to allow "gray flannel"—and the corporate success it now represents—to cross over to women continues. One large, fold-out advertisement for Stuart Weitzman in a 1998 *Vanity Fair* presented an enormous gray flannel high-heeled pump, set against the New York City skyline, and read, with each unfolding page, "The woman . . . in the gray flannel . . . shoe."

50. See Cornel West, *Race Matters* (New York: Vintage, 1994), 57, and especially the chapter "The Crisis of Black Leadership." Of course West, too, is renowned for his trademark three-piece suit, which he continues to sport in all public appearances.

51. Qtd. in West, *Race Matters,* 54. See E. Franklin Frazier, *Black Bourgeoisie* (1957; New York: Collier Books, 1962).

52. "Men's Fall Fashions: Well-dressed Males Take Color Cue from Nature," *Ebony,* October 1957, 105–7.

53. Botany 500 advertisement, *Ebony,* October 1958, 110.

54. Great Western Tailoring advertisement, *Ebony,* March 1957, 113; Progress Tailoring advertisement, *Ebony,* February 1958, 87; Stone-Field Corporation advertisement, *Ebony,* October 1958, 119. Thanks to Kathy Peiss and Judith Smith for help in teasing out some of the links between Jim Crow segregation and the phenomenon of these "Free Suit" ads.

55. See Barbara Ehrenreich, "Early Rebels: The Gray Flannel Dissidents," in *Hearts of Men,* 28–41; Graham McCann, *Rebel Males: Clift, Brando, and Dean* (New Brunswick, NJ: Rutgers University Press, 1993). See also Karal Ann Marling's discussion of Elvis in *As Seen on TV* (Cambridge: Harvard University Press, 1994).

56. See Packard, *Status Seekers.*

57. The *OED* notes a few usages prior to 1955 as well. See "Establishment," *OED online,* 2nd ed. (1989; Oxford University Press, 2002), www.oed.com.

58. Brando appeared as a rebel biker Johnny in *The Wild One* in 1953 (directed by Laszlo Benedek for Columbia Pictures). In his most famous line, when asked "What are you rebelling against, Johnny?" his response was, "Whaddaya got?" Nicholas Ray's *Rebel Without a Cause* was released in 1955 by Warner Brothers.

59. Farid Chenoune, *A History of Men's Fashion* (Paris: Flammarion, 1993), 236–37.

60. David Dalton, *James Dean: The Mutant King* (New York: St. Martin's, 1974), 333.

61. John Francis Kreidl, *Nicholas Ray* (Boston: Twayne, 1977), 92.

62. Dalton, *James Dean,* 229.

63. Dalton, *James Dean,* 332.

64. Dan Weiner, *Commuters, Park Forest, Illinois, 1953* (photograph), "Archive: Just Passing Through," rpt. in *Fortune,* 18 September 1995, 248. The original June 1953 *Fortune* cover story focused on suburbanization, and included versions of the articles Whyte would incorporate into *Organization Man* two years later.

65. Robert E. L. Faris, "The Middle Class from a Sociological Viewpoint," *Social Forces* 39.1 (October 1960): 1–5, 4–5.

66. Bohlke, "Social Mobility," 358.

4. From Queer to Eternity: Normalizing Heterosexuality in Fact and Fiction

1. The metaphor of postwar gender and sexual "containment" was proposed most convincingly by Elaine Tyler May in her 1988 study *Homeward Bound: American Families in the Cold War Era* (New York: Basic Books), and questioned most forcefully by Joanne Meyerowitz's 1994 edited collection *Not June Cleaver: Women and Gender in Postwar America, 1945–1960* (Philadelphia: Temple Universuty Press). Work on "sex panics" includes John D'Emilio, "The Homosexual Menace: The Politics of Sexuality in Cold War America," in *Passion and Power: Sexuality in History,* ed. Kathy Peiss and Christina Simmons (Philadelphia: Temple University Press, 1989), 226–40; Estelle B. Freedman, "'Uncontrolled Desires': The Response to the Sexual Psychopath, 1920–1960," in *Passion and Power,* 199–225; Lisa Duggan, "Sex Panics," in *Sex Wars: Sexual Dissent and Political Culture,* ed. Lisa Duggan and Nan D. Hunter (New York: Routledge, 1995), 74–79; Gayle Rubin, "Thinking Sex"; and Terry, *An American Obsession.*

2. See Jonathan Ned Katz, *The Invention of Heterosexuality* (New York: Dutton, 1995). To a large extent, Katz leapfrogs the post–World War II era, focusing his study on what he identifies as "two major periods in the history of heterosexuality": the late nineteenth century, when the concept was created, and the 1960s and 1970s, when heterosexuality was "destabilized." The postwar period, I would argue, is the major period in which heterosexuality was consolidated and normalized. This period coincides with sexologists' development of a taxonomy to distinguish transsexualism, hermaphroditism, and homosexuality, also known as "psychosexual orientation." See Alison Redick on the 1955 establishment of the Intersex Protocols: "What Happened at Hopkins: The Creation of the Intersex Management Protocols," *Cardozo Journal of Law and Gender* 12 (2005): 289–96. See also Joanne Meyerowitz's 2002 history *How Sex Changed: A History of Transsexuality in the United States* (Cambridge: Harvard University Press).

3. Bérubé, *Coming Out,* 1–7.

4. Alfred Kinsey's *Sexual Behavior in the Human Male* was published in 1948 (Philadelphia: W. B. Saunders), and his *Sexual Behavior in the Human Female* in 1953 (Philadelphia: W. B. Saunders). For more on the impact of the Kinsey Reports see Sarah E. Igo, *The Averaged American: Surveys, Citizens, and the Making of a Mass Public* (Cambridge:

Harvard University Press, 2007), esp. chap. 5, "Surveying Normal Selves," and chap. 6, "The Private Lives of the Public"; and Miriam G. Reumann, *American Sexual Character: Sex, Gender, and National Identity in the Kinsey Reports* (Berkeley: University of California Press, 2005). See also discussions of Kinsey in Paul Robinson, *The Modernization of Sex: Havelock Ellis, Alfred Kinsey, William Masters and Virginia Johnson* (1976; Ithaca, NY: Cornell University Press, 1989); Henry L. Minton, *Departing from Deviance: A History of Homosexual Rights and Emancipatory Science in America* (Chicago: University of Chicago Press, 2002); Karen Winkler, "Kinsey, Sex Research, and the Body of Knowledge, *WSQ: Women's Studies Quarterly* 33.3–4 (Fall/Winter 2005) 285–313; and in Katz, *Invention of Heterosexuality.* On Kinsey himself, see Jonathan Gathorne-Hardy's biography, *Sex, the Measure of All Things: A Life of Alfred C. Kinsey* (Bloomington: Indiana University Press, 1998).

5. Kinsey writes, "It is characteristic of the human mind that it tries to dichotomize. . . . Things either are so, or they are not so. Sexual behavior is either normal or abnormal, socially acceptable or unacceptable, heterosexual or homosexual; and many persons do not want to believe that there are gradations in these matters from one to the other extreme" (*Sexual Behavior in the Human Female,* 469). See Miriam Reumann, *American Sexual Character,* 52–53 and 155–56; Katz, *Invention of Heterosexuality,* 97.

6. James Jones, *From Here to Eternity* (1951; New York: Avon Books, 1975). All future references are to the Avon edition and will be cited in the text by page number. In his correspondence as well as in his novels, Jones enjoyed breaking the conventions of English grammar, spelling, and punctuation, in an attempt to work toward a more vernacular writing style. I have reproduced his spellings throughout.

The historian James H. Jones, a different James Jones altogether, is the author of a more recent, somewhat sensationalized biography of Kinsey—*Alfred C. Kinsey: A Public/Private Life.*

7. *Scientia sexualis* is Michel Foucault's term for the proliferation of scientific knowledge about sex and sexuality in the Victorian era. See *The History of Sexuality,* vol. 1, *An Introduction* (1978; New York: Vintage, 1990). John Updike has used the term "sexual realism" to refer to his own and others' writings of the 1950s and early 1960s: "My models in sexual realism had been [Edmund] Wilson and D. H. Lawrence and Erskine Caldwell and James M. Cain and of course James Joyce." The models he refers to—Caldwell, Lawrence, Cain—were also some of the top-selling paperbacks of the postwar years. See John Updike, "Updike's Rabbit," *Penguin Classics,* 5 July 2008, www.penguinclassics.co.uk/nf/shared/WebDisplay/0,,214908_1_0,00.html.

Eugenia Kaledin writes that "between 1952 and 1961 the sale of books actually doubled" in the U.S.; see her *Mothers and More: American Women in the 1950s* (Boston: Twayne, 1984), 13. For the full story of the impact of the paperback revolution, see Kenneth C. Davis, *Two-Bit Culture: The Paperbacking of America* (Boston: Houghton Mifflin, 1984).

8. Katz, *Invention of Heterosexuality,* 81. See Elizabeth Lunbeck's *The Psychiatric Persuasion: Knowledge, Gender and Power in Modern America* (Princeton: Princeton University Press, 1994) for a detailed history of the transformation of psychiatry into the study of the "normal." See also Mona Gleason, *Normalizing the Ideal,* for a comparative perspective on psychology's postwar construction of the "normal" Canadian family.

9. Bérubé, *Coming Out,* 19. Bérubé goes into great detail on this topic, noting the frequently poor training and inexperience of many of the thousands of military psychiatrists charged with this task. He also notes the influence of certain military psychiatrists who were more "sympathetic" than others, and who used their power to depathologize homosexuality: "It is an irony of history that the first public challenges to the military's antihomosexual policy came not from the homosexual rights movement but from psychiatrists who studied gay soldiers, sailors, and officers during World War II" (*Coming Out,* 174). See Bérubé's

chap. 1, "Getting In," for a fuller discussion of the new "Selective Service psychiatry." See also Minton, *Departing from Deviance,* 100.

10. See Adams, *Best War Ever,* 78.

11. Qtd. in Bérubé, *Coming Out,* 19; 2.

12. Bérube, *Coming Out,* 33; Adams, *Best War Ever,* 84. Both authors note that screening procedures could become more lax at times when more soldiers were needed, but were tightened again as the war ended.

13. Paul Starr, qtd. in Meyerowitz, *How Sex Changed,* 105.

14. See, for example, D'Emilio, "The Homosexual Menace"; Freedman, "'Uncontrolled Desires"; Terry, *An American Obsession.*

15. Bérubé, *Coming Out,* 259; see also D'Emilio, "The Homosexual Menace."

16. Bérubé, *Coming Out,* 6; 257–58.

17. For example, the lesbian butch/femme role-playing culture documented in Elizabeth Kennedy and Madeline Davis's study *Boots of Leather, Slippers of Gold: The History of a Lesbian Community* (New York: Routledge, 1993); the increasingly separate spheres of lesbian female and gay male nightlife documented by George Chauncey in *Gay New York;* the sexual politics of the postwar history of transsexualism—particularly the Jorgensen case—documented by Joanne Meyerowitz in *How Sex Changed* and David Serlin in *Replaceable You.*

18. John D'Emilio, *Sexual Politics, Sexual Communities: The Making of a Homosexual Minority in the United States, 1940–1970* (Chicago: University of Chicago Press, 1983), 38–39.

19. The Mattachine Society was organized by the gay activist Harry Hay and others in Los Angeles. A comparable lesbian rights organization, the Daughters of Bilitis, was founded in San Francisco in 1955. See D'Emilio, *Sexual Politics,* 58n2. As recently as 2003, in the celebrated *Lawrence v. Texas* Supreme Court case overturning anti-sodomy laws, Lawrence's attorneys cited Kinsey's statistics on homosexuality in their arguments.

20. Chauncey, *Gay New York,* 22, 13. John Howard's study *Men Like That: A Southern Queer History* (Chicago: Chicago University Press, 1999) contends that such imaginary gender status continued to be important in gay male sexual cultures of the U.S. South.

21. Chauncey, *Gay New York,* 15–16. Chauncey also notes that gay author Donald Webster Cory's 1951 book on homosexuality, *The Homosexual in America: A Subjective Approach* (New York: Greenberg), contains an aside from Cory to his "uninitiated reader" that *gay* and *straight* are "words in common usage in the world in which I move" (xiv). Qtd. in *Gay New York,* 379n44.

22. Mary Louise Adams, *The Trouble With Normal,* 8–9; Katz, *Invention of Heterosexuality,* 54–55.

23. This was the 1934 *Webster's* definition. See Katz, *Invention of Heterosexuality,* 92.

24. Katz, *Invention of Heterosexuality,* 55.

25. Bérubé, *Coming Out,* 6.

26. Katz, *Invention of Heterosexuality,* 96; see also 95, 226nn39–40. At a pivotal moment in James Jones's novel *From Here to Eternity* (discussed below), one character, grasping for language, says, "Hell, Bloom was no queer. . . . If I ever saw a *not-queer,* it was Bloom" (558; emphasis added).

27. Chauncey, *Gay New York,* 16.

28. Alexander Doty, "There's Something Queer Here," in *Out in Culture: Gay, Lesbian, and Queer Essays on Popular Culture,* ed. Corey K. Creekmur and Alexander Doty (Durham, NC: Duke University Press, 1995), 72–73. Queer theory has marked a paradigm shift in the way some scholars are thinking about homosexuality. As Caleb Crain notes, "It proposes that traditional notions of lesbian and gay identity may be as confining as homophobia itself." Michael Warner, whose 1993 anthology *Fear of a Queer Planet* helped to

crystallize queer theory as a movement, writes: "To liberalism's offer to tolerate lesbians and gays as just another minority, queer theory says no. Instead, queer theory declares it opposes all identity pigeonholes on principle and aligns itself with anyone who troubles gender or sexual norms, including drag queens, transsexuals, and sex workers.'" Warner qtd. in Caleb Crain, "Pleasure Principles: Queer Theorists and Gay Journalists Wrestle over the Politics of Sex," *Lingua Franca,* October 1997, www.linguafranca.com/9710/crain.html. See also Michael Warner, ed., *Fear of a Queer Planet: Queer Politics and Social Theory* (Minneapolis: University of Minnesota Press, 1993).

29. Warner, *Fear of A Queer Planet,* xxvi.

30. Sexual behaviors and sexual identity were more separate in the early twentieth century, according to the evidence in George Chauncey's *Gay New York.*

31. Bérubé and D'Emilio, qtd. in Chauncey, *Gay New York,* 10.

32. See Bill Osgerby, "Muscular Manhood and Salacious Sleaze: The Singular World of the 1950s Macho Pulps," in Abrams and Hughes, *Containing America,* 125–50.

33. See Bérubé, *Coming Out,* 272, 357nn38–41. While the shadowy urban "homosexual" was essentially a stock character of 1940s pulp crime and detective fiction, postwar novelists' engagement with homosexual characters began to function differently. Homosexual characters helped authors lay claim to a "writerly realism" and "sexual cosmopolitanism." See, for example, Judith E. Smith's discussions of Richard Brooks's 1945 novel *The Brick Foxhole* and Paddy Chayefsky's 1953 *Marty* in her study *Visions of Belonging.*

34. Jones's text was a "literary phenomenon," and—like *Peyton Place*—a publishing success story as well. The "blockbuster" novel was itself a postwar phenomenon. The very *size,* the heft of novels seemed new, and might have been, as Janice Radway suggests, a sign of "the larger culture's effort to . . . corral an ever-more-complex society apparently wheeling into incoherence." The novels from these years that Radway borrows from the Duke University library are "well thumbed and heavily used" which is "additionally striking because so many are astonishingly long and consequently very heavy. . . . *Marjorie Morningstar, Advise and Consent, The Wall, Hawaii, Stillness at Appomattox, Exodus,* and *The Agony and the Ecstasy* are all more than 500 pages" (313–14). See Janice Radway, *A Feeling for Books: The Book-of-the-Month-Club, Literary Taste, and Middle-Class Desire* (Chapel Hill: University of North Carolina Press, 1997), 308–51.

From Here to Eternity was promoted in *Publisher's Weekly,* with a large advertisement and a photograph of Jones on the cover, in December 1950. See Robert E. Cantwell, "James Jones: Another *Eternity?" Newsweek,* 23 November 1953, 106. George Garrett reports that the original hardback editions sold nearly half a million copies; and by November 1953 the paperback reprint had gone through five printings in six weeks. See George Garrett, *James Jones* (San Diego: Harcourt Brace, 1984), xix, 26–27, 97.

35. James Jones, letter to Lowney Handy, New York, 16 November 1947, qtd. in Hendrick, *To Reach Eternity,* 108. this same letter to Handey, Jones described how he paid special attention these scenes, discussing them with his editor, Burroughs Mitchell: "I took in the queer scene and the whorehouse scene and the stories. [We] had talked a lot about queers and about how they had written about them always with this *Weird Tales* effect. . . . [Mitchell] asked if I'd read Gide and I told him no and he said he'd read two of his books and that they were both concerned with homosexuality, but that he felt that Gide had sentimentalized it, had not written it truly." By attending to these scenes, Jones tries to treat gay characters and sexuality in general in a more honest way than past writers had—including Gide, although, as we will see, he also disparages *Forever Amber* and its "ilk" as well as scientific treatments of human sexuality such as the Kinsey Reports.

36. At the same time, Jones will also construct a female heterosexuality that is private, passive, and performative.

37. Jones himself acknowledged in correspondence that "the way in which I write (and deliberately calculate to make myself write, ahead of time) is to start out with certain people, types, with their particular conflicts and then to bring them into contact and after that to deliberately stay out as much as possible and let them and the book write itself. Because of this, I do not ever try to plot tightly. I do not plot a book at all, in the conventional sense." See James Jones, letter to Ben W. Griffith Jr., June 13, 1954, qtd. in George Hendrick, ed. *To Reach Eternity: The Letters of James Jones* (New York: Random House, 1989), 203.

38. Jones wanted his text to reveal what really goes on behind the facade of the U.S. Army, and in a brief prefatory disclaimer, labeled "Special Note," he made a point to emphasize the verisimilitude of the Stockade scenes above all: "This book is a work of fiction The characters are imaginary, and any resemblance to actual persons is accidental. However, certain of the Stockade scenes did happen. They did not happen at the Schofield Barracks . . . but at a post within the United States at which the author served, and they are true scenes of which the author had first-hand knowledge and personal experience." Reviewers indeed stressed his realism. Orville Prescott concludes his review with the observation that "when [Jones] describes the sadistic tortures inflicted in the punishment 'stockade' he leaves his sickened and enraged readers wondering how much American Army practices duplicate those of the totalitarian nations." See Orville Prescott, "Books of the Times," *New York Times,* 26 February 1951, 21.

39. Beth Bailey and David Farber, *The First Strange Place: The Alchemy of Race and Sex in World War II Hawaii* (New York: Free Press/Macmillan, 1992), 19.

40. James Jones, *Some Came Running* (New York: Scribner, 1957); James Jones, letter to Robert Cantwell, qtd. in Hendrick, *To Reach Eternity,* 227.

41. Only Jane Hendler fully discusses Jones's treatment of homosexuality in *Eternity,* in her chapter "Masculinity and Male Power in James Jones's *From Here to Eternity,*" part of her book-length study *Best-Sellers and Their Film Adaptations in Postwar America* (New York: Peter Lang, 2001), 29–68. Hendler's lens is more literary/psychoanalytic than historical, and she employs a "crisis of masculinity" frame that I find fails to describe the shifting ground of gender in any era. Nevertheless, she provides a rich analysis of many of the same tensions I map here, including "queer hunting," Bloom's suicide, and Clift's subtle re-encoding of sexual complexity into the film version. Although other scholars deal with Jones's risky sexual content and his theme of masculinity, they apply these discussions to his later novels, especially *Go to the Widow-Maker* (New York: Delacorte, 1967) and *The Merry Month of May* (New York: Delacorte, 1971). In discussing *From Here to Eternity,* they focus instead on themes related to the army, heterosexual romance, or individualism.

42. According to George Chauncey, the *punk's* status was ambiguous: "He was regarded by some [as] homosexual, by others as the victim . . . and by still others as someone whose sexual subordination was merely an aspect of his general subordination." See *Gay New York,* 88.

43. Cynthia Enloe argues that "military bases and prostitution have been assumed to 'go together.' But it has taken calculated policies to sustain that fit: policies to shape men's sexuality, to ensure battle readiness, to determine the location of businesses, to structure women's economic opportunities, to affect wives, entertainment and public health." See Enloe's *Bananas Beaches and Bases: Making Feminist Sense of International Politics* (Berkeley: University of California Press, 1990), 81.

44. Bérubé, *Coming Out,* 214.

45. See Bérubé, *Coming Out,* chap. 8, "Fighting Another War," esp. 218–22.

46. According to Chauncey, the metaphor of the "closeted homosexual" does not become historically meaningful in the United States prior to around midcentury (*Gay New York,* 6–7).

47. In contrast to the articulation of male homosexuality is the near absence of lesbianism. In one scene, Karen describes an encounter in which, while waiting on a bench for her scheduled rendezvous with Warden, she is propositioned by "a big tall wide-shouldered dyed-blonde woman," whom Warden recognizes as the woman the servicemen call the "Virgin of Waikiki" (310). The lone lesbian character in the text, this woman functions solely as a one-liner for Jones, though her nickname is telling: the soldiers either see this sexually aggressive woman as a "virgin" because she has not been sexually "conquered" by any man, or else because she remains the only woman in Waikiki who has escaped the "heterosexual menace" of an occupying army.

48. Tensions over this idea of "brotherhood" emerge in other texts of this period as well, particularly William Whyte's arguments about the Organization Man being "imprisoned in brotherhood," and the hypocrisies of "The Brotherhood" in Ellison's *Invisible Man*.

49. The "homosexual menace" was a common phrase in the 1950s. See D'Emilio, "The Homosexual Menace."

50. David Dempsey, "Tough and Tormented, This Was the Army to Mr. Jones," rev. of *From Here to Eternity* by James Jones, *New York Times Book Review*, 25 February 1951, 55.

51. See Osgerby, "Muscular Manhood"; Ehrenreich, *Hearts of Men*.

52. This concept and phrase comes from Michael S. Sherry's study of postwar militarization, *In the Shadow of War: The U.S. since the 1930s* (New Haven: Yale University Press, 1995).

53. Dempsey, "Tough and Tormented," 5; Prescott, "Books of the Times," 26 February 1951, 21.

54. James Jones, Letter to Burroughs Mitchell, 29 March, 1950, qtd. in Hendrick, *To Reach Eternity*, 163.

55. James Jones, Letter to Jeff Jones, 3 October 1950, qtd. in Hendrick, *To Reach Eternity*, 173–74.

56. See Robert B. Westbrook, "'I Want a Girl, Just Like the Girl That Married Harry James': American Women and the Problem of Political Obligation in World War II," *American Quarterly* 42 (December 1990): 587–614; see also Elaine Tyler May's "Explosive Issues: Sex, Women, and the Bomb," in *Recasting America: Culture and Politics in the Age of Cold War*, ed. Lary May (Chicago: University of Chicago Press, 1989), 154–70.

57. Jones uses this line from Rudyard Kipling's *Gentlemen Rankers* as an epigraph to open his novel: "Gentlemen-rankers out on a spree, / Damned from here to Eternity, / God ha' mercy on such as we, / Ba! Yah! Bah!" (6).

58. In the early 1930s, for example, Honolulu had been the site of the notorious Ala Moana or Massie rape/murder case, an event that threw into relief Hawaii's inability to mete out justice without the constant presence of U.S. military and state intervention. The Ala Moana case itself is fascinating and complex, and would likely have been recalled by many of Jones's readers: In 1931, Thalia Massie, the well-connected young wife of a Pearl Harbor Navy lieutenant, accused five local youths of abducting and assaulting her as she walked home along a secluded area of Ala Moana Road. When evidence exonerated these men (two Hawaiians, two Japanese, and one Chinese-Hawaiian) and a mistrial was declared, Thalia's mother, a prominent Virginia socialite named Grace Fortescue, with the help of Massie's husband and two Navy enlisted men, masterminded the kidnapping and murder of one of the accused, a month later. The trials that ensued featured the seventy-five-year-old Clarence Darrow, retained in support of the Massies, and provoked a media circus and much propaganda about who exactly was at risk in the Hawaiian islands: "It remains a fact that . . . no white woman is safe alone in or near Honolulu at night," claimed an article in the national magazine *Liberty* in 1932. In the face of U.S. congressional pressure, the Massie/Fortescue defendants were convicted only of manslaughter, and under further threats from

the mainland that Hawaii would be made into a military outpost and put under martial law, the islands' governor, Lawrence M. Judd, commuted the Massie/Fortescue defendants to one hour in custody. See Pamela Haag's discussion of the case in *Consent: Sexual Rights and the Transformation of American Liberalism* (Ithaca: Cornell University Press, 1999). See also Ronald T. Y. Moon, "The Case for Judicial Independence," Social Science Association Conference, 1 June 1998, rpt. *Honolulu Star-Bulletin*, 24 July 1999, www.starbulletin.com/1999/07/24/editorial/ special2.html; DeSoto Brown, "Tiki Time: Hawai'i in American Pop Culture, *Honolulu Weekly*, 10 October 2001, www.honoluluweekly.com/archives/coverstory%202001/10-17-01%20Tiki/10-17-01%20tiki.html.

59. DeSoto Brown, "Tiki Time."

60. See "Base Women," in Enloe, *Bananas Beaches and Bases*, 65–92.

61. See Westbrook, "'I Want a Girl, Just Like the Girl,'" 592, 599. See also Enloe, "Base Women."

62. See Frank MacShane, *Into Eternity: The Life of James Jones, American Writer* (Boston: Houghton Mifflin, 1985), 36–37.

63. In a letter to his editor, Jones wrote, "As far as movie rights are concerned, I have only two desires. The first, and main one, is that I get as much money out of the sale as I can, and to hell with how they butcher it up." The other desire was to "get a couple months work or so out there [in Hollywood] on the script," not to have control over the text, but in order to get experience for a planned novel about Hollywood, as well as to make "a little money in wages." Jones, letter to Burroughs Mitchell, 2 December 1950, qtd. in Hendrick, *To Reach Eternity*, 178.

64. MacShane, *Into Eternity*, 132.

65. *From Here to Eternity* (Columbia Pictures, 1953), directed by Fred Zinnemann, screenplay by Daniel Taradash.

66. The scene was parodied only a few months after the film's 1953 premiere, by Imogene Coca and Sid Caesar on *Your Show of Shows* as "From Here to Obscurity," and then again in the Billy Wilder film *Some Like It Hot* (United Artists, 1959). It has since seen innumberable appropriations, including a skit on the 1970s-80s hit *The Muppet Show*, print advertising campaigns in *Entertainment Weekly*, and most recently, a music video for the song "Bones" by the American alt-rock band The Killers.

67. Following the widely-publicized *Howl* obscenity trials in 1957, courts began to relax restrictions on the possession, sale, and distribution of "obscene" materials throughout the late 1950s and 1960s, though these moves would begin to reverse again by the early 1970s. As for film, the year 1956 was the first time since its 1930 inception that the Hollywood Production Code was revised: bans on drug traffic, abortion, prostitution, and kidnapping were lifted, but not those on "sex perversion" or venereal disease. Andrew Dowdy notes: "This move was a more formal recognition that movies now intended to claim the freedom in content previously allowed to other art forms. . . . The decline of original scripts in favor of films based on popular novels tied the larger studios to the increasing permissiveness of American fiction. . . . By 1958 less than half the industry's movies were from original scripts." See Dowdy, *Films of the Fifties*, 208.

68. Screenwriter Daniel Taradash "interlaced the two love stories 'so that there seemed a connection between them,' even though there was none." MacShane, *Into Eternity*, 129.

69. For more on the way the filmmakers navigated the military/historical elements of the story, see J. E. Smyth, "James Jones, Columbia Pictures, and the Historical Confrontations of *From Here to Eternity*," in *Why We Fought: America's Wars in Film and History*, ed. Peter C. Rollins and John E. O'Connor (Lexington: University of Kentucky Press, 2008), 283–317.

70. MacShane, *Into Eternity*, 129.

71. James R. Giles, *James Jones* (Boston: G. K. Hall, 1981), 28. Giles continues, "Filmed simply, in black and white, [*From Here to Eternity* is] credited with helping Hollywood see that it can produce nothing better than honest movies about believable characters."

72. In a letter to Burroughs Mitchell, Jones wrote: "[Clift] was the only one who really seemed to come alive to me. The rest, except Frank [Sinatra], who was fine, seemed to fade when they got off the screen with him and I suddenly realized they were actors." July 31, 1953, qtd. in Hendrick, *To Reach Eternity,* 193.

73. See MacShane, *Into Eternity,* 131. On the issue of Jones's sexuality, MacShane argues that "Jones . . . liked giving the impression of having had more sexual experience than most people. . . . It is almost certain that his remark about Clift was a put-on, for he enjoyed shocking other men by asking, in a matter-of-fact way, 'Do you mean to say you've never sucked cock?' While it is not impossible that he had had an occasional homosexual experience as a young man, it is unlikely. . . . His habit of talking knowingly about sex derived in all likelihood from his shyness and his sexual diffidence" (131). Although the evidence of Jones's own novel might trouble MacShane's reading, Jones's public comments do seem performative and posturing. On another occasion, he felt compelled to address his girlfriend/mentor Lowney Handy's jealousy by quelling any suspicions of "queerdom": "I had a late dinner with [author] Bill Styron and went to an Italian movie, and we sat in a bar and talked until after 3 way down town, then we walked, and talked. I got back here around 4:30. There were no women involved, and no queerdom—if you suspect that, too." Jones, letter to Lowney Handy, 13 February 1952, qtd. in Henrick, *To Reach Eternity,* 185. Ultimately, Jones's personal experiences with "queerdom" remain uncertain—and perhaps immaterial—but the ironies remain interesting: according to one source, Jones would later remark that "All my girlfriends said Monty Clift acted just like me in *From Here to Eternity.*" See Judi Hoffman, "Candidates for the National Film Registry: *From Here To Eternity,*" remarks before the *National Film Preservation Board,* Mary Pickford Theater, Library of Congress, 29 July 1998, www.loc.gov/film/judihoff.html.

74. Fred Zinnemann, qtd. in Hoffman, "Candidates for the National Film Registry."

75. Chauncey, *Gay New York,* 357.

76. MacShane, *Into Eternity,* 131.

77. John T. Frederick, "Fiction of the Second World War," *College English* 17 (January 1956): 197–204, qtd. in Garrett, *James Jones,* 100.

78. As mentioned above, the Mattachine Society was formed in Los Angeles 1950, the Daughters of Bilitis in 1955 in San Francisco. According to Allan Bérubé, these organizations emerged in a paradoxical social climate in which "antihomosexual campaigns terrorized gay Americans while the expansion of gay culture and the public discussion homosexuality opened up new possibilities." See *Coming Out,* 273. On the role of homosexuals as midcentury cultural producers see Michael Sherry, *Gay Artists in Modern American Culture: An Imagined Conspiracy* (Chapel Hill: University of North Carolina Press, 2007).

79. Chauncey's *Gay New York* focuses on the interwar period, though his evidence reaches well into the 1940s and so is relevant to this discussion. His companion volume, dating from World War II through the Stonewall years, is forthcoming.

5. Picture Windows and *Peyton Place:*
Exposing Normality in Postwar Communities

1. Grace Metalious, *Peyton Place* (1956; Boston: Northeastern University Press, 1999), 16. All subsequent references are to the 1999 edition and will be cited in the text by page number.

2. Michel Foucault, *Power/Knowledge: Selected Interviews and Other Writings, 1972–1977,*

ed. Colin Gordon (New York: Pantheon, 1980), 155. Foucault is discussing surveillance in the context of the eighteenth-century gothic novel.

3. John Keats, *The Crack in the Picture Window* (Boston: Houghton Mifflin, 1957), 18.

4. Friedan, *Feminine Mystique,* 233.

5. Benedict Anderson coined this notion of "imagined communities" in *Imagined Communities: Reflections on the Origin and Spread of Nationalism* (New York: Verso, 1983), 7.

6. Raymond A. Mohl, "Race and Housing in the Postwar City: An Explosive History," *Journal of the Illinois State Historical Society* 94 (Spring 2001): 8–30, dig.lib.niu.edu/ISHS/ ishs-2001spring/ishs-2001spring008.pdf. See also Nicholas Lemann, *The Promised Land: The Great Back Migration and How It Changed America* (New York: Vintage, 1991).

7. Degler, *Affluence and Anxiety,* 170.

8. Kenneth T. Jackson, *Crabgrass Frontier: The Suburbanization of the United States* (New York: Oxford University Press, 1985), 208–9. The practice of redlining was initiated by an earlier federal lending program, FDR's 1933 Home Owners Loan Corporation, which devised a rating system of four color-coded divisions, separating "desirable" from "undesirable" neighborhoods along class, race, ethnic, and other lines. See Jackson, *Crabgrass Frontier,* 197–98; Delores Hayden, *Redesigning the American Dream* (New York: Norton, 1986), 74. See also Gwendolyn Wright, *Building the Dream: A Social History of Housing in America* (Cambridge: MIT Press, 1983).

9. *Race: The Power of an Illusion* (documentary film), episode 3, "The House We Live In" (California Newsreel, 2003). Transcript available at www.newsreel.org/transcripts/race3 .htm. It is important to note that, from the start, efforts were also undertaken by individuals, activists, organizations such as the NAACP, Congress, and even the Executive Branch to confront racist housing practices. President Truman's 1947 Committee on Civil Rights included recommendations for an end to residential segregation in its report *To Secure These Rights* (New York: Simon and Schuster, 1947). In 1949 Congress declared a national policy of ensuring "a decent home and a suitable living environment for every American family." In 1955 the Congressional Committee on Race and Housing was formed, and in 1958 the committee issued *Where Shall We Live? Report of the Commission on Race and Housing* (Berkeley: University of California Press, 1958), as well as a final, comprehensive report, *Residence and Race,* in 1960. The 1958 report collected data primarily on blacks, Puerto Ricans, Mexican Americans, Chinese, and Japanese, and "found no significant improvement in housing conditions for nonwhites between 1940 and 1950," while whites "made gains in housing space per capita" despite the postwar shortage. The report also found that "segregation barriers were tighter in 1950 than they had been ten years earlier," with cities witnessing white flight to the suburbs. For this discussion, see Cindy I-Fen Cheng, "Out of Chinatown and into the Suburbs: Chinese Americans and the Politics of Cultural Citizenship in Early Cold War America," *American Quarterly* 58.4 (2006): 1067–90, esp. 1069–71. For another example of resistance to racist segregation policies, see Judith E. Smith's discussion of Lorraine Hansberry's father's activism in her chapter "Reracializing the Ordinary American Family: *Raisin in the Sun,*" in *Visions of Belonging,* esp. 285–88.

10. Qtd. in *Race: The Power of an Illusion.* See also Matthew Frye Jacobsen, *Whiteness of a Different Color: European Immigrants and the Alchemy of Race* (Cambridge: Harvard University Press, 1998).

11. Racist community "covenants" were outlawed by a Supreme Court decision in 1948, but continued to be used informally. According to the sociologist Dalton Conley, "Today, the average Black family has only one-eighth the net worth or assets of the average white family. That difference has seemingly grown since the 1960's, since the Civil Rights triumphs. And is not explained by other factors, like education, earnings rates, savings rates. It is really the legacy of racial inequality from generations past. No other measure captures

the legacy, the sort of cumulative disadvantage of race, or cumulative advantage of race for whites, than net worth or wealth." Qtd. in *Race: The Power of an Illusion.*

12. Degler, *Affluence and Anxiety,* 164–66.

13. Andrew Weise, *Places of Their Own: African American Suburbanization in the Twentieth Century* (Chicago: University of Chicago Press, 2003); Cheng, "Out of Chinatown"; Mohl, "Race and Housing," 8.

14. Degler, *Affluence and Anxiety,* 166; Max Herman, "Ethnic Succession and Urban Unrest in Newark and Detroit During the Summer of 1967," Cornwall Center Publication Series, Rutgers University, July 2002, 9, www.cornwall.rutgers.edu/pdf/Herman-July%202002-Report.pdf.

15. Katherine K. Gordon and Max Gunther, *The Split-Level Trap* (1960; repr., New York: Dell, 1961), 20.

16. Degler, *Affluence and Anxiety,* 164.

17. Joel Kotkin, "Suburban Development" [Levittown Turns 60], *Wall Street Journal,* 23 November 2007, www.opinionjournal.com/Taste/?id=110010895; Clifford E. Clark Jr., "Ranch-House Suburbia: Ideals and Realities," in May, *Recasting America,* 183; William Chafe, *The Unfinished Journey: America since World War II,* 2nd ed. (New York: Oxford University Press, 1991), 117. The secondary literature on American suburbs and suburban culture is voluminous. Among the most useful to me have been Jackson, *Crabgrass Frontier;* Lynn Spigel, *Welcome to the Dreamhouse: Popular Media and Postwar Suburbs* (Durham, NC: Duke University Press, 2001); and Jurca, *White Diaspora.* See also Kevin M. Kruse and Thomas J. Sugrue, eds., *The New Suburban History* (Chicago: University of Chicago Press, 2006).

18. Clark, "Ranch House Suburbia," 185.

19. According to the *OED,* the term *nuclear family,* coined by Bronislaw Malinowski in 1924 (see "Psychoanalysis and Anthropology," *Psyche* 4 [1924]: 293–332, 294), is an anthropological/sociological idea that predates the "nuclear age." But the idea was developed most fully by the American anthropologist G. P. Murdock in the midst of World War II, in a 1941 article in *Sociometry* and further again in his postwar book-length work *Social Structure* (1949). Murdock writes: "The nuclear or individual family, consisting of father, mother, and children, is universal; no exceptions were found in our 220 societies." See George P. Murdock, "Anthropology and Human Relations," *Sociometry* 4 (1941): 146.

20. Clark, "Ranch House Suburbia," 174, 179.

21. Keats, *Crack in the Picture Window,* 21.

22. Whyte, *Organization Man,* 389.

23. Witold Rybczynski, "The Ranch House Anomaly," from *Last Harvest: How a Cornfield Became New Daleville,* excerpted in Slate online, www.slate.com/id/2163970/?nav=navoa#b.

24. Lynn Spigel, *Make Room for TV: Television and the Family Ideal in Postwar America* (Chicago: University of Chicago Press, 1992), 32, 1.

25. Degler, *Affluence and Anxiety,* 174.

26. Spigel, *Make Room for TV,* 32.

27. Nancy Armstrong, *Desire and Domestic Fiction: A Political History of the Novel* (New York: Oxford University Press, 1987), 187.

28. Spigel, *Make Room for TV,* 158.

29. Nearly 72% of all Americans with TV sets (44 million) watched the episode "Lucy Goes to the Hospital," while only 29% tuned in to Ike. *I Love Lucy* ran from 1951 to 1957 (with sequels from 1957 to 1960), and was the most watched television show in four of its six original seasons. It has been in reruns (which Desi Arnaz is credited with inventing, so that Lucy could have time off in late pregnancy), without interruption, ever since.

30. Mary Beth Haralovich, "Sit-coms and Suburbs: Positioning the 1950s Homemaker," in *Private Screenings: Television and the Female Consumer,* ed. Lynn Spigel and Denise Mann (Minneapolis: University of Minnesota Press, 1992), 112, 114–15. Some of these popular sitcoms, in addition to *I Love Lucy,* included *The Goldbergs,* 1949–55; *The Adventures of Ozzie and Harriet,* 1952–66 (started on radio 1944); *Make Room for Daddy* (renamed *The Danny Thomas Show* after its third season), 1953–64; *The Honeymooners,* 1955–56; *Father Knows Best,* 1954–63; *Leave It to Beaver,* 1957–63; and *The Donna Reed Show,* 1958–66. Adding to the reproduction of "normality," many of the exteriors for these 1950s programs, built on a Burbank backlot, were used repeatedly for other domestic sitcom productions. For example, the *Father Knows Best* (1954) house was also used for *I Dream of Jeannie* (1965). The exterior used for *The Donna Reed Show* (1958) was used again in *Bewitched* (1964), as well as for *The Partridge Family* (1970). See Ben Glenn, "What Happened to the Classic Sitcom Houses?" www.tvparty.com/myshomes.html.

31. Lennard Davis makes a similar point about the normalizing function of the novel in *Enforcing Normalcy,* 49.

32. Clark, "Ranch House Suburbia," 183; Degler, *Affluence and Anxiety,* 164.

33. Sidonie M. Gruenberg, "Homogenized Children of New Suburbia," *New York Times Magazine,* 19 September 1954, 42, 47. The article inspired at least one letter to the editor: Allen Ward of New Hope, Pennsylvania, noted that the strongest homogenizing force of the new suburbia was whiteness: "The big drawback in Levittown, from a sociologist's viewpoint (and mine, too) is that Negroes are excluded. . . . This is a deplorable situation . . . I don't think Mrs. Gruenberg should worry about the children in Suburbia; she should, instead, worry about their prejudiced parents." See "Suburbia, Ltd.," *New York Times Magazine,* 10 October 1954, 4.

34. Gruenberg, "Homogenized Children," 47, 42.

35. Degler, *Affluence and Anxiety,* 164.

36. In terms of African American fiction, for example, interventions had been launched by protest writers of the 1930s and '40s. By the mid-1950s, works by Ralph Ellison (*Invisible Man,* 1952), Gwendolyn Brooks (*Maud Martha,* 1953), and James Baldwin (*Go Tell It on the Mountain,* 1953, and *Giovanni's Room,* 1956) had made a major cultural impact, leading some toward a better understanding the depths of black American alienation and *in*visibility ("I am invisible, understand, because people simply refuse to see me," as Ellison's protagonist announces).

37. Also at this time, major Beat writers such as Allen Ginsberg and Jack Kerouac were bursting into the national consciousness, using their lives and their words to rail against American middle-class life, work, marriage, and the postwar state that supported it. *Howl* was published in 1956; Kerouac's *On the Road* in 1957. See Ehrenreich, "The Gray Flannel Dissidents," in *Hearts of Men.* Although their critique was launched in the late 1950s, they did not find a mass readership until the early-to-mid-1960s.

38. Keats, *Crack in the Picture Window,* 24, 26, 61.

39. Keats quotes sociologist Harold Mendelsohn as saying, "Remember, when we talk of [suburban] developments, we're really talking about women." *Crack in the Picture Window,* 38. See also Keats's chap. 3 ("Life Faces Mary"), and Friedan, *Feminine Mystique.*

40. Keats, *Crack in the Picture Window,* 193.

41. Keats, *Crack in the Picture Window,* 193, 50–51, 47.

42. Gordon and Gunther, *Split-Level Trap,* 13, 20.

43. Qtd. in Clark, "Ranch House Suburbia," 186–87.

44. Carlos Baker, "Small Town Peep Show," rev. of *Peyton Place, New York Times Book Review,* 23 September 1956, 4. Baker continued, "Life behind the scenes in New Hampshire is not widely different, fictionally speaking from life in Winesburg, Ohio, Hecate County,

Conn., or Gibbsville, Pa. It is only. . . . a little more frankly detailed—and, perhaps, a little more widely inclusive than the small-town chronicles of Messrs. Sherwood Anderson, Edmund Wilson and John O'Hara. The late Sinclair Lewis would no doubt have hailed Grace Metalious as a sister-in-arms . . . and certified her as a public accountant of what goes on in the basements, bedrooms and back porches of a 'typical American town.'" Baker's acknowledgment of Metalious's social critique was representative of early reviews of the novel. Another reviewer, writing for *Time,* concluded that Metalious "captures a real sense of the tempo, texture, and tensions in the social anatomy of a small town." See "Outsiders Don't Know," *Time,* 24 September 1956, 100. Such responses confirm that although Metalious located her plot in an earlier time, her novel was emphatically *about* postwar America.

    45. Sterling North, "Shocker Written by a Village Wife," rev. of *Peyton Place, New York World Telegram,* 29 September 1956.

    46. George Metalious and June O'Shea, *The Girl from "Peyton Place"* (New York: Dell, 1965), 101. Metalious's husband recalled the tenor of the reader response: "She received letters in the mail with obscene threats in them [from angry locals]. Other letters were from readers in Massachusetts, Ohio, Florida, and California saying, 'I'm sure that you are writing about my town. I live in *Peyton Place.*' Other letters said, 'If you think *Peyton Place* is bad, you should live in my town.' Others got into arguments through letters written to the editors of hundreds of newspapers. . . . And through all the comments, good and bad, the book continued to sell and sell and sell."

    47. See Hackett, *70 Years of Best Sellers,* 202; Emily Toth, *Inside Peyton Place: The Life of Grace Metalious* (1981; Jackson: University Press of Mississippi, 2000), 187–96. The one-in-six figure comes from Jane Sterns and Michael Sterns, "Peyton Place," *Encyclopedia of Pop Culture* (New York: Harper, 1992), 381–83.

    48. Released in 1957, *Peyton Place* was filmed in Camden, Maine. Changes included the substitution of a miscarriage instead of an abortion, toned-down sexual content, and the editing out of the Samuel Peyton storyline and other ethnic/racial content in the novel. Lana Turner made her big-screen comeback portraying Constance MacKenzie.

    49. *Peyton Place* remained the all-time fiction best-seller until 1975, when Mario Puzo's *The Godfather,* with its "book auctioning and television advertising," became the first "super blockbuster," selling 11,750,000 copies. By the end of 1975, Harper Lee's *To Kill A Mockingbird* (1962) and Jacqueline Susann's *Valley of the Dolls* (1966) had also outsold *Peyton Place* by "only a few hundred thousand copies." Nevertheless, *Peyton Place* remains today one of the all-time best-selling American novels. See Ardis Cameron's introduction to the 1999 edition of *Peyton Place,* "Open Secrets: Rereading *Peyton Place*" (Boston: Northeastern University Press), viii, xxi, xxviin6. See also Patricia Carbine, "Peyton Place," *Look,* 18 March 1958, 108; "Obituary Notes," *Publishers' Weekly,* 9 March 1964, 44; Toth, *Inside Peyton Place,* 207; and Hackett, *70 Years of Best Sellers,* 12, 40, 201–3. Metalious died, her estate insolvent, before the television program debuted.

    50. In addition to being refused by thousands of libraries nationwide, the book was banned as "lewd and indecent" in the town of Fort Wayne, Indiana. It was the first novel to appear on the Rhode Island Commission's blacklist, and it was prohibited from import to Canada. See Toth, *Inside Peyton Place,* 131–32.

    51. I am not suggesting that *Peyton Place's* sexual content was not what got it passed around the nation's junior high bathrooms. But there appears to be a distinction between younger readers reading for the sex (like the latter-day rock singer Grace Slick, whose recollections of reading the book in bits are quoted by both Toth and Cameron), and the more middle-aged (and likely female) readers who read the novel more holistically, taking in the cultural critique and identifying with the broader themes. Significantly, the younger generation has written most of the published criticism on *Peyton Place,* which continues

to interpret its popularity in strictly sexual terms. This myopic reading has been changing in the wake of Ardis Cameron's excellent 1999 scholarly edition and the republication of Toth's biography.

52. Laura Secor, "Amazing Grace," *Lingua Franca*, April 1999, B59–B61, B60. In fact, in the final, climactic trial of Selena Cross, "talk" *becomes* the law. It is the word, the testimony of the respectable town physician, Matthew Swain, that turns the jury's opinion. In this scene, the doctor's word is more binding than the physical evidence he presents: "Not one man of the twelve looked down at the paper [confession] as it went from hand to hand" (348–49). On the pain/pleasure of surveillance, see Foucault, *Discipline and Punish*.

53. Metalious, herself French-Canadian, had experienced such attitudes when she married her Greek-American husband, George Metalious. Metalious's own mother's response to their engagement was, "I told you he was no good, Grace. . . . What has that black Greek done, got you pregnant?'" Qtd. in Metalious and O'Shea, *Girl from "Peyton Place,"* 36.

54. Metalious tells a convoluted tale about Samuel Peyton, full of twists that punish the reader for making any easy assumptions about his character. The town grouch, Clayton Frazier, narrates the story of Peyton, whom he repeatedly calls "a friggin nigger," to a curious outsider journalist named Delaney. When Delaney asks why Frazier uses that phrase, he learns that Peyton was a turncoat. Frazier reasons, "If Samuel's skin had been of a different color, I'd say he was a friggin rebel" (331–32).

55. There are other subtle examples of antiracist content in the text: the jokes Doc Swain tells the bigoted nurses at their own expense, and having the blonde Constance MacKenzie marrying the Greek Tom Makris, for example. In contrast, Leo Litwak reports that the television version of *Peyton Place* had "no discernible Negroes, no obvious Jews, no bigotry, no religious or political division. The problems in Peyton Place—murder, adultery dating, lonely widows, premarital sex, social status, illegitimacy—are perhaps manageable. Undoubtedly this innocence exists in a considerable part of America, especially that part which is rural or suburban." Just as the film version of *From Here to Eternity* had excised homosexuality and normalized heterosexuality, the television version of *Peyton Place* in the early 1960s excised race/ethnicity to normalize whiteness. During the final season, in a last-ditch effort to "politicize" the show for ratings, the producers did add a "negro family" to the show. See Leo E. Litwak, "Visit to a Town of the Mind," *New York Times Magazine*, 4 April 1965, 46–64, 54. These aspects of the text raise the question of the racial/ethnic make-up of *Peyton Place*'s readership. This information is of course very difficult to determine, although if one in twenty-nine Americans purchased the text, then "minorities" had to constitute at least part of that readership.

56. The blaming of mothers, especially over-mothering, or over-attachment to the mother, was a favorite pop-Freudian explanation for all problems of adjustment in children (or society) throughout the 1940s and '50s. The term "Momism" was first coined by Philip Wylie in his screed *Generation of Vipers* (1942; New York: Rinehart, 1959).

57. John A. McDermott explores the striking resemblance between Metalious's plot here and both Bloch's novel and Hitchcock's film. See "'Do You Love Mother, Norman?': Faulkner's 'A Rose for Emily' and Metalious's *Peyton Place* as Sources for Robert Bloch's *Psycho*," *Journal of Popular Culture* 40.3 (June 2007): 454–67. See also Randall D. Larson, "PSYCHO: An Interview with Robert Bloch," *Fandom Unlimited* 1.1 (1971), mgpfeff. home.sprynet.com/interview_larson02.html.

58. Cameron, "Open Secrets," ix.

59. Apart from Bloch, at least a handful of people may have consciously or subconsciously culled some of their famous postwar ideas or images from the pages of the ubiquitous *Peyton Place*. The "cup inverted over Allison" at the beginning and end of the novel is very like the image Sylvia Plath used seven years later to describe Esther Greenwood's

sense of being in the world in *The Bell Jar* (London: Heinemann, 1963; rpt., New York: Bantam, 1971). The ennui and frustration that Constance Mackenzie embodies, particularly the way her condition is translated into sexual terms, is—as Emily Toth also points out—very like Friedan's notion of the feminine mystique. Metalious doesn't use the phrase, yet she is putting her finger on it several years prior to Friedan. If "everybody" read *Peyton Place*—and by the early 1960s, millions of Americans had—Metalious should perhaps be credited as at least one of the sources for these radicalizing ideas to come.

60. Qtd. in Eric F. Goldman, *The Crucial Decade* (New York: Vintage, 1960), 324.

61. Simone de Beauvoir, *The Second Sex* (1949; New York: Bantam, 1965), 45.

62. David Riesman, Nathan Glazer, and Reuel Denney, *The Lonely Crowd: A Study of the Changing American Character* (New Haven: Yale University Press, 1950).

63. Whyte contrasts the "Social Ethic" with the "Protestant Ethic." See Whyte, *Organization Man*, 6, 12; Riesman, *Lonely Crowd*, 37.

64. "Normal Isn't as Normal Does," *America*, 8 September 1956, 520–21. See also Igo, *Averaged American*.

65. Chafe, *Unfinished Journey*, 120; Kaledin, *Mothers and More*, 12.

66. Qtd. in Chafe, *Unfinished Journey*, 121. See Gibson Winter, *The Suburban Captivity of the Churches* (Garden City, NJ: Doubleday, 1961) and Andrew Greeley, *The Church in the Suburbs* (New York: Sheed and Ward, 1959).

67. Qtd. in Kaledin, *Mothers and More*, 13. By the late 1960s, Robert Bellah and others would propose the idea of American "civil religion"—in which the nation substituted for God, and one's good citizenship as a member of that nation could substitute for moral goodness. See Bellah, "Civil Religion in America" (1968) in *Beyond Belief: Essays on Religion in a Post-Traditional World* (New York: Harper and Row, 1970).

68. The *Peyton Place* television series "radically repositioned *Peyton Place*" in popular memory," according to Ardis Cameron, "aggressively relocating it within a . . . [more] conservative politics of domesticity, social consensus, sexual conformity, and male privilege." See Cameron, "Open Secrets," xviii. The serial (1964–69) was the first long-running, prime-time soap opera, with a cast including Mia Farrow, Ryan O'Neal, Dorothy Malone, Gena Rowlands, Lee Grant, and Mariette Hartley. See Dan Einstein et al., "Source Guide to TV Family Comedy, Drama, and Serial Drama, 1946–70," in Spigel and Mann, *Private Screenings*, 266. See also Otto Friedrich, "Farewell to Peyton Place," *Esquire*, December 1971, 168. Friedrich noted that "if TV statistics are any more reliable than publishing statistics, which is uncertain, *Peyton Place* attracted an audience of 60,000,000 Americans—about one out of every three." Friedrich also notes the whitewashing of the televised version: Metalious's "Caldron of Sin" became producer Paul Monash's "Village of Innocence," and New York came to represent the "wicked city, the metropolis of temptation and vice." Dropping the film's, novel's, and pilot's "pivotal Cross family, claiming they were 'too sordid for television'; transform[ing] Michael Rossi from a schoolteacher into a medical doctor . . . ; and start[ing] the story with teen siren Betty Anderson single and pregnant," the televised town either reversed or erased most of the cultural critique Metalious had embedded in her story. See Mora Luckett, "A Moral Crisis in Prime Time: *Peyton Place* and the Rise of the Single Girl," in *Television, History, and American Culture: Feminist Critical Essays*, ed. Mary Beth Haralovich and Lauren Rabinovitz (Durham: Duke University Press, 1999), 75–97, 77.

69. This trope of false fronts can be seen in such disparate postwar texts as John Okada's *No-No Boy* (1957), Ralph Ellison's *Invisible Man* (1952), Sylvia Plath's *The Bell Jar* (1963), J. D. Salinger's *Catcher in the Rye* (1951), Harriet Arnow's *The Dollmaker* (1954), Walker Percy's *The Moviegoer* (1961), Gwendolyn Brooks's *Maud Martha* (1953), and John Updike's *Rabbit Run* (1961), among others.

70. Kurt Vonnegut, *Mother Night* (1961; New York: Dell, 1966), v.

Conclusion: Home, Normal Home

1. Streit, "Baffling Search," 18–19, 82–83.

2. De Beauvoir, *Second Sex,* 45.

3. Julian Carter makes the point that "normality" functioned as a kind of code for white heterosexuality in his work *The Heart of Whiteness,* 27–29.

4. Davis, *Enforcing Normalcy,* 6–27.

5. As Lennard Davis writes, "The word 'norm' in the modern sense has only been in use since around 1855, and 'normality' and 'normalcy' appeared in 1849 and 1857 respectively." See his *Enforcing Normalcy,* 24.

6. Davis, *Enforcing Normalcy,* 30. See chapter 2 of this study for further discussion of eugenics.

7. "Normality," *Oxford English Dictionary Online,* 2nd ed. (New York: Oxford University Press, 2001), www.oed.com.

8. While "normality" certainly remains a potent idea in the conceptualizing of disability, I would counter that normality has continued to be subject to history since 1890—it has changed, sometimes radically, to suit its times.

9. See Lois W. Banner, *American Beauty* (New York: Knopf, 1983), 255.

10. See Julian Carter, *Heart of Whiteness.*

11. Warren G. Harding, Inaugural Address, 4 March 1921, avalon.law.yale.edu/20th_century/harding.asp.

12. Gabrielle Studenmund, "Are Your Bodies Sexually Compatible?" *Mademoiselle,* June 2001, 98–102. My thanks to Mae Creadick for this resource.

13. Associated Press, "Palin Says She Represents 'Joe Six-Pack,'" 1 October 2008, *USA Today,* www.usatoday.com/news/politics/2008-10-01-473685378_x.htm. See also Jack Garigliano, "Column: GOP Stoops Too Low for Joe Six-Pack to Stomach," CBS News, 30 October 2008, www.cbsnews.com/stories/2008/11/01/politics/uwire/main4562692.shtml.

14. At one point Palin awkwardly promised to "put government back on the side of the people of Joe Six-pack, like me." See Associated Press, "Palin Says."

15. Among many, see Jacobsen, *Whiteness of a Different Color;* Gail Bederman, *Manliness and Civilization: A Cultural History of Gender and Race in the United States, 1880–1917* (Chicago: University of Chicago Press, 1995); and Katz, *Invention of Heterosexuality.* Work historicizing the twentieth-century middle class remains sparse, but see Burton Bledstein and Robert Johnson, eds., *The Middling Sorts: Explorations in the History of the American Middle Class* (New York: Routledge, 2001). See also Mary P. Ryan, *Cradle of the Middle Class: The Family in Oneida County, New York, 1790–1865* (New York: Cambridge University Press, 1983); and Stuart Blumin, *The Emergence of the Middle Class: Social Experience in the American City, 1760–1900* (New York: Cambridge University Press, 1989) on nineteenth century formations.

Index

Page numbers in italics refer to illustrations.